THE DIVINE COMEDY
IN ENGLISH

1782-1900

THE DIVINE COMEDY IN ENGLISH

A Critical Bibliography

1782-1900

GILBERT F. CUNNINGHAM
B.A., PH.D.

BARNES & NOBLE, INC. · NEW YORK

PUBLISHERS · BOOKSELLERS · SINCE 1873

Published in Great Britain by
Oliver & Boyd Ltd., Edinburgh & London

First Published 1965

Printed in Great Britain
by Robert Cunningham and Sons, Ltd., Alva

TO MY WIFE

...tra bella e bona
non so qual più.

Purg. XXIV.13-14

CONTENTS

PREFACE

Much of the material used in this book was originally included in a dissertation which was accepted by the University of Edinburgh in 1954 for the degree of Ph.D. It has, however, been rewritten to include the results of later research, and the first volume appears on the occasion of the seventh centenary of Dante's birth, thanks to the good offices of Oliver and Boyd, who have undertaken its publication in this country, and Barnes and Noble, who are sponsoring its sale in the U.S.A.

The present volume deals with translators prior to 1900, and although the date is an arbitrary one, it is suitable for several reasons. Not only does it divide the translators into two groups which are numerically nearly equal but, with inevitable allowance for a small degree of overlapping, it marks the end of the long succession of dismal attempts at terza rima characteristic of the second half of the nineteenth century, and also the point at which the vogue for prose versions, which began in 1880, showed signs of waning. The twentieth-century translators will be dealt with in the second volume, including some whose versions are not yet published, and an effort will then be made to sum up achievement and speculate on the future.

In the preparation of the original thesis I was indebted for advice and encouragement to two members of the staff of the University of Edinburgh: Professor W. L. Renwick, who then occupied the chair of Rhetoric and English Literature, and Professor M. M. Rossi, then Reader, and now first occupant of the recently instituted chair of Italian, and I again express my gratitude for their help.

I should like to make special mention here of what I owe to my old friend, the late Jethro Bithell, whom many other former students must still remember as Reader in German at Birkbeck College, University of London. His interests went far beyond the language in which he was a scholar of international repute. His knowledge of the Divine Comedy was considerable, and he himself was a practised translator of poetry from numerous tongues. During many long conversations, and throughout a correspondence spread over many years, I had the benefit of his counsel and experience, bestowed with the enthusiasm and energy which were so notable a feature of his character.

Over ten years ago I made the acquaintance of one of the translators of Dante, Professor G. L. Bickersteth, who then occupied the

ix

chair of English in the University of Aberdeen, and now lives in retirement at Chichester. Since then I have had the privilege of his
friendship and the advantage of his immense knowledge of Dante and
the Divine Comedy. He has smoothed out many difficulties for me,
and has done so with willingness and kindness in the best traditions of
scholarship. He will, moreover, undoubtedly be remembered among
the great Dante scholars of our country in the present age.

I would also like to express my thanks to Dr Wm. J. De Sua, now of
the University of North Carolina, for initiating the present enterprise.
I am glad that my earlier work, as he has most generously acknowledged,
was useful to him in the preparation of his *Dante into English*, recently
published by the press of his university. I read it in manuscript with
great interest and, like every new approach, it has brought me clearer
light on the subject of translation. Most of all, however, I am grateful
for the fact that his encouragement and interest caused me to turn to
the completion of this volume which will, I hope, prove a worthy
companion to his own study.

The services of libraries have, of course, been of the utmost importance in writing this book. I should like to begin by thanking the
County Librarian of Clackmannanshire, Mr W. McK. Murray, who
has been my link with many of the sources of information and who has
always entered enthusiastically upon the task of satisfying my needs.
Of no less service has been the Library of the University of Edinburgh,
from whose staff I have always had the fullest co-operation. The staff
of Mitchell Library in Glasgow also took a great deal of trouble for
my benefit, and I am likewise indebted to the John Rylands Library
in Manchester and the Athenaeum Library in London for privileges
extended to me. The copyright libraries have also been indispensable;
at the National Library of Scotland, at the Bodleian, and in the
Reading Room of the British Museum I have always been received
with efficient and courteous attention. The National Library of Wales
has likewise given me assistance, and the Library of Congress, Washington, has been invaluable, both in providing books and supplying
information. In addition, I have directed inquiries relating to local
matters to many city, county and university librarians both in Britain
and America, and have always received a prompt and helpful response.
I should like especially to thank Dr W. R. Aitken, now of the Scottish
School of Librarianship, Glasgow, for help and interest in this enterprise during our many years of friendship.

While on the subject of books, it is only right to mention the debt
of all English-speaking students of Dante to Paget Jackson Toynbee,

whose three bibliographical volumes, enumerated in the list of abbreviations, are truly monumental, and whose gifts to the Bodleian and the British Museum are a veritable treasure-house of Dante literature. Two of the most valuable modern books are named in the same list, and their authors, Dr Angelina La Piana and Dr Werner P. Friedrich, have been kind enough to supplement the contents of these works in correspondence. Dr La Piana's book has been invaluable for its summaries of American comment, and in several of the articles I have made further acknowledgment of my indebtedness. The bibliographies of Evola and Vallone, those of the *Giornale dantesco*, Ostermann's *Dante in Deutschland*, as well as the work of Scartazzini and Witte, Farinelli's *Dante in Spagna etc.*, have all furnished a great deal of useful information. Professor Arrighi of the University of Aix-en-Provence was kind enough to give me information regarding some of the French translations and to direct me to the rare but fascinating book by Hippolyte Topin who, in his *Paradiso* of 1862, gathered together a remarkable amount of out-of-the-way information regarding the Divine Comedy in French.

To many of the translators themselves I have been indebted for the supply of personal information, and I remember with special gratitude my all too brief personal acquaintance with the late Dr John D. Sinclair, whose prose version of the Comedy has been one of the most important additions to Dante literature in the last generation. I must also record my gratitude to a more recent translator of the Divine Comedy, Professor Thomas G. Bergin of Yale University, a scholar of repute from whose advice and interest I continue to benefit.

I have applied for information, seldom in vain, to a great many other sources: publishers, booksellers, local authorities and private individuals. To all these I am most grateful for their help. Further acknowledgments appear in the appropriate articles.

In the preparation both of the original thesis and of the present volume a great deal of editorial work and typewriting has been necessary. On both occasions I have been excellently and efficiently served by members of my own staff, and I am pleased to take this opportunity of thanking them.

In conclusion I would like to express my thanks to my wife who has had to share me with Dante for so many years, and to whom this book is appropriately dedicated.

G. F. C.

ABBREVIATIONS

B.T.D.   Paget Toynbee: *Britain's Tribute to Dante* (London, 1921)

D.A.P.   Angelina La Piana: *Dante's American Pilgrimage* (New Haven, 1948)

D.E.L.   Paget Toynbee: *Dante in English Literature from Chaucer to Cary*, 2 vols. (London, 1909)

D.F.A.   Werner P. Friedrich: *Dante's Fame Abroad 1350-1850* (Rome, 1950)

D.N.B.   *Dictionary of National Biography*

D.S.   Paget Toynbee: *Dante Studies* (Oxford, 1921), pages 156-280 of which contain a 'Chronological List of English Translations from Dante from Chaucer to the present day'

T.L.S.   *Times Literary Supplement*

CHAPTER I

FACTS AND FIGURES

THE Divine Comedy has been translated much oftener than any other post-classical work. Versions exist in all kinds of languages, ancient and modern, from Sanskrit to Volapük. The greatest activity has been in western Europe and in America. The English-speaking peoples have been the most prolific translators of all, although they were late starters. When the first major rendering appeared in English in 1782, Spanish (easily first in the field), French and German translators had all several versions to their credit. During the nineteenth century English writers went rapidly ahead, especially when American translators began to swell their numbers in the latter decades of that century and, eventually, predominated in the present one. During the 183 years since Rogers published his Inferno there have been 82 versions of one or more cantiche in English, 22 of which are by Americans. It so happens that the year 1900 is nearly the mid-point in the record, for 40 of these translations appeared before and 42 after that date. Of the former 4 and of the latter 18 were American. The trend is much more emphatic in recent years; out of 12 translators who have entered print since 1945, 9 are American. There are now about 60 versions of one or more cantiche in both French and German, and nearly 30 in the Hispanic languages.

In the foregoing computation, and in the analysis that follows, it should be noted that two translations of the Purgatorio, each counted here as a cantica, are incomplete, namely those of Parsons and Home. Details of their omissions are given in the articles dealing with them. Their versions are, however, so substantial that it does not distort the picture to regard them as complete.

Of the 82 translators 46 have completed the whole Comedy, 5 have rendered two cantiche each, 22 have confined themselves to the Inferno, 6 to the Purgatorio and 3 to the Paradiso, making 179 cantiche in all. Two contemporary translators are at present engaged in completing their so far partial renderings, and one new entrant to the field is known to be at work.

While the present volume deals only with translators the first edition of whose work was published prior to 1900, the tables include the translators whose versions have appeared subsequently. These tables will be repeated in the second volume, with the addition of any others who appear in print up to the date of publication.

Table 1 contains a list of the eighty-two translators in chronological order of first publication. It shows dates of birth and death and occupation where known, the part or parts translated with the date of their first appearance, and the form of the translation. The conventional term 'defective terza rima' is used to describe the Schlegelian pattern where the second line of each tercet is left unrhymed. When it corresponds with the terzine of the original an unrhymed translation is described as 'blank terzine', otherwise as 'blank verse'. A fuller prosodic description of verse translations will be found in the respective articles. American writers are distinguished by an asterisk and feminine translators (of whom there are 9) by an obelisk. Fuller details of publication will be found in the bibliographies annexed to each chapter.

With regard to occupation, holders of Anglican orders are described as 'C. of E. clergyman' except in two cases where, since these translators spent most of their lives in non-ecclesiastical posts, the designation '[C. of E.], scholar' is used. Men with legal qualifications are described as 'lawyer', although in quite a number of cases they probably did not practise their profession. The borderline between 'scholar' and 'author' is difficult to define, since the occupations often overlap; the former description is used for those who spent the greater part of their life in University or similar appointments. In the period before 1900 we find 10 lawyers, 9 clergymen and 8 scholars or authors among the translators; since 1900, 5 lawyers, 6 clergymen and 18 scholars or authors. This indicates the tendency for such work to be undertaken in recent times by professionals rather than amateurs. The pre-1900 list includes 5 civil servants, whereas there have been none since. Of the medical men 3 are pre-1900 (if we class Parsons with this group) and 2 since that date. The united achievement of the clergy is impressive when we consider that Cary (an Anglican) produced his minor masterpiece at the beginning of this history; Wicksteed (a Unitarian) was one of the greatest figures in Dante scholarship at the turn of the century; and Sinclair (Church of Scotland) published his notable prose translation almost in our own generation. It must be added, however, that members of the clergy have also been responsible for some very poor efforts. Carlyle among the medical men and Butler among the civil servants deserve to be remembered; none of the lawyers, except perhaps Dugdale, have attained distinction. Scholars and authors have much good work to their credit, particularly in the present century;

in the preceding one the names of two American scholars, Longfellow and Norton, stand out.

As to form, there have been fluctuations in fashion, as is indicated in more detail in the succeeding chapters. Table 2, however, gives a diagrammatic summary. Four broad classifications are made, viz. (*a*) terza rima (including the 'defective' or Schlegelian form); (*b*) other rhymed verse; (*c*) unrhymed verse (including both ordinary blank verse and blank terzine); and (*d*) prose. As a better indication of volume, each star represents a cantica, and is placed in the decade during which it first appeared. It will thus be seen that the 82 translators have among them produced 179 cantiche, and that terza rima, in spite of its difficulty, has been the most popular form of all.

Table 3 gives a picture of activity throughout the period in Britain and America. Again each star represents a cantica in the decade of its first appearance. It will be seen that the 60 British translators have produced 121 cantiche, while the 22 Americans with 58 show a higher average per translator. These figures are, of course, changing from time to time, and it must also be borne in mind that two recent American renderings of the complete Comedy, i.e. 6 cantiche, although in print, have not been published, and are only available in expensive limited editions. While on the subject of nationality it may be noted that of the 60 British translators at least nine are Scots, four Irish and two Welsh. The Scots have produced two notable versions, namely those of Carlyle and Sinclair, but have also been responsible for some of the worst. None of the Irish or Welsh translators have achieved distinction in this field.

Of the 9 women on the list only one, Dorothy Sayers, has achieved fame; but the wide circulation of her version in the Penguin Classics probably exceeds the sales of all the other versions put together, with the exception perhaps of Cary's and Longfellow's.

There have been, of course, during the period under consideration, many partial English translations, ranging from short passages to quite considerable selections; there are also several unpublished translations existing in manuscript, as well as records of other manuscripts which have been lost. The more important of these are described in the appropriate chapters; some are interesting rather than valuable. By far the most considerable and influential among them are the fragments of Charles Hall Grandgent, who will be dealt with in the second volume.

In the following pages the translations are considered in groups, similar forms being treated together, and occasionally a number of experimental or anomalous versions are collected for convenience in one chapter. The opening pages of each chapter outline the features of the group and relate it to others; they also contain references to minor translations and continental versions where these have some relevance. An article is then devoted to each translator, these being arranged in chronological order of first publication within each chapter. A brief biographical sketch is given, with fuller particulars in cases where the information is not readily available, and a record of the inquiries made where no positive identification of the author has been possible. Each chapter is followed by a bibliography which gives particulars of the first edition of each translation, and also of any subsequent editions containing revisions by the author.

In the appraisal of the translations themselves, function has been taken into consideration, since the qualities expected from a prose crib are very different from those looked for in a poetical rehandling. Where a translation contains such glaring inaccuracies as to suggest imperfect comprehension on the part of its author, some examples are given, but such lists are by no means exhaustive. It must be borne in mind, however, that what appear to be mistranslations in earlier versions may very well be due to the use of an inferior text, or the adoption of some less known variant. Critics who have failed to consider these possibilities have often erroneously accused a translator of inaccuracy, and thereby only displayed their own lack of knowledge.

References are made from time to time to verbal similarities between translations. These have often led to charges of plagiarism, but here again great caution must be exercised. Resemblances are inevitable when translators have a common linguistic and literary tradition, and very careful investigation is needed to support a charge of piracy. There are, it is true, some flagrant examples, like Peabody's plundering of Carlyle; but, as will be seen, there are also cases of verbal identity between translators who could not possibly have known of each other's work, such as Rossetti and Longfellow. This question will be frequently referred to in what follows.

When available, contemporary opinions have been quoted, especially in the case of the earlier translations, where journalistic comment is of historical interest. But although many excellent literary periodicals have devoted attention to translations of Dante during a great part of the period (the *Athenaeum*, for instance, seldom missed one), the vagaries of reviewers, especially when anonymous, are often puzzling. One suspects at times that the critic has read very little of the volume under examination, and at other times that he has some kind of bias for or against the author. However interesting such episodes as the war between the *Academy* reviewers and William Warren Vernon may be, they shed little light on the subject of Dante translation.

Quotations are verbatim and unless otherwise stated are taken from the last revised edition of the work in question. Where the translation is printed in terzine, the usual method of indenting the second and third lines of each has been used here, although some other system of division may have been employed in the printed version, and this arrangement is also adopted for the stanzas of Wright and Wilstach which were so printed. Those of Boyd and Shadwell are also reproduced as originally printed, but no indention has been used in the Spenserian stanzas of Musgrave and others, since this is confusing in shorter extracts. In continuous prose and verse the original paragraph indentions are preserved, and Wicksteed's prose is reproduced in the form used in the Temple Classics. Italian quotations are from the 1964 edition of the *Testo Critico della Società Dantesca Italiana* unless some other text is specified.

TABLE I

CHRONOLOGICAL LIST OF TRANSLATORS

* denotes translator of American nationality or domicile
† denotes female translator
Dates given are those of first edition of each part only

Name, year of birth and death, occupation	Part translated and date of first appearance	Form of translation
Charles Rogers, 1711-84, civil servant	Inferno, 1782	blank verse
Henry Boyd, c.1755-1832, C. of E. clergyman	Inferno, 1785 Comedy, 1802	rhymed six-line stanzas
Henry Francis Cary, 1772-1844, [C. of E.], scholar	Inferno, 1805-6 Comedy, 1814	blank verse
Nathaniel Howard, 1781-1834, schoolmaster	Inferno, 1807	blank verse
Joseph Hume, 1767-1843, civil servant	Inferno, 1812	blank verse
Ichabod Charles Wright, 1795-1871, banker	Inferno, 1833 Purgatorio, 1836 Paradiso, 1840	rhymed six-line stanzas
John Dayman, 1802-71, C. of E. clergyman	Inferno, 1843 Comedy, 1865	terza rima
*Thomas William Parsons, 1819-92, medical practitioner	Inferno I-X, 1843 Inferno complete, 1867 Purgatorio I-VIII, 1875 Comedy (incomplete), 1893	quatrains and irregular rhyme
John Aitken Carlyle, 1801-79, medical practitioner	Inferno, 1849	prose
Patrick Bannerman	Comedy, 1850	irregular rhyme
Charles Bagot Cayley, 1823-83, scholar	Inferno, 1851 Purgatorio, 1853 Paradiso, 1854	terza rima
E. O'Donnell, R.C. priest	Comedy, 1852	prose
Thomas Brooksbank, 1824-1902, lawyer	Inferno, 1854	terza rima
(Sir) William Frederick Pollock, 1815-88, lawyer	Comedy, 1854	blank terzine
Bruce Whyte, lawyer	Inferno, 1859	irregular rhyme
John Wesley Thomas, 1798-1872, Methodist minister	Inferno, 1859 Purgatorio, 1862 Paradiso, 1866	terza rima

Name, year of birth and death, occupation	*Part translated and date of first appearance*	*Form of translation*
William Patrick Wilkie, 1829-72, lawyer	Inferno, 1862	blank terzine (lines of irregular length)
†Claudia Hamilton Ramsay	Inf. & Purg., 1862 Paradiso, 1863	terza rima
William Michael Rossetti, 1829-1919, civil servant	Inferno, 1865	blank terzine
*Henry Wadsworth Longfellow, 1807-82, scholar	Comedy, 1867	blank terzine
James Ford, 1797-1877, C. of E. clergyman	Inferno, 1865 Comedy, 1870	terza rima
David Johnston, 1800-79, medical practitioner	Inf. & Purg., 1867 Paradiso, 1868	blank terzine
Charles Tomlinson, 1808-97, scholar	Inferno, 1877	terza rima
Arthur John Butler, 1844-1910, civil servant	Purgatorio, 1880 Paradiso, 1885 Inferno, 1892	prose
Warburton Pike, 1818-82, lawyer	Inferno, 1881	terza rima
William Stratford Dugdale, 1828-82, lawyer	Purgatorio, 1883	prose
James Romanes Sibbald, 1839-85, independent	Inferno, 1884	terza rima
James Innes Minchin, 1825-1903, civil servant	Comedy, 1885	terza rima
Edward Hayes Plumptre, 1821-91, C. of E. clergyman	Inf. & Purg., 1886 Paradiso, 1887	terza rima
Frederick Kneller Haselfoot Haselfoot, 1829-1905, lawyer	Comedy, 1887	terza rima
*John Augustine Wilstach, 1824-97, lawyer	Comedy, 1888	rhymed stanzas
William Warren Vernon, 1834-1919, scholar	Purgatorio, 1889 Inferno, 1894 Paradiso, 1900	prose
*Charles Eliot Norton, 1827-1908, scholar	Inf. & Purg., 1891 Paradiso, 1892	prose
Charles Lancelot Shadwell, 1840-1919, scholar	Purg. I-XXVII, 1892 Purg. XXVIII-XXXIII, 1899 Paradiso, 1915	Marvellian stanzas

Name, year of birth and death, occupation	Part translated and date of first appearance	Form of translation
(Sir) Edward Sullivan, 1852-1928, lawyer	Inferno, 1893	prose
George Musgrave, 1855-1932, lawyer	Inferno, 1893	Spenserian stanzas
Robert Urquhart	Inferno, 1895	terza rima
Eugene Jacob Lee-Hamilton, 1845-1907, author	Inferno, 1898	hendecasyllabic blank terzine
Philip Henry Wicksteed, 1844-1927, Unitarian minister	Paradiso, 1899	prose
Arthur Compton Auchmuty, 1842-1917, C. of E. clergyman	Purgatorio, 1899	octosyllabic terza rima
Samuel Home, 1842-1914, lawyer	Purg. I-XVI, 1899 Purg. XVII-XXXI, 1901	hendecasyllabic blank terzine
Thomas Okey, 1852-1935, scholar	Purgatorio, 1901	prose
John Carpenter Garnier, 1839-1926, independent	Inferno, 1901	prose
Edward Clarke Lowe, 1823-1912, C. of E. clergyman	Comedy, 1902	blank terzine
Edward Wilberforce, 1834-1914, lawyer	Inferno, 1903 Comedy, 1909	terza rima
(Sir) Samuel Walker Griffith, 1845-1920, lawyer	Inferno, 1903 Comedy, 1911	hendecasyllabic blank terzine
†Caroline C. Potter	Purgatorio and Paradiso, 1904	rhymed quatrains
Henry Fanshawe Tozer, 1829-1916, [C. of E.], scholar	Comedy, 1904	prose
*Marvin Richardson Vincent, 1834-1922, scholar	Inferno, 1904	blank verse
Charles Gordon Wright, 1854-1936, C. of E. clergyman	Purgatorio, 1905	prose
†Frances Isabella Fraser, 1836-1929	Paradiso, 1908	blank terzine
†Agnes Louisa Money, 1842-1910, independent	Purgatorio, 1910	blank terzine
Charles Edwin Wheeler, 1868-1947, medical practitioner	Comedy, 1911	terza rima

Name, year of birth and death, occupation	Part translated and date of first appearance	Form of translation
†Edith Mary Shaw, born 1846	Comedy, 1914	blank verse
*Henry Johnson, 1855-1918, scholar	Comedy, 1915	blank terzine
Edward Joshua Edwardes, 1852-1917, medical practitioner	Inferno, 1915	blank terzine
*Courtney Langdon, 1861-1924, scholar	Inferno, 1918 Purgatorio, 1920 Paradiso, 1921	blank terzine
*†Eleanor Vinton Murray	Inferno, 1920	terza rima
*Melville Best Anderson, 1851-1933, scholar	Comedy, 1921	terza rima
Henry John Hooper, 1844-1923	Inferno, 1922	unrhymed amphiambics
David James MacKenzie, 1855-1925, lawyer	Comedy, 1927	terza rima
Sydney Fowler Wright, born 1874, author	Inferno, 1928 Purgatorio, 1954	irregularly rhymed deca-syllables
*Albert R. Bandini, born 1882, R.C. priest	Inferno, 1928 Purgatorio, 1930 Paradiso, 1931	terza rima
*Lacy Lockert, born 1888, scholar	Inferno, 1931	terza rima
*Jefferson Butler Fletcher, 1865-1946, scholar	Comedy, 1931	defective terza rima
Geoffrey Langdale Bicker-steth, born 1884, scholar	Paradiso, 1932 Comedy, 1955	terza rima
Laurence Binyon, 1869-1943, scholar	Inferno, 1933 Purgatorio, 1938 Paradiso, 1943	terza rima
*Louis How, 1873-1947, author	Inferno, 1934 Purgatorio, 1938 Paradiso, 1940	terza rima
Ralph Thomas Bodey, 1863-1952, scholar	Comedy, 1938	blank verse
John Dickson Sinclair, 1865-1951, Church of Scotland minister	Inf. & Purg., 1939 Paradiso, 1946	prose
*Thomas Goddard Bergin, born 1904, scholar	Inferno, 1948 Purgatorio, 1953 Paradiso, 1954	blank verse

Name, year of birth and death, occupation	Part translated and date of first appearance	Form of translation
*Lawrence Grant White, 1887-1956, architect	Comedy, 1948	blank verse
*Patrick Cummins, born 1880, R.C. priest	Comedy, 1948	hendecasyllabic terza rima
†Dorothy Leigh Sayers, 1893-1957, author. (Paradiso XXI-XXXIII by Barbara Reynolds)	Inferno, 1949 Purgatorio, 1955 Paradiso, 1962	terza rima
*Harry Morgan Ayres, 1881-1948, scholar	Inferno, 1949 Purg. & Par., 1953	prose
Thomas Weston Ramsey, 1892-1952, master wire worker and poet	Paradiso, 1952	defective terza rima
*Howard Russell Huse, born 1890, scholar	Comedy, 1954	prose
*John Ciardi, born 1916, scholar	Inferno, 1954 Purgatorio, 1961	defective terza rima
*Glen Levin Swiggett, 1867-1961, scholar	Comedy, 1956	terza rima
*†Mary Prentice Lillie, born 1906, scholar	Comedy, 1958	hendecasyllabic blank terzine
Warwick Fielding Chipman, born 1880, lawyer	Inferno, 1961	terza rima
*†Clara Stillman Reed, born 1879	Comedy, 1962	prose

TABLE 2

FORMAL ANALYSIS OF TRANSLATIONS

(Each star represents one cantica)

Date	terza rima	other rhymed verse	unrhymed verse	prose	
1800 –		★	★		
–		★★	★★		
–			★★★		
–					
–		★★★			
1850 –	★	★★★		★	
–	★★★★★	★	★★★	★★★	
–	★★★★★★★★★★	★	★★★★★★★★		
–	★				
–	★★★★★★★★★★★	★★★		★★★★	
1900 –	★★	★★★	★	★★★★★★★★	
Sub-total	30	17	18	16	= 81
–	★★★	★★	★★★★★★★★	★★★★★★	
–	★★★★	★	★★★★★★★★★★★		
–	★★★★★★★★	★	★★		
–	★★★★★★★★★★★★★		★★★	★★	
1950 –	★★★★★		★★★★	★★	
–	★★★★★★★★	★	★★★★★	★★★★★★★	
Sub-total	42	5	33	18	= 98
Total	72	22	51	34	= 179

Note. – The 40 translators dealt with in this volume produced among them 82 cantiche, but since Shadwell's Paradiso was not published till 1915 the sub-total to 1900 in Tables 2 and 3 is 81.

TABLE 3

BRITISH AND AMERICAN TRANSLATORS

(Each star represents one cantica)

	British	*American*		
1800 –	★★			
–	★★★★			
–	★★★			
–				
–	★★★			
1850 –	★★★★★			
–	★★★★★★★★★★★			
–	★★★★★★★★★★★★★★	★★★★		
–	★			
–	★★★★★★★★★★★★★★★	★★★		
1900 –	★★★★★★★★★★	★★★★		
Sub-total	70	11	=	81
–	★★★★★★★★★★★★★★★★★★★	★		
–	★★★★★★★★★★	★★★★★★		
–	★★★★★	★★★★★★		
–	★★★★★★★★★★	★★★★★★★★		
1950 –	★★★	★★★★★★★★		
–	★★★★★	★★★★★★★★★★★★★★★★★★		
Sub-total	51	47	=	98
Total	121	58	=	179

CHAPTER II

THE BEGINNINGS

UNTIL 1782 not so much as a complete canto of the Divine Comedy had been printed in English translation. There had been a few versions of famous episodes, none of them of notable merit, and two quite extensive renderings are said to have existed in manuscript, but both are completely lost. One was by William Huggins (1696-1761) whose translation of Ariosto's *Orlando Furioso* appeared in 1755; from a few lines published in the *British Magazine* it seems to have been in heroic couplets and triplets. The other was by the celebrated Dr Charles Burney (1726-1814) and was in prose; there is also a version in couplets of a few lines from Purg. II in his *History of Music*. All the information available regarding these early versions has been sedulously collected by Toynbee, and will be found in his bibliographies. We begin here from 1782, in which year William Hayley published a version of Inf. I-III in terza rima, dealt with in Chapter III below, and Charles Rogers issued his Inferno in blank verse. Three years later Henry Boyd's Inferno was published, and by 1812 no fewer than five translations of one or more cantiche had appeared in English. At this point there was a momentary pause, and over twenty years elapsed before a sixth translator entered print. We shall therefore deal with these first five translators as a separate group; incidentally Cary is the only one of any consequence, the other four being of interest only as curiosities.

CHARLES ROGERS (1711-84)

Rogers is best known as an art collector and connoisseur. He entered the Custom House service in 1731, spent fifty years there, and reached the rank of Principal Officer. He acquired some knowledge of the fine arts from his superior, William Townson, on whose death in 1746 Rogers inherited his house and collection. Rogers is also known for his monumental *A Collection of Prints in Imitation of Drawings* (1778). He was a friend of Sir Joshua Reynolds and of Horace Walpole, to whose brother Edward he dedicated his Inferno in 1782. Although this volume was published anonymously, its authorship is well authen-

13

ticated. Rogers was over seventy years of age when the book was published, and might be thought to have shown some enterprise and energy in undertaking the task at all. Unfortunately Toynbee's judgment that 'the translation, while entirely devoid of any spark of poetry, has not even the merit of being faithful' is not too harsh.

Rogers' blank verse is so completely lacking in quality that most of it might be called indifferent prose, distorted here and there so that a word ends with each tenth syllable. An occasional line suggests an effort to raise the style, e.g. 'Struck dread into the circumambient air' (I.48), but these are jostled by prosaic ones like 'They're consequently totally unknown' (VII.54), or ridiculous ones such as (III.88-9):

> And you, Sir, there, who yet do live and breathe,
> Get hence from these, for they are now deceas'd.

Very thoroughly split infinitives are a feature of Rogers' verse, e.g. 'and drives again / His sheep to in their usual pasture feed' (XXIV. 14-15), and he is also fond of quite inexplicable inversions like 'that you may teach / Demolish how that I Praeneste may' (XXVII.101-2). He uses many slovenly contractions: 'and if our prayers / And sad and naked Forms by you're despis'd' (XVI.29-30) is typical. He gives us no information as to what text he used, and his methods are so slapdash that it is often difficult to say whether he understood the original or not. There are some bizarre interpretations such as (II.48):

> As frequently the shadow of a beast
> Appears more horrid than the form itself,

or 'Heaven expects not you e'er more to see' (III.85). There is really nothing to be said in favour of Rogers' version.

HENRY BOYD (c.1755-1832)

Our information as to Boyd's life is scanty. He was a native of Ireland, and is probably the Henry Boyd who graduated at the University of Dublin in 1776, which would suggest that he was born about 1755. After being ordained to the Anglican ministry he held various livings in County Down. Some of his title pages designate him Vicar of Drumgath; his obituary in the *Gentleman's Magazine*, to which he had been an occasional contributor, records his death at Ballintemple in 1832 'at an advanced age', and refers to him as Vicar of Rathfriland and Chaplain to the Earl of Charleville. Our further knowledge of him is gleaned mainly from Nichols' *Illustrations*, where, in the Anderson-Percy correspondence, he is spoken of as a poet, who was evidently well known to the writers, although his Dante is not mentioned. Boyd wrote eulogistic poems for the *Gentleman's Magazine* on the deaths of Bishop Percy and his wife; he refers to the fact that they had befriended him during the troubles of 1798-9 and again in the Rebellion of 1808. His grandiloquent compliments in the memorial poems suggest that he may at times have exploited the Bishop's known weakness for aristocratic connexions. In 1793 Boyd published a volume of verse, and a translation of Vincenzo Monti's *Penance of Hugo*, as well as a long poem in Spenserians in 1805. A translation of Petrarch's *Triumphs* which followed in 1807 has had the distinction of being reprinted twice during the present century in *de luxe* quarto and octavo format. In 1809 Boyd edited a three-volume edition of Milton's Works, to which several of his own essays were appended. From the Anderson-Percy correspondence he also seems to have translated Ercilla's *Araucana*, but this remained unpublished.

Boyd's rhymed translation of the Inferno appeared in 1785, and his complete Comedy in 1802, with only slight changes in the earlier part. The essays, notes and other supporting matter are voluminous. The Preliminary Essay to the Purgatorio is stated to be 'an Abridgement of a larger Discourse', but the author's promise to publish this at some future date remained unfulfilled.

Boyd's Divine Comedy is a literary curiosity of some interest, but quite worthless as a translation of Dante. It is written in six-line stanzas, rhymed *a a b c c b*. The author may have had some vague notion of making each stanza correspond to two terzine, but if so he soon abandoned it in favour of progressive expansion. He uses 4962 lines against Dante's 4720 in the Inferno, 5562 against 4755 in the Purgatorio and 5742 against 4758 in the Paradiso. This is partly due to the insertion of glosses, presumably for the unlearned reader's benefit, but also to the addition of a good deal of original and often undesirable ornamentation. In one of his footnotes he apologises for the 'flat, prosaic aspect' of Dante's style, and he was evidently doing his best to write it up. Boyd was too firmly rooted in the poetic tradition of the eighteenth century to capture anything of the manner or atmosphere of the Italian; he could only take Dante's matter and clothe it in the stiff and pompous verse characteristic of the less inspired Augustans. His essays show him to be a man of good education, high intelligence and genuine classical and theological attainments. He makes many perceptive remarks, but though he versifies competently enough in the style of Johnson, his poetic horizon is limited. His version of Par. XVII.55-65 is a good example of his style and methods:

You then must bid adieu to all delight,
This is the first keen shaft that wings its flight
  From dire affliction's bow, then soon thy taste
Shall learn the flavour of the niggard dole,
Thy tears shall mix with the penurious bowl,
  On thy lean board by haughty Patrons plac'd.
Then shall you know what steps of anxious care,
The houseless Man that mounts a stranger's stair
  Must count, but still more deadly stings remain,
The thankless hearts of those with whom you fled,
Dastards, by you in vain to glory led,
  Shall censure thee as cause of all their pain.

Boyd departs so frequently from the text that it is difficult to know how well he understood his original. Many passages are so chaotic as to suggest hasty reading and inadequate comprehension; in others his departures from Dante are doubtless efforts at 'improvement'. Boyd, probably himself a careless reviser, was ill served by his printers. Misspellings are frequent, punctuation is misleading, and quotation marks confusing. In the 1785 edition the first three stanzas of Inf. XXI and XXII are interchanged, with disastrous results to sense and sequence.

Contemporary reviews of Boyd's work were mildly complimentary; Dante was hardly known, and the translation was commended for various imaginary merits. Within twenty years it was forgotten, or recalled only to be mentioned with scorn. Although as late as 1841 a writer in the *Dublin University Magazine* (Vol. 17, p. 429) still praised him, remarking that 'Charles Lamb thought Boyd the best translation of Dante', most subsequent critics were uncompromisingly adverse. In his *Comment on the Divine Comedy* (1822) John Taafe trounced an unnamed translation which is almost certainly Boyd's:

> I believe that if the title page were cut out and the book handed to me, I should not be aware that it was intended for a translation of Dante.

This is, of course, an exaggeration, but there are certainly many stanzas in Boyd's translation which a student of Dante would have difficulty in recognising out of context.

HENRY FRANCIS CARY (1772-1844)

Cary was born at Gibraltar; a few months later his father, Captain William Cary, returned to England with the First Regiment of Foot and, resigning his commission, settled down in Staffordshire as a country gentleman. The poet's mother was Henrietta Brocas, his ancestry being Anglo-Irish on both sides and Anglican by religion; the forefathers of both parents included clergymen and soldiers. Henry went to Rugby in 1783, but after two years there was transferred first to Sutton Coldfield and then to Birmingham. He started early to write verses, an occupation in which he was encouraged by Anna Seward, the poetess, whose acquaintance he made in his teens; by 1787 his poems had begun to appear in the *Gentleman's Magazine*, to which he later contributed critical articles of some quality. In 1790 he went to Christ Church, Oxford. He became a thoroughly competent classical scholar, and also devoted much time to the study of modern European literature. His reading, both ancient and modern, was very wide, Pindar being his favourite among the classics, and Dante very early becoming his major enthusiasm among the later writers. He graduated in 1794 and after some hesitation, for he was attracted to a military career, he decided to enter the Church, and was ordained in 1796. His father's influence gained his presentation to the small living of Abbots Bromley in Staffordshire, to which that of Kingsbury in Warwickshire was added in 1800. In 1796 he married Jane Ormsby of Dublin; they had six sons and two daughters. The deaths of the latter, in 1807 and 1816, caused him overwhelming grief, and from the former date began the fits of melancholy and despondency which often interfered with his literary work. In 1808, having placed a curate in charge of his livings, Cary moved to London, which was his home for the rest of his life. Always somewhat straitened financially, though not in actual want, he eked out the proceeds of his writing, very meagre at first, by readerships and curacies; then in 1826 he was appointed Assistant-Keeper of the Printed Books in the British Museum. He discharged his duties satisfactorily, but found them onerous and irksome; and when his immediate superior, Baber, retired in 1837, Cary was bitterly chagrined by the appointment of his junior, Panizzi, to the post, and forthwith resigned. This was perhaps the best thing that could have happened; since his wife's death in 1832 Cary had felt increasingly the burden of years; he was now able to spend the rest of his life in quiet leisure. He died at Willesden in 1844, and was buried in the Poets' Corner of Westminster Abbey, where a brief epitaph immortalises him as 'The Translator of Dante'. His third son, the Rev. Henry Cary, published a memoir, including his father's literary journal and letters, in 1847; there is also a good modern biography and appreciation, *The Translator of Dante* by R. W. King (London, 1925), which contains a full account of Cary's domestic affairs, literary activities and friendships, and has been invaluable in preparing this biographical sketch.

It is certainly as the translator of Dante that Cary is remembered. His other work, though not negligible, has long been forgotten. Much of it was published in periodicals, especially the short-lived *London Magazine* of 1821-4; this included his continuation of Johnson's *Lives of the Poets*, essays on *Early French Poets*, and many critical articles and reviews. His translations of Aristophanes' *The Birds* (1824) and of the Odes of Pindar (1833) were well received, but have since been superseded. Cary, quiet and studious by nature, was disinclined to court publicity, and but for a happy accident even his Dante might have shared the fate of his Greek volumes.

As early as 1792 we find Cary corresponding with Miss Seward about Dante, whom she did not like, and trying, by means of short prose versions, to convert her. She, however, felt dubious 'of Cary's taste and feeling, since he now prefers Petrarch to Young's *Night Thoughts*'. Cary's devotion to Dante fortunately freed him from domination by the 'Swan of Lichfield', which would certainly have been harmful. He started to translate the Purgatorio into blank verse in 1797; after a lapse of a year or two he decided to complete the Inferno first, and he published it in two parts (1805-6) with the Italian text. In the preface he briefly set forth his principles:

> I have aimed at not only adding to the original text a translation so faithful, as, with the assistance of the notes, to enable one moderately skilled in the Italian tongue to understand my author, but at producing a work which shall not be totally devoid of interest to the mere English reader.

The reception of the volumes was varied; the *Literary Journal* rather unfairly found the blank verse 'harsh' and at times 'obscure'. The *Critical Review* was mildly favourable. So was the *Gentleman's Magazine*, but the article in the latter contained a celebrated misprint, in a quotation from Cary's own preface, resulting in the statement that Dante was 'certainly one of the most obscene writers in any language'! An encouraging notice in the *Monthly Review* praised his fidelity, his versification and his notes. Miss Seward was not to be conciliated; but she showed the book to Sir Walter Scott whom she reports as saying that 'there was power and skill in having breathed so much spirit into a translation so nearly literal'.

From the commercial point of view the venture was unsatisfactory; the sales were small, and when, by 1813, Cary had completed the whole Comedy, he was unable to find a publisher. He decided to issue the book at his own expense, which was a severe strain on his resources. In an effort at economy he dropped the Italian text, using a tiny page size and minute type, with the result that the three volumes, which appeared in 1814, were nearly unreadable. In this edition the well-known title, *The Vision*, was adopted for the first time. The *Monthly Review* and the *Gentleman's Magazine* noticed it kindly, though the former complained of the strain on the reader's eyesight. The *Critical Review*, however, was, in Cary's own words, 'contemptuous', and indeed very unfair. Personal friends were complimentary, but sales, the most important matter to Cary for the time being, languished.

Then in 1817 came Cary's chance meeting with Coleridge at Little-hampton, which completely changed his prospects. The story is fully told in King's biography. Until then Coleridge had never heard of Cary's translation; at their very first meeting he borrowed a copy, and by the following day was already enthusiastic. In February 1818 he referred, in the tenth lecture of his last course on European Literature, to Cary's translation, and in the same month an article dealing with it by Ugo Foscolo appeared in the influential *Edinburgh Review*. It found the translation 'a great acquisition to the English reader', 'executed with a fidelity almost without example', and even opined that Dante would have used blank verse had he written in English. The effect of such support was almost instantaneous; laudatory articles appeared in other journals; and best of all, a publisher was found willing to take up the unsold copies of the 1814 impression and to produce a new one. In 1819 Taylor and Hessey issued the second edition in three well produced octavo volumes, the preface to which paid due tribute to Coleridge.

Cary's work was now fully established in public favour. A third edition was published in 1831. Cary was anxious, however, to revise his translation thoroughly, and used his leisure after he retired to do so. His strength began to fail during the proof-reading stage but he lived to see the appearance of the new edition in March 1844.

Cary's translation is written in continuous blank verse, divided into paragraphs, with a preponderance of masculine endings. There is no attempt at line-for-line rendering, nor to preserve the terzine, except in a few instances, e.g. Inf. III.1-9; the acrostic of Purg. XII and the symmetrical structure of Par. XIX and XX are not reproduced at all. Sentences are remodelled in English idiom; there are none of the reflections of Italian syntax common in later versions.

Some stress was laid by contemporary critics on the literalness of Cary's translation, but it must be remembered that the standard of comparison at that time was a type of rendering very far from the letter. The term 'literal translation' today suggests treatment such as Longfellow's or Butler's; then it meant that the translator followed his original with tolerable closeness, and did not, like Boyd for instance, interpolate matter of his own. Cary followed the *via media* clearly and briefly defined in the sentence quoted above from his first preface. His matter is essentially that of Dante, with only negligible omissions or additions; the manner differs considerably from that of the original, for Cary was resolved to write English poetry.

On the score of accuracy Cary must be given high praise. It is true that his version contains quite a few examples of what we should today call mistranslations; but in almost every case these are due to inferior readings or interpretations which were current at the time when he wrote. His notes and his correspondence indicate his unflagging conscientiousness; he made every possible effort to arrive at the meaning of the original, and where he errs it is usually in good company so far as his own day is concerned.

Cary's translation has enjoyed a popularity far beyond any of its nineteenth-century rivals, among whom Longfellow has been the only serious competitor. For this reason its influence has been very great. Throughout these hundred years a large proportion of English-speaking students of Dante made their first acquaintance with him through Cary; in many cases chance acquaintance with *The Vision* proved to be the spark from which a great flame followed. In the present century, owing to changes in taste and the large number of new translations on the market, Cary's reputation has admittedly declined, but his historical importance remains.

Perhaps the most celebrated passage in *The Vision* is Inf. III.1-9:

> Through me you pass into the city of woe:
> Through me you pass into eternal pain:
> Through me among the people lost for aye.
> Justice the founder of my fabric moved:
> To rear me was the task of power divine,
> Supremest wisdom, and primaeval love.
> Before me things create were none, save things
> Eternal, and eternal I endure.
> All hope abandon, ye who enter here.

It has stood the test of time, and other translators have been content to borrow from it. It is easy to object to details, yet the lines strike one as remarkably 'right'. In other places Cary has met the rhetorical challenge of the original less directly, e.g. (Par. XIV.40-51):

> bright
> As fervent; fervent as, in vision, blest;
> And that as far, in blessedness, exceeding,

As it hath grace, beyond its virtue, great.
Our shape, regarmented with glorious weeds
Of saintly flesh, must, being thus entire,
Show yet more gracious. Therefore shall increase
Whate'er, of light, gratuitous imparts
The Supreme Good; light, ministering aid,
The better to disclose his glory: whence,
The vision needs increasing, must increase
The fervour, which it kindles; and that too
The ray, that comes from it.

Cary's blank verse is often described as Miltonic, and it is true that he has based his prosody to some extent on Milton. In his effort, however, to preserve the precision and simplicity of Dante, he wisely avoids musical rhythms. There is a strong resemblance between his style and Cowper's, including something of the uncertainty of Cowper's touch. The often quoted 'excoriate forks deform' of *Yardley Oak* has many parallels in *The Vision*: Geryon's 'retractile claws', the 'conflagrant mass' of the purgatorial fire, the stream that flows 'from rock to rock transpicuous'. An essential difference between Cary and his original is that for him, with few exceptions, the unit is never the line or the terzina, but the period or verse paragraph; and he goes to work very deliberately to break up those lines and groups of lines which are so vital a feature of Dante's prosody, e.g. (Inf. XXXI.16-18) where Cary has:

So terrible a blast
Orlando blew not, when that dismal rout
O'erthrew the host of Charlemagne, and quenched
His saintly warfare.

Critics have frequently complained of the monotony of Cary's verse as compared with the variety of the original, and it is certainly true that the translation suffers from an evenness of pace which prevents many of Dante's effects from being even suggested. When Coleridge said that Cary's blank verse was 'the most varied and harmonious to my ear of any since Milton' he was again probably comparing it with the lifeless products of some contemporaries. Unfortunately Coleridge does not refer to any specific lines or passages in Cary; but probably the ability to translate the Divine Comedy with such precision and restraint as Cary showed, and at the same time to write blank verse of sustained quality, impressed Coleridge more than we, looking back, can readily realise. It must be admitted, however, after making every possible allowance, that Cary is very far from reproducing the endless variety of Dante, and that he is lacking in that energy and inventiveness which make the original so astonishing a performance.

Cary's *Vision* is still so readily accessible that it does not seem necessary to quote any passages at length, but rather conclude by repeating the verdict of Saintsbury in the *Cambridge History of English Literature* which is a fair summing up by a perceptive critic.

> [Cary's translation is] a courageous, scholarly and almost fully justified recognition that attempts directly to conquer the difficulty by adopting rimed terza rima are doomed to failure; and that all others, in stanza or rimed verse of any kind, are evasions to begin with, and almost as certain failures to boot. It may even be said to be a further, and a very largely successful, recognition of the fact that blank verse, while 'nearest prose' in one sense, and, therefore, sharing its advantages, is almost furthest from it in another, in the peculiar qualities of rhythm which it demands. Cary does not quite come up to this latter requisition, but, unless Milton had translated Dante, nobody could have done so. Meanwhile, Cary's verse translation has gone the furthest and come the nearest. It is no slight achievement.

NATHANIEL HOWARD (1781-1834)

Toynbee was unable to discover more of Howard than that he flourished around 1800 and that James Northcote referred to him in his *Memoirs of Sir Joshua Reynolds* as a native of Plymouth and 'an ornament to his country'. He also gave a list of Howard's books as recorded in the British Museum Catalogue (D.E.L. 2, p. 58). A letter signed 'Jabez', a frequent pseudonymous contributor to *Notes and Queries*, says (5th ser., Vol. 8, 1877, p. 417):

> It is worth a note that Nathaniel Howard's translation of the Inferno was made when he was under twenty years of age. My copy was given by him to John Britton, and has the recipient's signature, and a note of the author's age in the same handwriting.

Much more information is now available, thanks to a Devon antiquary, Mr A. G. K. Leonard, who published an article on Howard in the *Western Morning News* (20 Mar. 1953), and was kind enough to supply some notes for the present article.

Howard was born in 1781 at Plymouth, and attended the old Corporation Grammar School there as a charity boy. The later course of his education has not been traced, but he obviously became a proficient classical scholar, and also studied such languages as Hebrew and Persian. In 1804 his first book, *Bickleigh Vale and other Poems*, was published at York; it was reprinted at London in 1806 and at Devonport in 1856. The title poem, reproduced in Wright's anthology of West Country Poets, is conventional but respectable blank verse in late eighteenth-century style. Howard also published a number of Greek and Latin schoolbooks, which seem to have enjoyed some popularity; and a long and learned paper by him, *On Persian Poetry*, was printed in the *Transactions of Plymouth Institution* (1830). In 1812 Howard became headmaster of Harwood House, Tamerton (near the spot where the Saltash railway bridge now crosses the Tamar), which is described in a contemporary directory as 'a respectable and prosperous grammar school'. Howard's son was a pupil at Eton, whence he went to Exeter College, Oxford, in 1836, and is entered in the Matriculation register as 'son of Nathaniel Howard of Tamerton, Devon'; on the other hand a list of honorary members of Plymouth Institution dated 1830 includes the name of 'Nathaniel Howard of Eton'. The family's later movements are uncertain; we know that Howard died at Margate in 1834, and that his widow resided for some years thereafter at Plymouth.

Howard was evidently a man of great ability, industry and determination; he was only twenty-six when his Inferno was published in 1807. We must discount the story of the translation being made before he was twenty; even for a young man of twenty-six the eighty pages of learned notes which accompany it are an achievement. Howard's preface, however, hardly commends his literary judgment to the reader. He regrets that 'national custom obliged Dante to confine his great genius to the shackles of rhyme' and feels that 'blank-verse seems more analogous to his sublime manner', and goes on to deplore the fact that Dante,

> like our immortal Shakespeare, hurried away by the effervescence of imagination, has been guilty of many extravagances, and ludicrous images . . . but these defects in both should be rather attributed, perhaps, to the vicious taste of the age in which they lived, than to the authors themselves.

He adds that he has translated the Inferno only, since he thinks it Dante's 'grandest production'. It can thus be seen that Howard was willing to be an improver as well as a translator. His blank verse makes no attempt to keep to the lines or terzine of the original; he expands or contracts at will, his cantos being on an average ten or twelve lines shorter than the Italian.

After such a prelude, Howard's translation is a sad disappointment. Not only is his blank verse flat and uninspired, but he has some irritating and motiveless mannerisms, especially the unnecessary repetition of words and phrases of the type (IX.122-3):

> while deep lament
> Forth issued, such as well might issue forth
> From victims in such torture.

Other passages are 'written up', evidently in an attempt to atone for Dante's shortcomings, e.g. (II.52-7):

> With those I dwelt
> Who feel nor pain nor pleasure after death,
> When to my dazzled gaze a virgin form
> Came gliding, fair in angel beauty, came;
> And all-commanding, call'd me near. Her eyes
> Like stars a living lustre stream'd. She spake;
> Words, sweet as nectar, melted on her lips.
> Seraphic flow'd her voice and thus began.

Howard can, however, on occasion, do much better. In his notes he bestows judicious praise on the simile of the storm (IX.64-72), and he makes a fairly good attempt at translating it:

> Now deafening o'er the turbid surge
> Came Terror, full of crashing sounds; his voice
> Shook either shore; as if a whirlwind roar'd
> Impetuous, warring with fierce elements;
> Which bursts the blustering forest, smites away
> The branches, shattering, hurling them afar:
> Then, sweeping clouds of dust, it proudly rears,
> Driving before its fury herds, and flocks,
> And flying shepherds.

In other places he finds it necessary to 'write down' Dante's extravagances. The *nuovo ludo* of cantos XXI and XXII is very restrained; XVIII.114, 'che dalli uman privadi parea mosso', is omitted altogether; XXV.115-7 are omitted and replaced with two lines of his own.

Howard is on the whole accurate, although his padding often obscures the meaning. In quite a few places he does not seem to have taken sufficient trouble to master the meaning of the text. One strange line is (XX.28), 'Pity tho' dead, here mostly seems alive', which, in the Mitchell Library copy of the book, has been cancelled in ink and replaced by 'Rather thou shouldst be dead to pity here'. The worst piece of confusion is at XXXIV.4-7 which is rendered:

> As when heavy clouds
> Breathe darkness, or dense shades converging round
> Benight our hemisphere, what far descried
> Appears a towering windmill whirl'd by blasts,
> Such seemed the wondrous fabric to my gaze.

In a note to XXXI.31 he says 'Dante here mistakes giants for towers, and, in the thirty-fourth canto, a windmill for a giant', quoting Henley's notes to *Vathek* in support, but evidently failing altogether to understand the point of either Dante's lines or Henley's comment.

Howard's eighty pages of notes are over-learned and diffuse, and do little to clarify Dante. He quotes freely in all languages, ancient and modern, including Hebrew, which evidently gave the printer some trouble and involved several entries in the errata.

The *Monthly Review* noticed Howard's book (Oct. 1807) briefly but unenthusiastically. A year later the *British Critic* (Apr. 1808), in a longer article, compared some lines in the earlier cantos with Cary, slightly to the latter's advantage, and concluded rather chillingly:

> We should not, indeed, on the whole, find any material fault with Mr Howard's translation, except that the other having been published before, it appears to be rather superfluous.

The remark is amusing in the light of after-events. In any case the critic could not have examined the two books very carefully, or he would have seen the marked inferiority of Howard in every respect.

JOSEPH HUME (1767-1843)

Hume might well be dismissed in a few lines, but for the century-long confusion of his identity with that of his more famous namesake, which requires a few words of elucidation. The truth about the matter must have been well enough known to contemporaries, but fifty years later, when the fashion of compiling bibliographies began, his memory, like his work, had sunk into oblivion. It was therefore not unnatural that Hume's Inferno, published in 1812, should in the latter part of the century have been attributed to Joseph Hume 'the Radical' (1777-1855). The mistake did not go altogether unquestioned. In *Notes and Queries* (5th ser., Vol. 9, 1878) a correspondent inquired if the Joseph Hume who translated Dante was in fact 'the well-known M.P. of that name', but he gave no reason for his doubt, nor was there any reply. The Mitchell Library, Glasgow, has a copy of Hume's Inferno containing a quaintly worded note beginning: 'Start not reader! this is not the great Joseph lately defunct . . . the Senator was anything but a poet', but it offers no further clue. The seal of authority was set on the wrong attribution by the D.N.B. in 1900, when it included among the Radical's works 'a blank verse translation of Dante'. Paget Toynbee not surprisingly followed this lead (D.E.L. 2, p. 80), and from his bibliography the mistake found its way into others. Meantime, however, the editors of the D.N.B. had discovered the error, which was corrected in a Supplement, and eventually in the 1908 and subsequent editions. Amusingly enough, now that the prestige of the supposed author was removed, they added an adjective to qualify his translation. The new entry reads:

> Another Joseph Hume (1767-1843), a clerk at Somerset House, published in 1812 a bad blank-verse translation of Dante's Inferno, and in 1841 *A Search into the Old Testament*. At his residence, Montpelier House, Notting Hill, there met Lamb, Hazlitt, Godwin and other literary men. One of Hume's daughters was mother of Mrs Augusta Webster, the poetess, and another married Isaac Todhunter, the mathematician.

In 1910 a letter in the *Westminster Gazette* drew attention to the wrong attribution in Toynbee's book, and in the next issue Toynbee himself acknowledged and agreed with the correction, rectifying the error in his subsequent publications. This correspondence is recorded by Arturo Farinelli in his *Dante in Inghilterra* (1922), but in spite of all this the mistake is still current and has been repeated by various writers down to the present day.

Hume's *Search into the Old Testament* is a strange mixture of fundamentalism and rationalism. Though he discourses at great length on the physical events of the Creation, and tries hard to construct a logical genealogy of the patriarchs from their ages as recorded in Genesis (all of which he interprets literally), he asserts unequivocally that the story of Eve and the serpent is allegory, not history, and he discusses the four principal traditions combined in the Pentateuch with almost modern detachment.

Although the original article in the D.N.B. treated the supposed work of 'the Radical' gently, Toynbee had always been outspoken; in the article already cited he says that 'it is probably the worst translation of any portion of Dante's works ever published', and he repeated this statement in his letter to the *Westminster Gazette*. No defender of Hume has, so far as one can find, ever challenged this verdict, although there have been translators since who might well rival him for the lowest place. By whatever standards translations are judged, Hume's must always be one of the worst. His blank verse is appalling, and indeed not worthy of the name. Much of it defies scansion of even the most liberal kind, e.g. (I.22-4):

> As he who wreck escapes and treads breathless
> The shore, his danger distanc'd, turns gazing
> At the terrific sea.

The most baffling and exasperating feature of Hume's verse is the way in which he divides his lines; there are hundreds of examples like the following (XXXI.19-24):

> Raising mine eyes, before them seem'd, and near,
> Huge Tow'rs. 'What country this?' besought I from
> My Bard. 'Thro' such obscurity, and thro'
> A space so long, mis-sent all objects.' (His
> Reply.) 'When nearer . . . '

Hume's cantos are some 20 to 30 lines shorter than Dante's; his most drastic cut is in canto XXIX where he gets 139 lines of the original into 97 of his own. This is not done by omitting any passage, but by leaving out words and phrases, with frequent mutilation of the sense. On the other hand, although he gets the 151 lines of canto XIII into 129 of his own, he uses 10 of these to render the first 6 of Dante's.

As to Hume's accuracy, as can probably be judged even from the short quotations above, he departs so far and so often from the text that it is difficult to know whether he understood it or not. There are some obvious mistakes of comprehension; some of the similes are quite incoherent. Hume's inaccuracy reaches its climax in the last canto which is chaotic. It begins:

> Banners were in the distance waving high
> 'Look forward (said my Guide) th' Infernal King
> Approaching.' Like a huge mill on ev'ning
> Seen obscurely, or in black storm, onward
> He strode.

Hume's footnotes are brief, seldom illuminating, sometimes inaccurate, and occasionally misleading. His sole reference to Beatrice is as 'the poet's mistress'. He is severe on Dante in dealing with the episode of Filippo Argenti, suspicious of his motives in naming Aldobrandi, Rusticucci and others, and censorious of his 'exultations and ejaculations' over the fate of Vanni Fucci. In what appears to be a general statement at the beginning of the footnotes, the translator says:

> The poet is supposed to have aimed at an allegory, which was to refer to his own conduct. But it would be difficult to prove its correctness: and if proved neither the poem nor the reader would probably receive much benefit.

The phraseology of the above is typical of Hume's style, which is very similar in his later *Search into the Old Testament*.

There is really no redeeming feature in Hume's performance. He went mercifully unnoticed alike by contemporary and mid-century critics, and is only of interest as a curiosity.

BIBLIOGRAPHY TO CHAPTER II

ROGERS

The Inferno of Dante Translated. London: Printed by J. Nichols; and sold by
T. Payne and Son, J. Dodsley, B. White, J. Robson, P. Elmsly, C. Dilly, Leigh
and Sotheby, P. Molini and T. Evans. 1782

BOYD

A Translation of the Inferno of Dante Alighieri in English Verse with Historical
Notes, and the life of Dante to which is added, A specimen of a new translation
of the Orlando Furioso of Ariosto. By Henry Boyd, A.M. London: printed
by C. Dilly. 1785, 2 vols.

The Divina Commedia of Dante Alighieri consisting of the Inferno – Purgatorio –
and Paradiso. Translated into English Verse, with preliminary essays, notes,
and illustrations, by the Rev. Henry Boyd, A.M., Chaplain to the Right Honour-
able the Lord Viscount Charleville. London: Printed by A. Strahan for T.
Cadell Jun. and W. Davies. 1802, 3 vols.

CARY

*The Inferno of Dante Alighieri, with a translation into English blank verse, notes
and a life of the author by the Rev. Henry Francis Cary, A.M. London: printed
for James Carpenter. 2 vols, 1805-6

The Vision: or, Hell, Purgatory, and Paradise, of Dante Alighieri. Translated by
the Rev. H. F. Cary, A.M. London: Printed for the author by J. Barfield.
1814, 3 vols.

The Vision: or Hell, Purgatory and Paradise, of Dante Alighieri. Translated by the
Rev. Henry Francis Cary, A.M. The second edition corrected. With the life of
Dante, additional notes, and an index. London: Printed for Taylor and Hessey.
1819, 3 vols. (This edition was reprinted in 1831 without revision under the
imprint of John Taylor.)

The Vision; or Hell, Purgatory and Paradise, of Dante Alighieri. Translated by
the Rev. Henry Francis Cary, A.M. A new edition, corrected. With the life
of Dante, chronological view of his age, additional notes and index. London:
William Smith. 1844. (Simultaneously with the above a cheaper edition,
with two columns on each page, was issued by the same publisher.)

The above are the editions published during the translator's lifetime. There
have been many since in Britain, America and elsewhere, in a wide range of
sizes and styles; it has also been included in many popular series.

HOWARD

The Inferno of Dante Alighieri, Translated into English blank-verse, with notes,
historical, classical, and explanatory, and a life of the author by Nathaniel
Howard. London: Printed for John Murray; and A. Constable & Co., Edinburgh. 1807

HUME

Inferno: A Translation from Dante Alighieri into English blank verse by Joseph
Hume Esq. London: Printed for T. Cadell and W. Davies. 1812

* includes Italian text

CHAPTER III

FIRST EFFORTS AT RHYME

IT was inevitable that before long some translator would attempt the task of reproducing Dante's original rhyme scheme in English. It was not till 1843 that a complete cantica was published in this form, but there had been numerous earlier experiments. A few months before Rogers' Inferno in blank verse appeared, William Hayley (1745-1820) published his *Essay on Epic Poetry* (1782) which contained an English version of Inferno I-III in terza rima. Hayley, a minor poet, a friend of Cowper, an encourager of Cary, and an intimate of the 'Swan of Lichfield', was undeservedly maligned for his genuinely kind-hearted efforts to help Blake. In addition to poetry he wrote biographies of Milton, Cowper and Romney. He is perhaps best known from Southey's remark that 'there is nothing bad about the man except his poetry', a verdict which Saintsbury confirmed later; but if he was a failure from the literary point of view he had other qualities that gained him respect and affection, for Cary, writing to the *London Magazine* after his death, said of him:

> In one respect he is deserving of most honourable notice. During the course of a long literary life, I doubt whether he was ever provoked to use a single word of asperity or sarcasm towards any of his contemporaries.

Justice has recently been done to him in a biography, *Blake's Hayley* (1951), by Morchard Bishop (pseudonym of Oliver Stonor). Toynbee remarks of Hayley's cantos that they are 'not without merit', and they are certainly as good as those of some later practitioners. Inf. II.1-9 is quoted as a specimen, but it will be seen that Hayley has quite misunderstood line 6.

> The day was sinking, and the dusky air
>   On all the animals of earth bestow'd
>   Rest from their labours. I alone prepare
> To meet new toil, both from my dreary road,
>   And pious wish to paint in worthy phrase
>   The Unerring Mind, and his divine abode.
> O Sacred Muses! now my genius raise!
>   O Memory, who writest what I saw,
>   From hence shall spring thy ever-during praise.

Byron and Shelley were both interested, but their contributions to Dante translation were slight. The former composed his indifferent terza rima version of Inf. V.97-142 in 1820, but it was not published till ten years later. Shelley in the same year made a draft of Purg. XXVIII.1-51, also in terza rima, which Medwin published in 1834. The rendering of the Ugolino episode printed in Shelley's works is mainly by Medwin.

In 1836 there was published a terza rima translation of Inferno I-X; the title page gives the author's name as Odoardo Volpi, but his real name, Edward N. Shannon, is disclosed in a postscript. An introduction of 33 pages is devoted to criticism of his predecessors, especially Cary. His tone is carping and his style impudent. Quoting Cary's Inf. I.22, 'And as a man, with difficult short breath . . . ', he asks: 'Did Mr Cary wish us to think that the poor man was asthmatic before he got into the sea?' Shannon's own translation is, however, worthless.

Much more interesting and meritorious are the terza rima fragments of John Herman Merivale (1779-1844), a native of Exeter, and a lawyer by profession. He was a good scholar, and a volume of translations from the Greek Anthology, published in 1806, in collaboration with Robert Bland, brought the authors a tribute from Byron in *English Bards and Scotch Reviewers*; later Byron said of Merivale's *Orlando in Roncesvalles*: 'You have written a very noble poem.' In 1838 Merivale published two volumes of *Poems Original and Translated*; these contained terza rima versions of thirteen portions of the Divine Comedy, including three complete cantos (Inf. III, X and XIII). This work was well reviewed; several writers expressed the hope that the author would complete the whole Comedy, but no more appeared. Merivale's fragments read well, though they are Augustan in style and conventional in phrasing and vocabulary. He had observed in his preface that Cary's 'Miltonic style' was at variance with 'the true character of the Divine Comedy', but he was not averse to borrowing from it, as the following specimen (Inf. III.1-9) shows:

> Through me ye pass into the realm of woe;
> > Through me ye pass, eternal pain to prove;
> > Through me amidst the ruin'd race ye go:
> Justice my heavenly builder first did move;
> > My mighty fabric Power Divine did rear,
> > Supremest Wisdom and Primaeval Love.
> None but eternal things created were
> > Before me; and, eternal, I endure.
> > All hope abandon, ye who enter here!

Merivale's collaborator, Robert Bland, teacher and clergyman, who died young in 1825, was also interested in Dante. In an article in the *Quarterly Review* (Apr. 1814, pp. 10ff) he included seven fragments of the Divine Comedy, but these correspond closely to Merivale's, and the two may have worked on them together.

James Henry Leigh Hunt (1784-1859) may be dealt with here. He had a good knowledge of Italian and considerable interest in Dante, as is evidenced by his *Story of Rimini* (1816) based on the episode of Francesca in Inf. V. Hunt's works are interspersed with quotations from Dante, in blank verse, couplets, terza rima and prose. These are collected, together with a prose summary of the Comedy, in his *Stories from the Italian Poets* (1846). But although he praised Dante often and discerningly, some aspects of the Comedy filled Hunt with a disgust and horror that he could not conceal, and at the end of the Inferno he wrote:

> At the close of this medley of genius, pathos, absurdity, sublimity, horror and revoltingness, it is impossible for any reflecting heart to avoid asking, *Cui bono?* What is the good of it to the poor wretches, if we are to suppose it true? and what to the world – except, indeed, as a poetic study and a warning against degrading notions of God – if we are to take it simply as a fiction?

Equally strong language is used regarding Purgatory and Paradise – so many pages of it indeed that mere quotation will hardly do it justice. It is interesting to observe that a fitting rejoinder to this outburst was made, not by a theologian, or even by a Christian, but by a young agnostic, Charles Bagot Cayley, who wrote in the preface to his own translation that Hunt

> evidently translates Dante with a peculiar reluctance and disrelish . . . for a utilitarian philanthropist must always have a mean idea of the Singer of God's righteousness, . . . who proclaims a principle of retribution to overrule the 'greatest happiness of the greatest number'.

Although no British translator of this period refers to them, the Germans had already produced several translations of Dante in terza rima. A. W. von Schlegel, between 1791 and 1799, rendered selections amounting to some 1,500 lines in 'defective' terza rima, i.e. with the middle line of each tercet unrhymed, a system followed by some later translators and known in Germany as 'Schlegelische terzine'. Karl Edmund published selections from the Inferno in full terza rima in 1803, and during 1803-5 August Bode produced a terza rima version of Inf. I-XXIV. Then came two complete Comedies, fully rhymed: Kannegießer's in 1809-21 and Streckfuß's in 1824-6. By the time Dayman's Inferno appeared in England, there were still two more in

Germany: a complete Comedy by von Berneck in 1840 and Graul's Inferno in 1843.

The pioneers in English were I. C. Wright, Dayman and Cayley. The former was first in the field, but he used a simplified system of rhyme which earned him some obloquy. Dayman's Inferno was published in 1843, so that although his complete Comedy was delayed till 1865, when there were many others in print, his proper place is with the founders of the terza rima tradition. Cayley started a few years behind Dayman, but he worked quickly, so that by 1854 he had acquired the distinction, by a margin of nine years, of being the first writer to render the entire Comedy in English terza rima. By the 1860s the 'mass production' of terza rima versions was in full swing, and the consideration of these other practitioners, from 1854 onwards, is deferred to a later chapter.

ICHABOD CHARLES WRIGHT (1795-1871)

Wright was born at Mapperly Hall, Nottinghamshire, being the son of the owner of a banking business in the county town. He was educated at Eton and Christ Church, Oxford, and from 1819 to 1825 he held a fellowship at Magdalen. In the latter year he married and became partner and joint manager in the family business. Banking was his primary occupation for the remainder of his life; the extent of his knowledge is evidenced by several books and pamphlets, one of which, *Evils of the Currency* (1847), went through six editions in eight years. In 1833 Wright published a rhymed translation of Dante's Inferno, followed by the Purgatorio in 1836 and the Paradiso in 1840. A second revised edition in three volumes followed in 1845, and in 1854, the third edition, further revised, was published as a single volume in Bohn's Library. In 1859 Wright began to issue a blank verse translation of the Iliad, which reached Book XIV in 1864 but was not continued. Matthew Arnold said of it, in his essay 'On Translating Homer' (1861) that it 'had no proper reason for existing', a criticism which Wright resented and contested.

Wright's version of Dante was printed just as the Italian usually is, continuously, indented in terzina form, the number of lines corresponding exactly with the original. The rhyme scheme, however, is *a b a c b c*, so that in effect it consists of a series of six-line stanzas with no rhyme linkage between them. It was thus only necessary to find two rhyming words instead of three in each sound, and also each group of six lines could be dealt with separately. The only place where a triple rhyme had to be found was at the end of a canto containing an even number of terzine; in that case there is an odd terminal line which rhymes with the middle lines of the two preceding groups of three. Where the number of terzine is odd the last four lines form a quatrain rhymed *a b a b*. At first sight there is a fair resemblance to the rhyme scheme of the Comedy, but the difference is soon detected. Though it may not be readily noticed in a series of isolated terzine, or where Wright's group of six corresponds to a similar group in the original, in many other cases the complete break in the rhymes becomes obvious and gives a sense of incompleteness and dissatisfaction. Nowhere in his various prefaces did Wright make any reference to his metrical scheme; this probably led many readers to assume that he had reproduced that of the original. It also caused some critics to hint at deliberate deception on the translator's part. It would certainly have been better if he had frankly defended his choice; he must have been conscious of the desirability of some reference to so important a matter.

When Wright's Inferno first appeared the *Athenaeum* (23 Mar. 1833, pp. 177-8) gave him high praise, finding him 'as exact as the most scrupulous admirer of the great Florentine could desire' and successful in preserving Dante's 'grandeur and force'. The *Monthly Review* (Mar. 1833, pp. 428-9) was only slightly less complimentary: it found 'the measure adopted . . . well suited to the nature of the subject' and the whole handled 'with great ease and simplicity of expression'. The *Edinburgh Review* (July 1833, pp. 413ff) not only noticed the rhyme scheme but commended it; Wright had 'very luckily solved the problem of the English terza rima' and secured freedom 'by throwing off one of the rhymes (which nobody will miss)'. Reviewing Wright's Paradiso the *Dublin University Magazine* (Nov. 1840, pp. 590-1) went further and thought Wright's rhyme scheme an improvement on Dante's. But a very different note was sounded in the *Quarterly Review* (July 1833, pp. 449ff) when it dealt with Wright's Inferno; not only his ability, but his honesty, were impugned in terms no less effective because of their urbanity. As literary criticism this article is really worthless, for it is merely one of the manoeuvres which distinguished the war between the *Quarterly* and the *Edinburgh*, and Wright's political affiliations, which were well to the left, though not mentioned, are the real target. The *Edinburgh* had concluded its review with the hope that Wright would proceed to complete his translation. The *Quarterly* began:

> The most cursory perusal of Mr Wright's Inferno will satisfy every one that, had there been no Cary, this work would have been a valuable addition to the English library. But with every disposition to encourage

any gentleman in an elegant pursuit, it is our duty to ask, in how far, Cary's volumes being in every collection, it was worth Mr Wright's while to undertake a new version?

This polite contempt is continued for a page or so and then, Wright's literary reputation having been undermined, his character is attacked by suggesting that his translation is a wholesale plagiarism of Cary's, to which end a great array of italicised words is used, but not a single concrete instance given. There is then an attack on the metrical form, and the concluding sentence is:

> The result, then, is not an English Inferno in the measure of Dante, instead of the measure of Milton; but only the sense of Cary twisted out of blank verse into a new and anomalous variety of English rhyme.

A careful examination shows, however, that there is no substance whatever in the *Quarterly*'s allegation that 'Cary has been in the main the Dante of Mr Wright'. Such resemblances as exist are much less striking than those observed between other translations where no borrowing could possibly have taken place.

Wright was an indefatigable reviser, and the alterations to the text in the second and third editions show that he had gone through the whole poem very carefully. The Inferno, in particular, contains nearly one fourth of new matter in the second edition. One reason for this is that he had been criticised for repeating sets of rhymes at too frequent intervals; he had avoided this fault in the Purgatorio and Paradiso, and now he rectified it in the Inferno. Apart from this he remodelled many stanzas in all three cantiche, and in the 1854 edition there was a further series of minor changes.

Even greater alterations were made in his introductory matter and his notes, all of which were completely rewritten for each successive edition. One effect of this was to make their sturdy Protestantism progressively less belligerent. References to the papacy, the Roman Catholic Church, Mariolatry, and so on, disappear almost entirely from the revised notes; there are still some side-thrusts in the second edition, but these have all gone by 1854. There are similar modifications in the introductory matter. These modifications may well be due to pressure from his publishers, rather than to any change in Wright's opinions.

Wright's metrical scheme can hardly be regarded as a success. Its effect in emphasising six-line units which often do not correspond to any such division in the original is irksome, and breaks the continuity even more than does the complete omission of the middle rhyme in the Schlegelian scheme. Moreover, the advantages conferred by the simplification of the task for the reasons already referred to seem to have encouraged a fatal fluency so that, although the verse flows smoothly, it often lacks vigour.

Whatever we may think of Cayley's taste in criticising his predecessors by way of introduction to his own translation, he had a knack of hitting the nail on the head. His remarks are quoted on p. 41; not only does he very neatly expose Wright's 'counterfeit' prosody, but he lays his finger on the other fundamental weakness of the earlier version when he speaks of its 'boarding-school or family-Shakespeare etiquette'. Doubtless Wright felt justified in toning down such things as the mutilations of Inf. XXVIII and the references to Pasiphae in Purg. XXVI. He may likewise have considered that his 'Let him wince who feels himself reproved' was an elegant substitute for 'e lascia pur grattar dov'è la rogna' (Par. XVII.129). But his failure or unwillingness to render the vigour of Dante's expressions goes far deeper than the avoidance of what he may have thought occasional crudities. Again and again he uses some commonplace or cliché to replace Dante's direct forcefulness, and examples like the above, or 'In envy's full blown sighs they ever end' for 'Invidia move il mantaco a' sospiri' (Purg. XV.51), could be culled from every canto.

Wright must have read a good deal of poetry, for he is constantly echoing the words and manner of earlier writers, sometimes deliberately, oftener perhaps subconsciously, and seldom discriminatingly. His borrowed plumage is rather obvious when he renders the simple 'se fossi morto' of Purg. XI.104 by 'whether . . . thou shuffle off thy mortal coil'. Dante apostrophises Virgil as 'Or living man, or melancholy ghost' (Inf. I.66). The fiends on the walls of Dis inquire 'who is this, that . . . / Stalks through the dusky regions of the dead?' (Inf. VIII.84-5). It is unlikely that anyone could place the line 'Waving the wreath of glory round my head' as representing Purg. XXI.99. In Par. V.16-17 Beatrice 'poured along / The holy strain in smooth unbroken course'. One of the worst lapses is Inf. XXI.68-9 where 'il poverello' becomes 'one of squalid looks / Who begs a pittance at some rich man's door'. Wright has a sprinkling of savourless archaisms, and often uses forms like 'I ween', 'eyne', 'hight', 'dight', etc. for the sake of the rhyme.

Wright has not many direct mistranslations. He had an advantage over Cary in the availability of improved readings and commentaries; he corrects some of Cary's mistakes, preserves others, and occasionally introduces a new one of his own. In the more involved passages he is often obscure and inaccurate, but this is no doubt partly due to the difficulty of working the meaning into the verse.

Wright has some good terzine, e.g. Inf. X.34-6:

> Already on his face my eyesight fell;
> And he upreared his forehead and his breast
> As if he felt supreme contempt for Hell.

To illustrate one of the better sustained passages, we quote Wright's version of Par. XVII.106-20.

> 'Sire,' I began, 'I mark how time for me
> Prepares a blow that heaviest falls on those
> Who look for it with most despondency:
> Therefore with foresight let me arm my breast,
> That if I lose the place I cherish most,
> The boldness of my verse lose not the rest.
> Down in the world of endless misery,
> And on the mountain, from whose beauteous coast
> The eyes of Beatrice exalted me; –
> And as through heaven I passed from sphere to sphere,
> That did I learn, which, were I to disclose,
> To many would of bitter taste appear.
> But if the truth I timidly unfold,
> I fear to die in the esteem of those
> To whom the present time will soon be old.'

Wright's translation, though popular in its day, has not survived the test of time like Cary's. At its best it is smooth and easily read, but it lacks fidelity and vigour. Wright was a disciple of the Augustans, and he followed a convention rather than a tradition. Yet his achievement, considering he had few predecessors to fall back on, commands respect; and in fairness it must be recorded that, though he touches no heights, he maintains on the whole a respectable level.

JOHN DAYMAN (1802-71)

The translator was the eldest son of another John Dayman, who belonged to St Columb in Cornwall. The younger John graduated at Corpus Christi College, Oxford, where he was elected a Fellow in 1825, and he was presented to the College living of Skelton, Cumberland, which he held till his death. His Inferno, published in 1843, was the first version of a complete cantica in English terza rima. By the time he published his completed Comedy in 1865 several other renderings in triple rhyme had appeared.

Dayman's 1843 preface is very short. He mentions that:

> In justice to myself, no less than others, I have rightly abstained from
> making any acquaintance with the English translations which have pre-

ceded this; and hence the candid reader will refer whatever coincidences he may discover to our common original.

In the much longer preface to the 1865 volume he sets forth, briefly and well, the poetic qualities of Dante's Comedy. He goes on to justify his use of terza rima, arguing that the 'organic' form of a work of art is an essential part of it, and thence that terza rima is an indispensable element in the 'ternary' structure of the original. He repeats his disclaimer as to knowledge of other translations, and then gives a brief outline of Dante's life.

There seems to be no valid reason for doubting Dayman's assertion that he had abstained from making acquaintance with the work of his predecessors. Indeed the point need not have been raised, were it not for the remarks of Ichabod Charles Wright, placed on record by Toynbee (D.E.L. 2, p. 680n), and thence copied by other writers. These remarks were not published, but written in the margins of a copy of Dayman's Inferno belonging to Wright. They include such expressions as 'my word', 'my rhyme', 'my line', 'suspicious', 'most suspicious'; while against the preface he notes: 'Pretends ignorance of my translation, though it had been published ten years, – reviewed in almost all the reviews – and quoted in numerous works.' He refers to Dayman's work as 'a burlesque upon Dante; rhyme without either sense or poetry, a mere verbal translation'. These peevish remarks are indicative rather of Wright's pettiness than Dayman's duplicity. A careful examination shows that the accusations are quite groundless. It must be remembered too that Wright took no steps to make them public, and these notes were perhaps just a way of 'letting off steam' when he was smarting under equally unjust charges of plagiarism made against himself.

Both Dayman's volumes were well received by the reviewers. The *Spectator* (19 Aug. 1843) thought his extreme literalness 'not only fair, but useful, as bringing the translation closer to the text', and concluded that 'Dayman gives the English reader a better idea of Dante, his matter and manner, than any previous translator'. The *Athenaeum* (23 Mar. 1844, pp. 267-8) found Dayman a worthy successor to Cary and Wright, 'a sincere, earnest and laborious effort; sufficiently learned and accurate, with the additional advantage of its being in the measure of the original'. Dealing with the complete Comedy (3 Feb. 1866, pp. 170-1) the same paper said that it possessed 'many beauties of style which still improve upon acquaintance'. A less favourable view of the Inferno was taken by the *Westminster Review* (Jan. 1861, pp. 201ff) when it surveyed English versions of Dante from Cary onwards; while agreeing that the version was 'on the whole, decidedly good' the critic added: 'He fails, however, very often in detail, and misses both the sense and the spirit of the Italian.' In June 1867 (pp. 736ff) *Blackwood's Magazine* published a long article on 'Dante in English terza rima' which considers Cayley and Dayman 'incomparably the best terza rima translators of the Divine Comedy', going on to demonstrate the final superiority of Dayman. It is lavish in its admiration, and quotes numerous passages as worthy of high praise. One of these (Inf. III.1-9) might, strangely enough, have been picked to show Dayman at his worst, for it is sheer doggerel:

> Through me the path to city named of Wail;
> Through me the path to woe without remove;
> Through me the path to damned souls in bale!
> Justice inclined my Maker from above;
> I am by virtue of the Might Divine,
> The Supreme Wisdom, and the Primal Love.
> Created birth none antedates to mine,
> Save endless things, and endless I endure:
> Ye that are entering – all hope resign.

The other passage (Purg. VIII.1-18) is definitely Dayman at his best; indeed it is a favourable example of the average achievement of the mid-century terza rima translators, and of some of their successors as well:

> 'Twas now the hour the longing heart that bends
> In voyagers, and meltingly doth sway,
> Who bade farewell at morn to gentle friends;
> And wounds the pilgrim newly bound his way
> With poignant love, to hear some distant bell
> That seems to mourn the dying of the day;
> When I began to slight the sounds that fell
> Upon mine ear, one risen soul to view,
> Whose beckoning hand our audience would compel.
> It joined both palms together and upthrew,
> The fixed eyes eastward bent, as though it said
> To God, 'With other I have nought to do.'
> *Thee ere the light fail* from the lips was sped
> In tones so dulcet, so devoutly sung,
> As me from out myself entrancing led;
> And with as dulcet and devout a tongue
> Followed the rest through all that hymn complete,
> Their eyes upon those orbs supernal hung.

The verdict of posterity has been heavily against Dayman, and his translation is forgotten. The most we can say in its praise is that it is slightly better than some others of the period. Dayman may have appreciated the poetic value of his original, but for the most part he fails to convey any notion of it into English; and he often obscures Dante's direct vigour by the shifts and turns to which he is driven in the search for rhyme. He also fails to preserve the ternary structure on which he lays such stress; over-running is frequent, sometimes with very awkward enjambement. He is less profuse in his archaisms than Cayley, but his work is sprinkled with such words as 'ween', 'wot', 'meseems', 'bespake' (very frequent), 'hight', etc., and quite a few more recondite expressions like 'a teacher well ared', 'our limbs 'gan upward hoise', 'devoir', 'chode', 'mansionry', and such a desperate rhyming expedient as 'to support my smile unshent' (Par. XXIII.48). Often he puts an accent on a word to denote an unfamiliar pronunciation, e.g. 'sùccessor', 'spirìtual', and he is fond of forms like 'upcome', 'uprush', 'upthrust'. His rhymes are on the whole good, but sometimes he is hard put to it, as in Inf. IX.16-18:

> Came ever one to this profounder cave
>   Of the sad shell, from that first-entered room,
>   Whose only curse, to be for hope a grave?

There is much awkwardness and obscurity, and often passages can only be unravelled by reference to the Italian, e.g.

> And I could tell how – but for arrowy sleet
>   Of native flames shot hence – it more became
>   Thyself than these with eagerness to meet.   (Inf. XVI.16-18)

> Of Peter hold I them, who bade ward ill,
>   When souls abased themselves my feet before,
>   Rather by opening than by closing still.   (Purg. IX.127-9)

> Lost Cleopatra yet hath cause to mourn
>   Those deeds, preferring (while she fled before)
>   The aspic's fell and sudden death to scorn.   (Par. VI.76-8)

Even more depressing is the frequency with which Dayman spoils a notable line by using a wrong word, e.g. (Par. XX.10-12):

> Since all those living lustres, while they flushed
>   More brilliant yet, prelusive warblings quired,
>   That gliding all too fleet for memory gushed.

Now and again Dayman has some really good verses. Majestic gloom seems to suit him, as in Inf. VI.94-9:

> 'Henceforth he wakes no more,' the master said,
>   'Until the angelic trumpet burst the gloom;
>   When He shall come, the Avenging Power they dread,

These shall revisit each his joyless tomb,
Put on his flesh and form, and hear the sound
That thunders through eternity his doom.'

Dayman is in general accurate, and seems to have studied and understood his text adequately. He has corrected some of the inferior readings and interpretations which occur in Cary and Wright, and the revision of his Inferno in the 1865 edition shows that he made some further improvements in this direction. There are some obvious errors, hardly worth enumerating, and also some apparent mistranslations which are probably misprints, of which there are too many. Although the errata list (not itself free from error) contains 32 entries it is by no means complete. Faulty line numbering is also a cause of confusion in many cantos from the point of view of reference.

The words of the *Athenaeum* reviewer, 'a sincere, earnest, and laborious effort; sufficiently learned and accurate', are, if we cut them off at that point, as just an epitaph as could be devised for Dayman.

CHARLES BAGOT CAYLEY (1823-83)

Cayley was born near St Petersburg where his father was in business, but educated in Britain. From Blackheath he went to King's College, London, and thence to Trinity College, Cambridge, where he gained a second class classical tripos in 1845. From that time onward he settled down to 'the quiet and unpretentious life of a scholar' as one of his obituaries put it. He was long a familiar figure in the reading room of the British Museum, and he had his lodgings in Bloomsbury near by. The first volume of his translation of Dante appeared in 1851, when he was only twenty-eight, and the whole, together with a 400-page volume of Notes, was completed by 1855. Other books followed: a volume of verse, *Psyche's Interludes* (1857), a metrical Psalter (1860), various translations including *Prometheus Bound* (1876) and the *Iliad* (1877), and finally the *Sonnets and Stanzas* of Petrarch (1879).

Cayley sought instruction in Italian and aid in the study of Dante at the fountainhead, for in 1847 he was one of the few pupils whom Gabriele Rossetti, by that time in failing health, still received at Charlotte Street. Here Cayley met Christina Georgina, then only seventeen, and probably fell in love with her immediately; but he was shy and diffident, and it was not till many years later, after the Collinson episode, that he declared himself. Christina left it on record that Cayley had 'much endeared himself' to the family, and William Michael indicates that she took a great interest in the translation of Dante. Eventually a formal proposal of marriage by Cayley was rejected, evidently on account of religious scruples such as had preserved her from a union with Collinson. This time it was the fact that Cayley was not a member of any Christian church that deterred her – did she see herself in the role of her brother's Blessed Damozel? William Michael did his best to encourage the match, even offering the couple the hospitality of his house, but Christina remained inflexible. There can be no doubt that there was deep mutual affection, and when Cayley died Christina, in accordance with his will, became his literary executor and heir. Eleven years later, in her own last days, she spoke of him with deep contrition and regard, and it is likely that expressions of love in some of her poems refer to him.

Cayley's translation of Dante was introduced by a brief but vigorous preface, couched in tones that seem aggressively out of character with what we know of his quiet nature; it may well be that he did not realise that such a prelude to his own translation was in questionable taste. Having deplored the present 'public state of apathy and uncertainty on the canons and value of translation', and the need for reform, he says frankly that the reasons for his own venture are to be sought 'among the defects attributable to our chief predecessors'. He allows some merit to Merivale and Dayman, although he has abstained from reading more than a few pages of the latter, but he is severe in his criticism of Cary, Wright and Carlyle. Here occurs his celebrated retort to Leigh Hunt already mentioned. Cayley feels that Cary, in trying to give the poem a uniformly dignified tone, has 'adulterated all its franker style with the pomp and stiffness of our traditional epic poems'. As for Wright,

> he seems chiefly to have rivalled his predecessor by persuading the public that he had imitated the versification of Dante's poem, which he has indeed counterfeited to the eye, although the reading of a few triplets will show that he has adopted a much poorer and looser metre. . . . Besides Wright's language is sometimes terribly weakened by a boarding-school or family-Shakespeare etiquette.

Of Carlyle's version he says that 'there is something in its language or style that reminds us more of the writer's celebrated brother, the author of *Sartor Resartus*, than of the style of Dante'. And he adds:

> Many passages have required, under Mr J. Carlyle's treatment, to be doubly rendered, that is literally in the text, and more perspicuously in the notes, or vice versa . . . whereas a decided literary version should require no notes that are merely exegetic, and its text should be 'in seipso totus, teres atque rotundus'.

Cayley then remarks that

> all the allegorical proper names in the poem which are of Italian forma-
> tion should be replaced by English, or, if need be, by Greek or Latin
> equivalents intelligible in a classical day-school,

and he refers to Inf. XXII for an illustration of his method in this
respect. He ends confidently by appealing to the judgment of

> the ermine-robed great world, for whose approval I am but provisionally
> encouraged to hope by the kind criticisms ... of Signor Rossetti, and by
> other gentlemen of known literary attainments and no shallow acquain-
> tance with this subject.

The *Athenaeum* reviewer (6 Sep. 1851, pp. 941-2) regretted the style
of the preface:

> It is by no means well written; and it breathes a tone of more pretension
> than would be expected from one who had been walking with the august
> Florentine in the right way.

Nevertheless he finds that the translation itself is

> to our mind by far the most effectual transcript of the original that has
> yet appeared in English verse. One main ground of his superiority to
> previous translators lies in the true perception that nothing but plain and
> bald language in the copy can represent the bold plainness of the original.

The *Dublin University Magazine* (Sep. 1853, pp. 253ff) thought that
Cayley was 'meritorious, but has many awkward and inelegant inversions and transpositions'. The *North British Review* (Aug. 1854, pp.
541ff) found his use of terza rima 'not very successful' and objected to
his archaisms. As late as 1867 the article already mentioned on 'Dante
in English terza rima' in *Blackwood's* placed Cayley next to Dayman,
but took exception to his archaisms and colloquialisms, over-Latinis-
ation and loose rhymes.

Cayley has all these faults, but the worst feature of his translation is
the one hinted at by the Dublin reviewer: his inversions and contor-
tions in fitting sense to metre and rhyme effectively squeeze out all the
poetry. He is, indeed, more unscrupulous than Dayman in this respect,
as the following examples show:

> He shall this humble Italy deliver,
>   For which Euryalus, Nisus, Turnus, fell
>   Bewounded, and Camilla knew man never.   (Inf. I.106-8)

> Is breach so made in statutes of the deep,
>   Or change of new decrees in heaven enrolled,
>   That damnèd you upon my bulwarks peep?   (Purg. I.46-8)

No farther ever climbeth arid gas,
    Than by the topmost of the stairs before-
    Named, where his feet St Peter's vicar has. (Purg. XXI.52-4)

The rhymes are indeed very loose, as *Blackwood's* noticed; we have
such pairs as 'kept – intellect', 'firm – discern', 'attend – condemned',
'lament – exempt'. We also have a numerous and often astonishing
variety of double rhymes, a feature, as we shall see, developed even
further by some of Cayley's successors. Thus to suit 'Lucca – Gen-
tucca' he has 'which makes them each to look a / Grape with its husks
out' (Purg. XXV.39). In Par. XV.125-6 we have 'and amongst her
maidens tell a / Tale of the Romans . . . ' to rhyme with 'Salterello –
Cianghella'. A curious case arises in Purg. XXVI.37ff:

    Then from the friendly greeting all again
        Dispart themselves, and take not leisure for a
        Step only, when they call, with might and main,
    The later comers, 'Sodom and Gomorra',
        The former gang, 'Pasiphae,   *   *
    *   *   *   *   *   *   *

The next line is 43, which ends in 'haste'. Whether Cayley had words
in his mind which he did not print is hard to tell. There are two other
instances where words are replaced by asterisks, viz. line 87 of the
same canto, 'che s'imbestiò nelle 'mbestiate schegge', and lines 100-2
of Par. XII, which refer to Dominic's attacks on heretics. There is no
remark in the notes, and it is strange that Cayley, who objects to Wright
translating 'la meretrice' as 'that wicked meretricious dame', should be
squeamish about putting these lines into English.

There are a number of unintentional omissions, later detected and
supplied in the notes. The worst is in Inf. X where lines 106-14 are
missing; the others are single terzine. In all cases but one a rhyme
change has to be given to link up, and of course the omissions throw out
the line numbering of the cantos, to the confusion of references. Otherwise the printing is accurate, with quotation marks correctly placed.

In fulfilment of his promise in the preface, Cayley performs some
strange feats with proper names. The defiant thief of Inf. XXIV is
John Futchi. Malebolge is Evilpits, and the demons are anglicised to
names like Mammock-hound or Hellenised to others like Choeroides.

As a representative specimen of a sustained passage we quote Cayley's version of Inf. XXVI.106-20:

    And I and all my crew were age-opprest
        And stiffened, when we reached that narrow strait,
        Where Hercules his bounding columns placed,

That man should never further penetrate;
And passing Seville now upon the right,
And Ceuta towards the left of ocean's gate,
'O comrades, who to this far-west, in spite,'
Said I, 'of danger's million threats have run
For this brief gloaming of perception's light
That we inherit still, ere life is done,
Be loth to abdicate the experience
Of yon unpeopled world behind the sun;
Consider that original from whence
Ye spring, to live not like the beasts, but strain
After all knowledge and all excellence.'

Cayley's volume of Notes is a testimonial to his industry and thoroughness. The notes are mainly factual, giving information as to the persons and incidents in the poem; occasionally they deal with allegory and interpretation; literary judgments are rare. Cayley does not show much interest in Dante as a poet. Sometimes he is betrayed into observations that seem to reflect his personal problems, the most remarkable of which is appended to Purg. XXVII.49:

In representing himself to have tasted the torments of this circle, Dante is said to have avowed, in a marked manner, his proneness to unchaste desires. Yet as he apparently intimates that there is no gap in the flames, – whence we must conceive that every soul, in emerging from Purgatory, passes through them however rapidly, as does on this occasion the grave Virgil with the modest and conjugal Statius, – shall we not say that the poet convicts mankind in general, rather than his individual self, of lewdness in deeds, words, or thoughts? We must allow, of course, that there are some spirits who do not go through Purgatory, and among these, for the sake of women's honour, let every gentle reader include his Beatrice.

To the Purgatory is appended a discussion of the interpretation of the poem, based on the 'four senses' referred to in the Convito. Various authorities are quoted, showing that Cayley had read widely, and several pages are devoted to the role of Beatrice in cantos XXX-XXXIII.

Cayley's translation of Dante is scarcely readable today. He never seems really to have faced the task of devising an English vehicle for the poem; he is content to twist the literal meaning into a frame of recurring stresses and rhymes, perhaps without realising what this distortion involves. The dates of publication suggest too that he may have worked too fast. Had he not embarked on the task so young he might have done better; his last work, Petrarch's sonnets, shows some improvement in technique, and is better than his Dante.

BIBLIOGRAPHY TO CHAPTER III

WRIGHT

The Inferno of Dante, translated by Ichabod Charles Wright, M.A. London: Longmans. 1833

The Purgatorio of Dante, as above. 1836

The Paradiso of Dante, as above. 1840

Dante. Translated by Ichabod Charles Wright, M.A. A new edition revised and corrected. London: Longmans. 1845

Dante. Translated into English Verse, by I. C. Wright, M.A. Third edition. London: Henry G. Bohn. 1854. (There were several subsequent impressions of this edition, the later ones bearing the imprint of G. Bell & Sons, but all were from the original plates.)

DAYMAN

The Inferno of Dante Alighieri, translated in the terza rima of the original with notes and appendix by John Dayman, M.A. London: William Edward Painter. 1843

The Divine Comedy of Dante Alighieri, translated in terza rima by John Dayman, M.A. London: Longmans. 1865

CAYLEY

Dante's Divine Comedy, translated in the original ternary rhyme by C. B. Cayley, B.A. London: Longmans, 4 volumes: The Vision of Hell, 1851; The Purgatory, 1853; The Paradise, 1854; Notes on the Translation, 1855.

CHAPTER IV

FIRST TRANSLATIONS IN PROSE

D URING a period of nearly a hundred years after the appearance of Rogers' Inferno only two versions of one or more complete cantiche of the Divine Comedy were published in English prose. There were, of course, numerous prose renderings of passages, occurring in critical works by way of illustration. We know also of at least one eighteenth-century prose translation that has been lost. Madame d'Arblay in her *Memoirs of Dr Burney* says that her father, Charles Burney, as a distraction for his grief after the death of his first wife, made a prose version of the Inferno. No trace of it has ever been found, and all that is known of the matter is recorded by Toynbee (D.E.L. 1, pp. 323-5). Toynbee also mentions (D.S. p. 206) a prose translation of Inf. I-XVII by P. Hawke, who was a professor of drawing at Angers *c.* 1830-48. The unpublished manuscript is said to be in the Bibliothèque d'Angers, but no further information is available. In 1842 Charles Hindley published his *Plain and Direct Translation of the Inferno of Dante* which, however, ends at IV.57. Nothing is known of the writer. Toynbee's account of him (D.E.L. 2, pp. 666-9) includes a specimen of the translation which is neither accurate nor elegant. A highly unfavourable press mention of it is quoted in the article on O'Donnell later in this chapter.

Meanwhile both French and German readers were well supplied with prose translations. Prose was the natural vehicle in French, where terza rima presented great difficulties. There were already three renderings of the Inferno and one of the whole Comedy in French by the end of the eighteenth century, and an even larger number was published during the first half of the nineteenth. Although no German prose version has appeared during the last hundred years, there were several in the preceding century. Johann Nikolaus Meinhard's selections (1763-4) was a minor classic; Lebrecht Bachenschwanz published a complete Comedy in 1767-9; while another Comedy by Hörwarter and Enk appeared in 1830-1. Thomas Carlyle was doubtless familiar with some of these, and may have influenced his brother's decision to use prose for his Inferno.

Since a prose translation of poetry can convey little of the original form, one of its main functions has always been to assist the student who requires guidance in reading the original. Carlyle, as we shall see, had this need very much in mind, and provided for it so successfully that his Inferno is still one of the best known versions of Dante. Unfortunately it must be stated that the other prose translator considered in this chapter can only, despite his pretensions, be dismissed as a charlatan.

JOHN AITKEN CARLYLE (1801-79)

John Carlyle was born at Ecclefechan, Dumfriesshire, being six years younger than his more famous brother Thomas, who outlived him by nearly two years. John was both assisted and influenced by Thomas, and shared some of his literary enthusiasms. After taking his M.D. at Edinburgh in 1825, John went to London, but was unsuccessful there so far as medicine was concerned, although he had literary articles published in *Fraser's Magazine* and similar periodicals. In 1831 an appointment as travelling physician to the Countess of Clare enabled him to reach financial independence, and later he held a similar appointment with the Duke of Buccleuch. From about 1844 he seems to have occupied himself entirely in study and literary work. He had earlier interested his brother Thomas in Dante, and in 1840 the latter's *The Hero as Poet* was given in lecture form, and published the following year in *Heroes and Hero Worship*.

The aim and scope of John Carlyle's prose translation of the Inferno, published in 1849, can best be defined by quoting from the original preface.

> The object of the following Prose Translation is to give the real meaning of Dante as literally and briefly as possible. No single particle has been wittingly left unrepresented in it, for which any equivalent could be discovered; and the few words that have been added are marked in Italics. English readers, it is hoped, will here find a closer, and therefore, with all its defects, a warmer version than any that has hitherto been published for them.

The Italian text, he explains, has been carefully collated from the best editions; the arguments and notes are either original or based on the most reliable Italian commentators and historians.

> Now this simple statement will sufficiently shew that the present undertaking is upon a plan quite different from that of the other English translations; and therefore enters into no competition with them, and requires no apology. I am persuaded that all who know anything of the manifold

significance of the Original, or of its old and recent history, will be glad to see another faithful effort made to bring the true meaning of it nearer to English readers.

Carlyle says that he had originally thought of publishing a correct edition of the Italian text with English arguments and notes, but decided to add a literal translation and 'to send forth this first volume by way of experiment'. Repeating these words in the preface to the second edition in 1867 he says that 'the experiment has been successful in the best sense', also that 'the greater part of the Purgatorio had been translated when the Inferno was first sent forth', and concluding with the hope that though hitherto 'other occupations have stood in the way' he will soon 'send forth' the two remaining volumes. Although he lived twelve years longer, the hope was not fulfilled, nor has the manuscript of the Purgatorio ever come to light. It has been suggested that one of the reasons that deterred Carlyle from completing his work was the publication of a complete prose Comedy by O'Donnell. This seems unlikely; the Irish priest's version was so shoddy a piece of botchwork that every reviewer who handled it abused it roundly. More probably the reason was that his experiment, however 'successful in the best sense', made little headway with the public, and it was eighteen years before a second edition was called for. By then he was in his later sixties, and we know that about this time he told A. J. Butler that he did not intend to proceed with the Purgatorio.

Carlyle's Inferno was one of the most valuable and influential translations ever published in English. The book itself was well arranged, having the Italian in the upper part of each page, the translation immediately below it, and the notes at the foot. Many people might laugh at the ideas and the idiom of the Carlyles; but they possessed the ingrained capacity of the Scot for distinguishing between the real elements of genius and its tinsel accompaniments. Their attitude is well summed up in Thomas's essay, *Characteristics*, and it was the same clear-sighted, if sometimes awkwardly expressed, idea of a mission to interpret the works of genius from within that actuated John. His concern for a direct approach to Dante led him to preface his translation with an account of the most important manuscripts, editions and commentaries, a most valuable addition in those days when precise information was not readily accessible and many ill-supported readings were current in contemporary reprints of the text.

Carlyle's translation was well received by the reviewers, although almost all of them included a pleasantry on the Carlyle mannerisms. Many years later, in 1861, the article in the *Westminster Review* already referred to, summed up what was the general opinion, quoting incidentally from Cayley's preface sentences which we have already cited in Chapter III.

> Mr Carlyle's translation of the Inferno is a work of very rare merit, though we are inclined to acquiesce in Mr Cayley's estimate of it, as reminding the reader, in its manner of expression, less of Dante than of the author's celebrated brother. The introductory preface, in particular, is open to this criticism, and conveys, so far, an erroneous impression about the nature and object of the poem. The scholarship is first-rate throughout, and the translation so scrupulously literal, that those who have only the very slightest knowledge of Italian may enjoy by its assistance the treat of reading the original.

In reality the language of the translation has little in common with *Sartor Resartus*, but there are two pages in the preface which were probably responsible for provoking critics to the comparison. They are too long for quotation in full, but a few sentences will give a sufficient indication of their style.

> And to those amongst ourselves, who, with good and generous intentions, have spoken lightly and unwisely concerning Dante, one has to say – not without sadness: Study him better. His ideas of Mercy, and Humanity, and Christian Freedom, and the means of attaining them, are not the same as yours, but unspeakably larger and sounder. He felt the infinite distance between Right and Wrong, and had to take that feeling along with him. And those gentle qualities of his, which you praise so much, lie at the root of his other heroic qualities, and are inseparable from them. All anger and indignation, it may safely be said, were much more painful to him than they can be to you. The Dante you have criticised is not the real Dante, but a mere scarecrow – seen through the unhealthy mist of your sentimentalism. Why do you keep preaching your impracticable humanities, and saying Peace, peace; where there is no peace?

This passage, if not written by Thomas, must have been inspired by him, and is aimed mainly at Hunt and Landor; the former's *Stories from the Italian Poets* had appeared in 1846; the latter's *Pentameron* (1837) had been followed by more *Imaginary Conversations* on the same subject. It was a somewhat injudicious addition to a preface of only eight pages, otherwise written in a sober and matter-of-fact tone.

The translation is not, as some of the comments might suggest, a Carlylean tour-de-force. Its main resemblance to the works of Thomas lies in its battery of capital letters and its sometimes eccentric punctuation. It is doubtful whether, had it been published anonymously, without the preface and the capitals, it would have been connected with the Carlyles at all. Admittedly it is not written in straightforward

literary English, but most of its inversions are due to an effort to reproduce as nearly as possible the word order of the text. This sometimes
produces effects that are clumsy without being illuminating, e.g. 'yet
not so, but that I feared at the sight, which appeared to me, of a Lion'
(I.44-5). There are other phrases like 'Good there is none to ornament
the memory of him' (VIII.47) where the last four words, representing
'sua memoria', are merely a stylistic device; while 'and he made the
great endeavours' for 'e fece le gran prove' (XXXI.94) is pedantic. It is,
however, this effort to follow the original, together with the background
of biblical language which is the heritage of the Scot, that gives the
translation its strongly individual flavour, rather than any attempt to
reproduce the idiom of Weissnichtwo. As it was, Carlyle fell between
two stools. The *Athenaeum* thought he was too literal:

> To those who know nothing of Italian we fear this literal version will,
> however, be meagre fare. The vital spark of poetry is absent – the cinders
> of prose are left. Its very literality kills.

On the other hand Cayley, always an acute observer, had seized on one
weakness genuinely present:

> Furthermore many passages have required, under Mr J. Carlyle's treat-
> ment, to be doubly rendered, that is literally in the text, and more per-
> spicuously in the notes, or vice versa.

It is true that Carlyle here and there is obliged to compromise between
an idiomatic and a literal translation. Thus (V.102) his text reads 'of
which I was bereft; and the manner still afflicts me' and his footnote
'which was taken from me; and in a way that continues to afflict me',
where in each case one half of the line, 'che mi fu tolto; e 'l modo ancor
m'offende' is literal and one half transposed. Similarly the next line,
'Love, which to no loved one permits excuse for loving', is given a
footnote: 'Lit.: "pardons or remits loving" in return'. At VII.91 'tanto
posta in croce' is rendered 'so much reviled', with a footnote 'so oft
put on the cross'; while in line 99 'quand' io mi mossi' is translated
'when we entered', but a footnote tells us: 'Lit.: "when I moved myself" to lead thee in'.

It is clear, from Carlyle's own remarks, that he had much more in
mind the convenience of those who were anxious to make a translation
their bridge to the original than that of the casual reader. With a few
reservations, he succeeded in this purpose; moreover, with some allowance for his mannerisms, his version can be read with pleasure by those
who cannot benefit from the Italian. Some typical specimens are given
below.

When he had ended, the dusky champaign trembled so violently, that the remembrance of my terror bathes me still with sweat. The tearful ground gave out wind, and flashed with a crimson light, which conquered all my senses: and I fell, like one who is seized with sleep. (III.130-6)

'Now it behooves thee thus to free thyself from sloth,' said the Master; 'for sitting on down, or under coverlet, men come not into fame; without which whoso consumes his life, leaves such vestige of himself on earth, as smoke in air or foam in water. And therefore rise! Conquer thy panting with the soul, that conquers every battle, if with its heavy body it sinks not down. A longer ladder must be climbed. To have quitted these is not enough. If thou understandest me, now act so that it may profit thee.' (XXIV.46-57)

I sorrowed then, and sorrow now again when I direct my memory to what I saw; and curb my genius more than I am wont, lest it run where Virtue guides it not; so that, if kindly star or something better have given to me the good, I may not grudge myself that gift. (XXVI.19-24)

As to Carlyle's scholarship, it was acclaimed by all critics as first-class, and so it certainly was for that date. He had studied his text thoroughly, as well as numerous commentaries. His notes show that he was familiar with most of the alternative readings and interpretations; once or twice he chooses one which has since been rejected as inferior, but in general his judgment is excellent. There is not what one could call a serious mistranslation in the book; and in some places Carlyle is the first English translator to get a passage right, e.g. the much abused 'tanto che solo una camicia vesta' of XXIII.42.

The most notable tribute to Carlyle's translation is Oelsner's revision, which now forms the first volume of the Temple Classics edition of the Divine Comedy. Gollancz says in his editorial note:

Carlyle's translation has been edited by Dr Oelsner with all the reverence due to an English classic; alterations have been made only where a faulty Italian reading had been adopted, or in the case of actual errors.

At a rough count, less than a hundred changes have been made, many of them very slight, and quite a number merely transferring the wording of Carlyle's footnote to the text. There is also some normalisation of the punctuation. That Carlyle's work should emerge so triumphantly from an overhaul by a competent scholar more than half a century after its publication, a half century, too, crowded with Dante research and overcrowded with other translations, suffices to disarm criticism. Like Cary and Longfellow, Carlyle has earned the right to have his name permanently linked with that of Dante among the English-speaking peoples.

E. O'DONNELL

So far nothing has been discovered regarding O'Donnell beyond what he tells us in his preface. Neither Toynbee nor other bibliographers give any particulars regarding him; and inquiries from Church authorities and from the National Library of Ireland have elicited no information. All we know is that he was a priest of the Roman Catholic Church, and we can infer his nationality from his name and the fact that his prose translation of the Divine Comedy, published in 1852, includes a Dublin address in the imprint. In his preface he tells us that he began it in 1848 at the monastery of Santa Trinità in Florence and finished it at the monastery of Vallombrosa, while other parts convey the impression that he had long resided in Italy and knew the language well. In 1855 he published a translation of Chateaubriand's *The Genius of Christianity*, the preface to which is dated from the College of the Assumption, Clichy, near Paris. This was followed by a *Compendium of Saint Thomas's Theology in English* (1859) and *Sermons on the Gospels of all the Sundays* (1863).

The preface is aggressively worded, and it is supplemented by a few hundred words headed 'To the Reader', the following extract from which will suffice to indicate O'Donnell's attitude.

> I here present to you the labour and fruit of my long and hard study, and hope you will derive some literary advantage, and mental entertainment from it. I must say without vanity or exaggeration, that no translator has ever done more justice to the author than I have in every respect. What some translators are deficient of in spirit of the Poem, or in their knowledge of the Italian language, they strive to supply with pompous, bombastic quotations from others, and often give erroneous interpretations of many passages of the work. I have diligently studied the Text in all its poetic and figurative styles, consulted the most intelligent commentators, and deduced in a true Catholic spirit, in accordance with the Poet's Christian principles, moral, religious, and philosophic allegories, which are a considerable acquisition to the work. I have translated, as far as the original text would allow, a few of the first cantos, as literally as possible. The Italian scholar alone is capable of judging of its almost insurmountable difficulties. Whoever is ignorant of the language cannot possibly do so. To please both is the most critical task. A literal translation of the Poem is morally impossible; a loose, paraphrastic one would completely distort and disfigure the natural beauties of the original. I have therefore observed the medius terminus throughout, in order to satisfy all.

In the preface the same claims are repeated, and the difficulties of Dante are further insisted on. The translation of Homer and Virgil 'is but child's amusement, in comparison to the complicated and intricate composition of the Divina Commedia'; even O'Donnell's shoulder trembled beneath 'the weight of this arduous, and I may say, presumptuous task', but he had the 'kind approbation and flattering encouragement' of some learned friends. He draws particular attention to his arguments and to 'what has not yet appeared in any translation of the poem, interesting allegories at the end of each canto'. 'The youth of Great Britain and Ireland', to whom the volume is dedicated, might well be excused for feeling somewhat discouraged by the preface, for O'Donnell, remarking that his aids to comprehension should suffice for the classical scholar, adds:

> As for the others, it would be labour in vain, as it is not in the power of man to make the work intelligible to those who are not well versed in history and other sciences.

These claims to something approaching infallibility are in no way vindicated by the translation itself, which is definitely among the worst ever made. It is neither literal nor literary; moreover it abounds in errors, some of them suggesting that O'Donnell was either extremely careless or by no means so proficient in the Italian language as he claimed. Nowhere does he say what text he followed, or who were his authorities, but even after the most generous allowance for an inferior original, he must be convicted of often writing what is obvious nonsense. In Inf. VI.103-4 he has: 'Master, will these torments cease after the general judgment', having evidently read 'cresceranno' as 'cesseranno', which is absurd in the context. Inf. VII.72 reads 'Now I wish to make my opinion known to all', as though he took 'tu' as standing for 'tutto'. Fraud, says O'Donnell (Inf. XI.52-4) 'can be committed by a breach of confidence, or want of confidence', and the explanation that follows is quite chaotic. Inf XIV.25-7 reads:

> Those lying were more numerous, and those sitting, exposed to torments, were less in number, but their tongue was more apt to express their grief and torture,

a confusion which suggests extreme slovenliness, which is continued in lines 38-9 of the same canto, and misses the point completely:

> in like manner to increase their torments, the eternal fire fell there, which inflamed the sand like a match.

Inf. XIX.47 reads 'tossed upside down like a pail'; even if we suppose this should be 'pale' it is hardly perspicuous. O'Donnell's rendering of Inf. XX.16-18 introduces a novel idea: 'It might have been perhaps that some of them had the neck dislocated from the effect of a palsy in their lifetime.' Inf. XXI.1-2 rather disconcertingly represents the poets as 'talking of things not fit to be inserted in my comedy'. Inf. XXVIII. 86-7 reads 'which a certain ghost here with me would not be over-anxious to see'. Inf. XXX.136-8 is hopelessly confused: 'As one who dreams of some misfortune, and in his dream wishes to dream what he fears should not be'. The explanation of the sun's position in Purg. IV is very hazy, and ends with the Hebrews seeing it 'in the hot western clime'. In Purg. V.38-9 the sun darts through the August clouds. The arc of the second circle in Purg. XIII.6 'inclines less'. Purg. XVII.59-60 reads absurdly:

> for he that waits to be prayed to, and sees his neighbour in distress, unfortunately exposes himself to a refusal in time of want.

The tree in Purg. XXII.134 increases downward instead of upward. The syntax of Purg. XXVII.76-8 has not been understood, producing:

> As light-footed wanton goats lie ruminating on the side of a hill, before they take their last meal . . .

The pearl of Par. III.14-15 'would not appear quicker to the sight'. In Par. XVII.33 we read of 'the angel of God, who taketh away the sins of the world', perhaps a mere slip, but one which O'Donnell's superior knowledge should surely have avoided. We must hasten the tale, however, and quote from the last canto what should perhaps be called an Irishism (Par. XXXIII.58-60):

> Like one who sees something in a dream, and when it is over retains some impression thereof, and then completely forgets it . . .

This brief summary is indicative of the kind of error strewn throughout O'Donnell's translation. Apart from this his language is often clumsy and stilted, and he has a predilection for polysyllables that tends to obscure rather than clarify, e.g. (Inf. II.37-42):

> And like one who no longer desires what he wished for before, and, on a second consideration, changes his mind, so as to have abandoned what he had commenced, such was my case on approaching this gloomy region, for I accomplished my enterprise merely in imagination, whereas, at the very commencement it was forsaken.

This, incidentally, is from one of the early cantos in which he professes to be very literal. From the later we may quote Purg. X.10-13:

> We must here use some dexterity, said my guide, keeping close alternatively to each side that opens hollow. This critical position retarded our journey . . .

'Il gran rifiuto' of Inf. III.60 is made by one 'who through false deli-

cacy rejected the great offer'. In Inf. XIV.99 Ida is 'in a state of
abandonment through antiquity'. The spirits in Purg. VI.27 desire 'to
accelerate their sanctification'. The gate of Purgatory (X.2) is 'seldom
passed on account of the culpable concupiscence of souls'. And so on,
ad nauseam. Perhaps, however, the most astonishing line of all is
Par. XIII.84: 'thus the pregnant Virgin preserved her virginity'.
There are other oddities which may be left to the imagination. The
contraction 'Mr.' is frequent (presumably=Monsignor), but Mr. Bru-
netto and Mr. Adam seem rather out of place in Inferno. An annoying
feature is the complete absence of quotation marks or paragraphing to
represent direct speech, which would be most confusing to the novice.

O'Donnell's notes are brief and mainly factual; sometimes ambiguous
and even misleading. In Purg. XIV he mixes Guido and Rinier in a
confusing fashion. The 'Allegories' appended to the cantos are pedestrian affairs, with no sign of the profundity promised in the preface.
That to Inf. XV will serve as an example.

> By Dante's difficulty in recognising his old preceptor, is shown how that
> horrible crime contrary to nature renders one more like a brute than
> human being; by his not descending with him through fear of the fire,
> is intimated how one should avoid the company of such vicious men, so
> that he should not be subject to the same brutal state and punishment.
> By bending down his head at such an awful sight, is meant how one should
> bend his head and shut his eyes against every temptation and concupi-
> scence, prejudicial to his health, honour, and salvation.

The article in the *Westminster Review* of January 1861, surveying
English translations of the Divine Comedy to date, dismisses O'Donnell with the verdict he deserves.

> With Mr Hindley's and Mr O'Donnell's prose versions we may complete
> the list of those 'ove non è che luca'. They display so few evidences of
> either spirit or accuracy, that we will not rashly undertake to decide
> between their respective merits. We have certainly detected the graver
> errors and inaccuracies in Mr O'Donnell's; but his translation extends
> over the whole poem, and has thus afforded him more opportunity of
> distinguishing himself; whereas Mr Hindley has more prudently confined
> himself to the rendering of four cantos.

BIBLIOGRAPHY TO CHAPTER IV

CARLYLE

*Dante's Divine Comedy: The Inferno. A Literal Prose Translation, with the text of the original collated from the best editions, and explanatory notes. By John A. Carlyle, M.D. London: Chapman and Hall. 1849. (A second edition was issued by the same publishers in same format, with a few revisions and corrections, in 1867. A third edition, identical with the above except for the insertion of a leaf to carry prefaces to the second and third editions, was issued by G. Bell & Sons in the Bohn's Library series in 1882.)

*The Inferno of Dante Alighieri. London: J. M. Dent & Sons. 1900. (This is a volume in the Temple Classics series and is now in its 25th edition. The translation and arguments are Carlyle's, revised and corrected by Hermann Oelsner, with new notes by the latter and additional matter by Philip Henry Wicksteed.)

O'DONNELL

Translation of the Divina Commedia of Dante Alighieri. By the Rev. E. O'Donnell. London: Thomas Richardson and Son; Dublin; and Derby. 1852

* includes Italian text

CHAPTER V

BLANK TERZINE

THE blank verse translations which we have so far considered made little or no attempt to reproduce Dante line for line, or to keep intact the terzina which is the characteristic unit of the Comedy. Cary, the only blank verse translator so far of any importance, wrote in verse paragraphs somewhat after the Miltonic style. There are, however, a number of fragments of this period in which the ternary structure is to some extent reproduced.

Leigh Hunt, for instance, to whom we have already referred, and who translated numerous passages in different styles, kept close to the line and terzina arrangement of the original. Creditable mention must also be made of James Montgomery (1771-1854), a native of Irvine in Scotland. He was a minor poet of some merit, and is still remembered for his hymns; these are above the average level of such compositions and still in regular use. His activities as editor and proprietor of the *Sheffield Iris*, which we have no space to describe here, gained him respect and admiration. He interspersed numerous blank verse passages from Dante in his writings; most of them reproduce the original triplets, and are on a competent level. The following are a few lines from his version of the Farinata episode in Inf. X, to the original of which he gives high praise:

> Meanwhile that other most majestic form,
> Near which I stood, neither changed countenance,
> Nor turn'd his neck, nor lean'd to either side:
> 'And if,' quoth he, our first debate resuming,
> 'They have not well that lesson learn'd, the thought
> Torments me more than this infernal bed.'

A much less favourable verdict must be passed on the first American experimenter in this style. J. C. Peabody, a clergyman of Newburyport, Massachusetts, and a zealous Protestant, published at Boston in 1857 a slim volume entitled *Dante's Hell*, containing cantos I to X in blank terzine, with a second version of canto I only in terza rima. He explains that he had started in rhyme, but 'changed his design' when Cayley's translation appeared. He claims in his preface that 'by labor and plodding' he has made a 'more literal, and perhaps, therefore, a

57

better translation than them all', but his version is a flagrant plagiarism of Carlyle's prose, which is forced into decasyllables by the occasional change of a word or phrase. Charles Eliot Norton exposed it in the *Atlantic Monthly* (I, 1858, pp. 382ff, quoted D.A.P. p. 82) as 'nothing more than a poor versification of Carlyle's prose translation of 1849, from which Peabody has also copied the notes', adding that it was evident that he was entirely unfamiliar with the Italian language. An examination amply confirms this view.

Ernest Ridsdale Ellaby (1834-96), Fellow of Wadham and barrister of Lincoln's Inn, published a version of Inf. I-X, with cantos I-III in terza rima and the remainder in blank terzine with occasional rhyme. The first edition appeared in 1871 and a second, with considerable revision, in 1874. The translator, who acknowledges the help afforded by the work of his predecessors, opines that his system of connecting the triplets 'by means either of a final rhyme or half rhyme or of some internal harmony' combines 'something of the freedom of Miltonic verse with . . . the separation of the triplets and their connexion by a common sound'. His version is, however, very pedestrian, with frequent padding and distortion, nor do his rhyming devices enhance the effect.

The most notable pioneer of blank terzine as a medium for the translation of the Divine Comedy was King John of Saxony who, under the name of Philalethes, published a German version between the years 1828 and 1849. In this the ternary divisions of the original are strictly adhered to, and the verses are hendecasyllabic throughout. The system has proved popular in Germany, and there has been a steady stream of such versions down to the present day. Some writers have followed the example of Philalethes by using hendecasyllables, while others have mixed masculine and feminine endings, notably Karl Vossler whose Comedy (1942) is one of the best. Witte used the system of Philalethes in his version (1865), as also did a well-known contemporary Dante scholar, Hermann Gmelin, whose translation began to appear in 1950. Although hendecasyllables are more feasible in German than in English, the effect is very monotonous. Philalethes received high praise in his day; but his merit lay in a correct reproduction of Dante's meaning rather than of his poetry. The mechanical repetition of the unrhymed triplets, with frequent awkward line endings to maintain the hendecasyllables, quickly palls. English lends itself still less to such a succession of final disyllables though, as we shall see, their use has been adopted by quite a few translators. For the most part, however, the users of blank terzine in English have used decasyllables, with only occasional feminine endings, and this is true of those in the mid-nineteenth century with whom we are about to deal.

The work of Philalethes was well known throughout Europe and its fame reached America. George Ticknor, Longfellow's predecessor at Harvard, made the royal translator's acquaintance during a visit to Europe and was present at one of the sessions during which the King discussed Dante with his friends and helpers. Longfellow, who wrote no introduction to his translation, makes no direct mention of Philalethes, but was doubtless acquainted with his work and perhaps to some extent influenced by it. Although none of the other users of blank terzine in English during the period refer to the German version, they probably knew of it, and the system was perhaps 'in the air' at the time. It may be noted, however, that while the four major versions in blank terzine dealt with in this chapter all appeared during the short space of fourteen years, no other translation of Dante in English blank verse of any kind was published between 1868 and the very end of the century. This was doubtless partly due to new fashions: first that of terza rima, and later of prose; perhaps also the immense popularity and prestige of Longfellow's rendering deterred possible rivals from entering the field.

SIR WILLIAM FREDERICK POLLOCK (1815-88)

Pollock was a member of a brilliant family; his father and two uncles, sons of David Pollock, saddler to King George III, achieved baronetcies; while the translator's two brothers and his two sons all made their mark in English jurisprudence. William Frederick himself, who succeeded to his father's title in 1870, was educated at St Paul's School and Trinity College, Cambridge, being a young member of the 'band of youthful friends', including Tennyson, Thackeray, Hallam and Trench, who, as *In Memoriam* records, 'held debate . . . on mind and art'. He reached the bar in 1838 by way of the Inner Temple, was appointed a Master of the Exchequer in 1846 and a Queen's Remembrancer in 1874. Apart from his translation of the Divine Comedy, published in 1854, he edited Macready's *Reminiscences* (1876) and published his own *Personal Remembrances* in 1887.

In a short preface to his translation he states his intentions:

It has been my endeavour in the present version of Dante's great Poem to be strictly literal in the rendering of the original Italian into English of our own times, so far as I found it possible, regard being had to the idioms of the two languages, and to the preservation of a metrical form. To a

certain extent also I have tried to represent to the Reader the actual
arrangement, as well as the true English equivalent of the original, and
I have made it a condition to retain the order and identity of the lines,
except where this could not be done without violating more essential
requirements.

The translation is in blank verse, printed continuously and divided
into paragraphs, but it corresponds very closely to Dante's terzine, the
whole poem containing exactly the same number of lines, although in
two places wrongly printed numerals cause an apparent discrepancy.

The volume had a lukewarm reception from the reviewers. The
Athenaeum (8 July 1854, pp. 843-4) conceded the merit of 'studious
adherence to the words of the text and the elucidation by footnotes of
difficulties and allusions', going on to say:

> The skeleton of the piece is exhibited with more verbal felicity, perhaps,
> than has hitherto been attained by any previous translator in verse: but
> of the poetic substance of these living features on which the especial type
> of power and character is outwardly impressed, the resemblance has not
> been adequately preserved.

The reviewer censures gravely Pollock's lack of prosodic skill, quoting
numerous lame or clumsy lines, and concluding that

> Pollock's work shows industry and care, but the spirit, colouring, and
> beauties are unfelt or at least not conveyed . . . owing to his reliance on
> the method of verbal instead of virtual translation.

In its 1861 article the *Westminster Review* praised him very faintly:

> Mr Pollock's work, in blank verse, in spite of occasional grave inaccuracies,
> presents a pretty literal version of Dante. He has preserved the matter,
> however, at the expense of a total loss of the form of the original.

It must be admitted that Pollock's version contains numerous mistranslations, some obviously due to incomprehension, others probably
to carelessness. Thus we have (Inf. X.73-5):

> That other of great soul, at whose request
> I had remained, nor silently looked on,
> Nor turned his neck, nor moved in any part,

where 'non mutò aspetto' seems to have been read as 'non muto
aspettò' which is both meaningless and metrically impossible. In Purg.
XXIII.84 'tempo per tempo' has been misunderstood and the line
rendered 'Where gradually is restoration worked'. Faults of this kind
are frequent, but it must be remembered that Pollock, pinning his
faith to Ciardetti's text of 1830, had little help from predecessors or
commentators, and his standard of accuracy is fairly respectable.

His poetic sense and his word values, however, are poor, so that we have much awkwardness and weakening. It is difficult to know how to read a line like 'Shown by thee in earth, heaven, and in hell' (Inf. XIX.11), while 'So more and more the dogs to wolves turned finds' (Purg. XIV.50) is both obscure and cacophonous. 'Which all the ills of all the world confines' (Inf. VII.18) or 'Such an access of desire came on / To be above' (Purg. XXVII.121-3) are typical of the weakening process. On the whole, however, Pollock does better than Wright in preserving the vigour of the original, and has some good terzine like Inf. XII.28-30:

> So we our way took through the scattered waste
> Of rocks that often were to motion stirred
> Under my feet, by the unwonted weight.

On the whole, however, Pollock's besetting sin is dullness. He is content through most of the poem to string his words together to form suitable metrical groups with little regard for the total effect, and his vocabulary is selected on the basis of verbal equivalence rather than evocative value. He manages to maintain a respectable level within these limits, with rather frequent lame lines or descents to bathos, but seldom jarring by reason of oddness or bad taste. Bearing in mind his chronological position, he is entitled to some credit as a pioneer. Occasionally a sustained passage stands out, and perhaps Par. XXIII. 49-69 is as good as he ever produced.

> Like to a man was I, what time he wakes
> From unremembered visions, and who tries
> In vain to bring them back into his thoughts,
> When I this proffer heard, that worthy was
> Of such acceptance, as will never fade
> From out the volume which reviews the past.
> If all the languages could sound again
> Which Polyhymnia with her sisters made
> With their most sweet milk more luxuriant,
> To aid me, to a thousandth of the truth
> They could not reach, singing the holy smile,
> And how it perfect made her sacred face.
> And thus, as I prefigure Paradise,
> My sacred poem here must take a leap,
> Like one who finds his road is cut away:
> But whoso thinks upon the weighty theme,
> And on the mortal shoulders charged with it,
> Will not upbraid, if under it they tremble.
> No voyage is it for a little bark,
> This which is opened by my daring prow,
> Nor for a sailor who himself would spare.

A word may be said about the illustrations in this volume which the *Westminster Review* with unnecessary asperity described as 'mere blots on the page, and had far better be omitted'. Volkmann in his *Iconografia* also dismissed them with a slighting reference: 'und endlich ist eine illustrierte Dante-Ausgabe von George Scharf (1820-95) nichts weiter als eine Kopie nach Flaxman.' Actually 31 of Scharf's 50 drawings *are* reproductions of Flaxman's sketches, and do not profess to be anything else, as the list of illustrations shows. The other 19 are various but all, except two original ones, are referred to their origin. They may not be to the taste of many readers, but 'blots' is a very inept description of their rather spidery texture.

WILLIAM MICHAEL ROSSETTI (1829-1919)

This member of a famous family, second son of Gabriele Rossetti, was the younger brother of Dante Gabriel and elder brother of Christina Georgina. During a very long life he combined many interests. At the age of sixteen he entered the Excise Office (later the Inland Revenue Board) from which he retired after fifty years service. Before he was twenty he was one of the six original members of the pre-Raphaelite Brotherhood, and he acted as editor of *The Germ*, contributing a sonnet to the first number. He was also well known as an art critic; he wrote for the *Spectator* and other periodicals, and was responsible for some articles on art in the *Encyclopædia Britannica*. He did much miscellaneous editorial and literary work, and was one of the early collaborators in the compilation of the *Oxford English Dictionary*. His interest in Dante was lifelong; his translation of the Inferno appeared in 1865, and his *Dante and his Convito* as late as 1910.

Rossetti published his Inferno on the occasion of the Dante sexcentenary in 1865, but in his preface he says it had been made some seven or eight years earlier. He had delayed publication with the intention of completing the whole Comedy, an intention which he repeats in his preface, but no more appeared; Longfellow's success on similar lines may have deterred him. Rossetti's translation is in blank terzine, following the original line for line, but it is printed continuously in paragraphs like Pollock's, which at first sight obscures the ternary form.

Rossetti's preface sums up the situation to date, and clearly states his own object.

The aim of this translation of Dante may be summed up in one word – Literality. Numerous are the translations already existing. Some may be passed in silence . . . but there are four of which no fresh translator can assume to be unheedful – Cary's, Cayley's, Carlyle's, and Pollock's. Each of these has a distinct aim, and none is done less than creditably.

After some praise and a little criticism of these four, and mentioning Brooksbank, Thomas and Mrs Ramsay in a footnote, he proceeds:

> My attempt is of precisely the same class as Pollock's. Like him, I have aimed at unconditional literality in phraseology, and at line-for-line rendering; and, like him, I have kept to the metre, which is the same as in blank verse, but not to the rhyme (the so-called terza rima). That I am not entirely satisfied with his success in substance and spirit is implied in the attempt which, with a consciousness of its numerous imperfections, I now submit to the reader. The aim appeared to me the best that remained to be pursued, after Cayley. To follow Dante sentence for sentence, line for line, word for word – neither more nor less – has been my strenuous endeavour; various shortcomings in form, from a literary point of view, are the result. Some readers will probably be disposed to consider that singularity, or even oddity, of phrase is one of my chief shortcomings. Where that fault is my own, I must simply plead guilty; but I would ask my reader (if unacquainted with Italian) to believe me when I say that generally I am odd to the English reader for one reason only – that Dante also is odd to the Italian reader in the same passage.

It may be mentioned here that there are numerous resemblances, amounting to identity of line and phrase, between Rossetti's version and Pollock's, but these are all cases where the translation is severely literal, and there is no reason to suppose that they were not arrived at independently. There are similar resemblances between Rossetti's rendering and Longfellow's, where neither could possibly have any knowledge of the other's work; and indeed it seems obvious that such resemblances and identities will always exist in translations based on similar principles and using a common literary idiom.

Rossetti, however, clings to his principle of literality with what often seems mere perverseness. For instance, VI.1-3 reads:

> On the returning of the mind, which shut
> Before the pity for the cognate twain
> The which with mournfulness confused me all . . .

This, although it follows the words of the original with painful exactness, is neither a good translation, nor even a good crib, because the sense of the original is obscured rather than revealed, in spite of a footnote which informs us that 'this word (*cognati*), besides the general sense which I have rendered by "cognate", expresses in Italian the exact relationship of brother and sister-in-law'. The habit of departing from normal English idiom seems to grow on Rossetti, and we get many such lines as 'But, when thou art to be in the sweet world' (VI.

88), 'To get the sand and flamelet fully ceased' (XVII.33), 'He is along
the path crossed o'er and nude' (XXIII.118), and such a puzzling
terzina as XXX.22-4:

> But neither Trojan furies nor of Thebes
> Were ever against any seen so fierce,
> Nor beasts be stabbed – (I say not human limbs) –
> As I beheld . . .

The use of etymological equivalents also tends to produce obscurity
or distortion of sense, as when we learn that the sinners in the vestibule
of hell 'were stimulated much / By the great flies' (III.65), or that at
Pola 'The sepulchres make various all the place' (IX.115). This habit
also seems to grow, producing such a strange rendering of 'dietro alle
poste delle care piante' (XXIII.148) as 'After the cherished footsoles'
vestiges'. We even find an un-English reflection of an Italian form
in V.121-3:

> There is no greater grief
> Than to remember one of happy time
> In misery.

Many critics commented on these 'oddnesses', and were by no means
satisfied with the translator's suggestion that the blame for them should
rest with Dante.

There are a few archaic words, of which 'whenas' is the worst
offender. The prepositions 'of' and 'with' are frequently contracted,
for no apparent reason, to 'o'' and 'wi'' which, being out of character,
increases the oddness. Monosyllabic lines are often cacophonous, e.g.
'I put in purse pelf there, and here myself' (XIX.72). XVIII.98-9 is
rather ugly:

> And of the foremost vale be this enough
> To know, and eke of them it in it gores.

On the other hand there are lines and passages which please by their
vigour and forcefulness, such as the onomatopoeia of IV.9, 'Which
gathers thunder of unnumbered wails', or the neat rendering of VII.18
as 'Which bags entire the universe's bane'. Rossetti follows Cayley in
giving the 'Evilclaws' new names which, if not so recondite, are more
effective than the latter's, e.g. Barbariccia is Bristlebeard, Libbicocco
is Play-the-trick, and Rubicante is Ruddyflare.

As might be expected from one of his family, Rossetti is in general
accurate. He knew the original well, and he explains in his preface
that, while he chiefly used Venturi's text, he adopted from others
readings thought preferable, 'without, I must acknowledge, any curious

inquiry as to authority'. His footnotes often give variant readings and alternative interpretations. There are one or two slips which may be misprints.

The *Athenaeum* reviewer (1 Apr. 1865, pp. 452-3), taking up the sentence in Rossetti's preface, remarked:

> We cannot admit that there is any necessity in the nature of things for a translation of the Divine Comedy to read oddly.

He also criticised some of the etymological equivalents. Charles Tomlinson, severe towards most of his predecessors in his preface (dealt with in Chapter VII), speaks more kindly of Rossetti and Longfellow, finding that the former has 'a more Dantesque spirit' than the latter, but objecting to frequent discordant lines and lack of poetic sense.

Rossetti's footnotes are brief and useful. The general exposition, besides containing a list of every individual mentioned in the Inferno, and relating each to his respective circle and sub-division,

> aims particularly at giving (what, so far as I am aware, has not been given before) a connected view of the moral relation between the sins punished in Hell, and the punishment.

There is no reflection anywhere in the book of the elder Rossetti's notorious theories about Dante's esoteric significance.

HENRY WADSWORTH LONGFELLOW (1807-82)

Longfellow was born in Portland, Maine; he was the second son of Stephen, whose great-great-grandfather, William Longfellow, had come to America from Yorkshire in the latter part of the seventeenth century, and of Zilpah Wadsworth, who was descended from John Alden, one of the company who had crossed even earlier in the *Mayflower*. Stephen was a lawyer by profession and a Unitarian by religion, to which faith the poet remained loyal throughout his life. The Longfellows upheld the best traditions of their ancestry; they were of high character, broad culture and genuine piety. Stephen had been educated at Harvard, but having become a trustee of Bowdoin College, recently established by the State of Maine at Brunswick, it was there that he sent his son in 1822; and there three years later young Henry graduated with such distinction that he was offered, subject to the completion of further studies in Europe, the professorship of modern languages which the trustees had decided to establish. He took up the appointment in 1829 being, as a biographer puts it, 'one of the youngest scholars, probably the most accomplished scholar, in America'. Five years later he succeeded Ticknor as Professor of Modern Languages at Harvard, where he remained till 1854, when he resigned to devote himself entirely to literary work, and was succeeded by James Russell Lowell.

There are numerous biographies of Longfellow, so that details of his life and writings need not detain us here. It must be remarked that during his quiet, studious and prosperous life he knew more than one crushing sorrow. He lost both his wives in tragic circumstances; his friends were saddened by the fact that his avoidance of all allusions to these losses was a sign of acute inward suffering which they were helpless to relieve. It was during the period that followed his second wife's death in 1861 that he found distraction in the translation of the Divine Comedy, begun much earlier, but progressing very slowly at first. Nor was Longfellow's academic life free from vexations, and in this connexion the reader may be referred to an interesting volume by Carol L. Johnson, *Professor Longfellow of Harvard* (Oregon University Press, 1944).

Longfellow's stature as an original poet will always be a matter of controversy. His immense reputation with his contemporaries was inevitably short-lived; those very elements in his style which ensured his immediate popularity in a land whose self-consciousness was still only developing – his blend of homely simplicity, facile ornament and sentimental pathos, and above all his fatal fluency – did him most discredit with the age that followed. His studies, spread over seven or eight languages, tended to disperse his energies and weaken his concentration. His undoubted gifts of sensibility and expression never quite focused themselves; his work contains many admirable fragments and striking experiments, but as a whole it lacks direction and cohesion.

With translation the case is different. Longfellow's verbal competence stood him in good stead in the hundred or so poetic versions which he made from a dozen different languages. His first published translation was of the famous *Coplas de Don Jorge Manrique*, and was recently praised by Roy Campbell in his preface to Ramsey's Paradiso. Longfellow was also successful with German lyrics and Spanish sonnets. His experiments with Virgilian hexameters and Ovidian elegiacs are good in parts; his attempts to make French Alexandrines into English ones as hopeless as those of others.

His interest in Dante began early. In 1839 he included in *Voices of the Night* five passages from the Purgatorio, all in the unrhymed terzine in which his complete Comedy was later written. He changed his style in the direction of literality during the years that followed, but his phrasing and vocabulary remained essentially the same in the final form. He embarked on a translation of the Purgatorio in 1845; his diary records that it was completed in 1853, but it remained un-published. He went to work much faster after the tragedy of 1861, and completed the Comedy in 1863, after which he gave it a thorough revision. The Inferno was hurried through the press in order that advance copies could be sent to Italy for the sexcentenary celebrations of 1865, but publication was delayed till 1867 when the complete Comedy appeared. A British edition was issued in London during the same year, as well as a continental one by Tauchnitz in Leipzig. Long-fellow's was the first blank verse translation in which the terzine were distinguished by indention in print.

During the final revision of the translation Longfellow enjoyed the advice and co-operation of a number of accomplished friends, including Lowell and Charles Eliot Norton. The story of their weekly meetings at which the translation was read and discussed canto by canto recalls Ticknor's account of how, thirty years earlier, he was the guest of Philalethes at a similar gathering. Thus even before it reached the public Longfellow's translation had already been the means of inter-esting the men who were making Dante known to the younger Ameri-can generation, and in Norton he found an enthusiastic disciple and successor.

It was unfortunate that Longfellow, after expending such effort on his translation and the explanatory notes and 'illustrations' that accom-panied it, should have published it without a single word of intro-duction. He may have desired to avoid falling into the error of some predecessors by enunciating a theory of translation; but it was soon obvious that many critics failed to understand his aims. Later Long-fellow wrote:

The only merit my book has is that it is exactly what Dante says, and not what the translator imagines he might have said if he had been an English-man. In other words, while making it rhythmic, I have endeavoured to make it also as literal as a prose translation. . . . In translating Dante, something must be relinquished. Shall it be the beautiful rhyme that blossoms all along the line like a honeysuckle on the hedge? It must be, in order to retain something more precious than rhyme, namely, fidelity, truth, – the life of the hedge itself. . . . The business of a translator is to report what the author says, not to explain what he means; that is the work of the commentator. What an author says, and how he says it, that is the problem of the translator.

Dr Werner P. Friedrich (D.F.A. p. 548) comments:

Longfellow saw his task similar to that of a witness in court: to tell the truth, the whole truth, and nothing but the truth, to give the facts as they were, and not to try to interpret and twist them for his readers.

Lowell referred to Longfellow's translation as 'not the best possible, by any means, but the best probable'; William Dean Howells, another member of the company who assisted Longfellow in his revision, wrote: 'Opening the book, we stand face to face with the poet, and when his voice ceases we may well marvel if he has not sung to us in his own Tuscan.' W. C. Bryant, in a letter of 1867, said:

> Mr Longfellow has translated Dante as a great poet should be translated. After this version, no other will be attempted until the present form of the English language shall have become obsolete, for, whether we regard fidelity to the senses, aptness in the form of the expression, or the skilful transfusion of the poetic spirit of the original into the phrases of another language, we can look for nothing more perfect.

Others were equally laudatory. Norton himself was the most active panegyrist of all. The translation, he said, was 'the best that has ever been made of the Divine Comedy into English' and 'hardly likely to be superseded or surpassed'. In a long article in the *North American Review* (July 1867), of which he was joint editor with Lowell, he set forth his theories of translation and demonstrated that Longfellow's was 'the most faithful of Dante, that has ever been made', comparing it, to their disadvantage, with several earlier versions.

It will be noted that many of these favourable comments came from those who were members of the Longfellow circle, and therefore familiar with the system on which the translation was constructed. Opposition came from outside, but there was a tendency on the part of adverse reviewers to criticise Longfellow for having failed to do something which he was not trying to do, and there was also perhaps something of a bias against New England which made some of them deliberately unfair. The most vocal opponent was Edward J. Sears, the Irish editor of the *National Quarterly Review*, who, not content with criticising the translation, attacked Longfellow's scholarship and character as well. John Fiske, who reviewed the book in the *New York World*, thought it a failure owing to the system used; he admitted that the rendering was faithful in a sense, but objected to the syntax and vocabulary. T. W. Hunter, writing in the *Philadelphia Press*, averred that all the poetical flavour of the original had vanished. All these and others were vigorously answered by Norton, who did not hesitate to criticise the critics. A full account of contemporary American reaction to Longfellow's translation is given by Dr La Piana (D.A.P. ch. V).

The first reaction in Britain was somewhat cool. The Inferno was reviewed in the *Athenaeum* (18 May 1867, pp. 655-6) in terms which suggested that the blank terzina form was found puzzling:

> It is not prose – we can scarcely call it poetry – but it is rather poetic-prose in a tripartite arrangement.

The reviews of Purgatorio (29 June 1867, pp. 845-6) and Paradiso (10 Aug. 1867, pp. 171-2), evidently by a different writer, were much more favourable. Though it was remarked that the 'divine harmony' was missing, the first of the two articles says:

> We know of no translation in English in which the beautiful and profound thoughts of Dante in his Purgatorio are rendered with a more conscientious, loving regard, and laudable desire to do him honour, than in this very literal version of Professor Longfellow, which will remain a standard of comparison among English readers, and will be of advantage also to those who are equally familiar with both languages, for here is the production of a master in each.

To come to the translation itself, little fault can be found in the matter of accuracy. There are certainly readings and interpretations since recognised as inferior, but Longfellow was a careful scholar, and thoroughly familiar with his original. It is true that he errs, like Rossetti, in sometimes pinning faith to cognate words which really make the meaning less clear, e.g. 'That of all pause it seemed to me indignant' and 'These did their faces irrigate with blood' do not convey the sense of 'indegno' and 'rigavan' (Inf. III.54, 67) into English. 'Evil comfort' is not quite the same as 'mai conforti' (Inf. XXVIII.135), nor 'puerile conceit' as 'pueril coto' (Par. III.26). We have many passages overloaded with such words, e.g. (Purg. XVIII.40-2):

> 'Thy words, and my sequacious intellect,'
> I answered him, 'have love revealed to me;
> But that has made me more impregned with doubt.'

Moreover Longfellow often prefers a polysyllabic Latin word to the commoner native one when there seems to be nothing to gain by the change, so that 'danno' is rendered by 'detriment', 'subitana' by 'instantaneous', 'dape' by 'aliments', 'lettura' by 'prelections', and so on, which gives some jarring effects like Inf. V.136: 'Kissed me upon the mouth all palpitating'. On the other hand Longfellow often uses his polysyllables to good effect, giving us strong lines like 'Can traverse the illimitable way' (Purg. III.35) or 'With affirmation that compels belief' (Purg. XXVI.105).

Longfellow's method, aiming at line for line rendering, necessarily involves frequent inversion and consequently awkwardness. This is, of course, helpful to the student who is working through the Italian, but the casual reader may be brought up with a jerk by such lines as (Purg. XXII.130-1):

> But soon their sweet discourses interrupted
> A tree which midway in the road we found.

So with unfamiliar constructions like 'That Frederick used to put them on of straw' (Inf. XXIII.66) or 'I think with wonder I depicted me' (Purg. II.82). There are, too, some lame and cacophonous lines which seem to have been missed in revision, like 'And if they were before Christianity' (Inf. IV.37), 'Within we entered without any contest' (Inf. IX.106), or 'Thus are not wont to do the feet of dead men' (Inf. XII.82). Incidentally, although Longfellow uses a fair proportion of hendecasyllables, he is very sparing in ending them with two words (as in the last example quoted), a usage whose regular recurrence in the versions of Philalethes or (later) Lee-Hamilton becomes very tiring.

Having mentioned most of Longfellow's faults we must emphasise that his translation has many virtues. It is accurate, conscientious, dignified, the work of one who was a poet himself, and who loved, valued and honoured the greater poet whom he was translating. As a student and teacher he did his utmost to make his original available and comprehensible to others; he attempted no remodelling, no fusing of the original with his own individual contribution. We might say that his translation contains, in addition to the reflection of Dante, an unconscious touch of his own best genius, restrained from its wonted vagaries through being tied to the text of a master with a surer touch. It is noticeable that commentators writing in English often quote Longfellow's version because he so regularly manages to get an expression just right, with a flavour which is lost in prose, and a fidelity seldom possible in rhyme.

The following are one or two attractive terzine from various parts of Longfellow's Comedy. Further passages from his translation will be reproduced in Vol. II, where his influence on his successors is discussed.

> Thus they returned along the lurid circle
> On either hand unto the opposite point,
> Shouting their shameful metre evermore.   (Inf. VII.31-3)

> Thus was descending the eternal heat,
> Whereby the sand was set on fire, like tinder
> Beneath the steel, for doubling of the dole.   (Inf. XIV.37-9)

The dawn was vanquishing the matin hour
Which fled before it, so that from afar
I recognised the trembling of the sea.   (Purg. I.115-7)

Even as the Blessed at the final summons
Shall rise up quickened each one from his cavern,
Uplifting light the reinvested flesh . . .   (Purg. XXX.13-15)

Light intellectual replete with love,
Love of true good replete with ecstasy,
Ecstasy that transcendeth every sweetness.   (Par. XXX.40-2)

In his attack on Longfellow Sears alleged that his notes were taken mainly from those of earlier translators, 'omitting often the most valuable, and substituting in their stead the platitudes of friends' (the last probably a tilt at Norton, who was quoted once or twice). There does not appear to be any substance in this indictment: Longfellow's notes are mainly factual, intended to help readers to understand the allusions. They contain information drawn from a great variety of sources, showing the width of the translator's own reading. Sears also says that the 'illustrations' at the end of each cantica consist of 'indifferent' passages from the writings of his friends, who in return bestow their praises on him. This charge is equally without foundation. The Illustrations provide valuable information, not readily available to the reader in those days when literature on Dante was much scarcer than it is now. Norton and Lowell certainly figure among the writers quoted, but there are also such various source passages as the Odyssey, the Aeneid, St Patrick's Purgatory and St Brandan, and extracts from Carlyle, Macaulay, Leigh Hunt, Milman, Ruskin, Schelling and more than half a dozen French authors.

Longfellow's translation was one of the most influential ever made of Dante, and played a great part in laying the foundation for later American achievement in the field. Its popularity in its own time was in a large measure due to the author's personal prestige. Longfellow was the poet of the American 'man in the street' in a way that his more gifted rivals were not. Indeed, had all his poetry been on his best level, his influence with the general public would have been less. He was also one of the foremost academic figures of his age, and therefore commanded the confidence of scholars and men of letters. He has merited the respect and affection of subsequent generations, and although in many respects his work has been superseded, it is by no means forgotten.

DAVID JOHNSTON (1800-79)

Johnston was a native of Corstorphine, then a Midlothian village detached from the capital. He was evidently proud of his origin, for after he became resident in Edinburgh he continued to describe himself as 'of Corstorphine' in the directories, and the words 'formerly of Corstorphine' appear in his death notice in the *Bath Chronicle* of 23 October 1879. He graduated M.D. at the University of Edinburgh in 1821, on which occasion he submitted a thesis entitled 'De quibusdam Lucis effectibus'. Thereafter he practised in the city, first at 34 Queen Street, then at 21 Charlotte Square. His name disappears from the Edinburgh directory in 1843. By the time the *Medical Directory* began to appear in 1849 he was evidently no longer practising, since his name is not recorded. He was resident in Bath from about 1867 until his death. He must have been a man of substance, because he produced and distributed free of charge seven handsomely printed and bound volumes of translations. The foregoing facts have been established with the co-operation of the City Librarian of Bath, whose help in the matter is greatly appreciated.

Johnston's translation of the Divine Comedy in blank terzine was issued in three volumes: Inferno and Purgatorio in 1867 and Paradiso in 1868. These were followed by Corneille's *Le Cid* (1873), *Cinna* (1874) and *Polyeucte* (1876), translated into rhymed Alexandrine couplets, and finally by *Translations literal and free of the dying Hadrian's address to his soul*. The books are excellently produced, printed on thick paper, well bound in heavy boards, bevelled and tooled, with the monogram D.J. on the spine. Edinburgh University possesses presentation copies of the three Dante volumes, with the name of the Library and the translator's autograph boldly written on the half-title page. The National Library of Scotland has copies of these and of two of the Corneille plays, all inscribed as gifts to the Advocates' Library, Edinburgh.

Johnston's generosity seems to have been equalled by his modesty, for contemporary inquiries regarding his identity remained unsatisfied. A letter in *Notes and Queries* (4th ser., vol. 2, 1868) from R. Wilbraham Falconer, M.D., asks about Johnston's translation, saying that the writer believes him to have been a M.D. of Edinburgh or Glasgow, but no direct response was forthcoming, although later in that year William Michael Rossetti wrote to the same periodical to say that he had managed to obtain a copy of Johnston's translation. He mentioned that it was 'not, strictly speaking, published', but, though he praised it, he gave no information as to the author's identity. The *Athenaeum*, reviewing Johnston's Comedy (10 July 1869, pp. 48-9), after referring to the recently issued Vernon quarto, said:

> We have now to record a similar act of generosity in an English gentleman, Mr David Johnston, of Bath, who, to promote the study of Dante among his friends, has translated the poem, and printed it in three handsome volumes as a present, to encourage this laudable pursuit.

The quality of Johnston's work shows that he was a man of intelligence and, remembering the subject of his M.D. thesis, it is interesting to note that his version of the optical experiment in Par. II is well expressed and clear, although from his rather woolly rendering of Purg. IV it would seem that his researches had not extended to astronomy. It may be mentioned that Johnston's Purgatorio is dedicated to 'my very kind friend, the Rev. James Ford'. The latter, who is dealt with in Chapter VII, spent his years of retirement in Bath; he published a terza rima translation of the Inferno in 1865, and of the complete Comedy in 1870.

Johnston's Inferno was issued without any introductory matter whatever; in a short foreword to the Purgatorio he speaks of his 'deep admiration of Dante' and thanks his friends for their kind reception of the first volume. He says nothing of his choice of metre, but no doubt the form could be considered well established by then. He prints his translation in terzine, corresponding line for line with the original. There are arguments at the head of each canto, but no notes.

Internal evidence suggests that Johnston's translation may have been begun many years earlier and resumed after a lapse of time. There are irritating mannerisms in the first half of the Inferno which disappear almost entirely in the remainder of the poem. In the earlier part the unnecessary repetition of words, with no reference to any such repetition in the original, is frequent, e.g. 'with a loud cry I cried' (Inf.I.65). Often this tendency is carried to an absurd extent as in Inf. IV.86-90:

> Take note of him who with that sword in hand
> Before the other three comes as their lord.
> Homer the Poet Sovereign is he! –
> Next Horace comes, the satirist, and then
> Ovid the third, and lastly Lucan comes.

In this part of the poem there are also many 'conceits' of the type (Inf. II.34-5):

> For if I fearless should the venture dare,
> I fear the venture may my folly prove,

and grandiloquent paraphrases like 'Whose coward blood renounc'd

his lofty state' (Inf. III.60). At the same time Johnston often misses
Dante's own repetitions, e.g. the 'dura ... durerà' of Inf. II.59-60
which is rendered:

> Whose fame embraces the wide world's expanse,
> And shall endure so long its movement lasts.

Later in the poem he makes more use of his ingenuity to obtain parallels to Dante's word effects when he cannot render them directly.
Word order does not escape him. He preserves the chiasmus of 'Born
in Siena, in Maremma slain' (Purg. V.134) and of 'Which made the
earth to quake and opened heaven' (Par. VII.48).

Although he translated the poem terzina by terzina Johnston did not
aim at the same kind of literal accuracy that Longfellow and Rossetti
did; he often replaces an Italian expression with a familiar English one.
Inevitably this leads to weakening, e.g. 'Which evil universal all involves' (Inf. VII.18), or 'And let him feel the pain who owns the wound'
(Par. XVII.129). Often he remodels phrases or sentences, deliberately
substituting effects of his own instead of those in the original, e.g.

> Nought it avail'd him, for give rein to fear
> And wings then lose their pow'r.   (Inf. XXII.127-8)

> But does as nature doeth in the flame,
> Which spite of thousand efforts riseth still. (Par. IV.77-8)

On the whole Johnston's reconstruction is well done, and he maintains
a very competent level of language and versification, avoiding archaism
and colloquialism, with a minimum of distortion and padding. His
version would be no use as a crib, but it would give the uninitiated
reader a very fair idea of Dante's content and meaning.

Unfortunately there are too many inaccuracies which indicate that
Johnston did not always take the trouble to understand his original,
since many of them suggest carelessness. One of the strangest is in
Purg. X.46-8 which reads:

> 'Let not one place alone thy thoughts absorb,'
> My gentle master said, who by me stood
> Close to the part where beat the hearts of men.

The mistake might pass almost unnoticed had not Johnston, evidently
visualising the scene as misunderstood by him, inserted in lines 100-1
a gratuitous indication of direction:

> 'Lo! from the right with steps sedate and slow,'
> The poet murmured, 'many people come.'

This reverses the whole scene, and makes nonsense of XIII.10-21 and other succeeding passages. Doré, whose misrepresentations of the text reach the height of their absurdity in Purgatorio, made the same mistake, but Johnston could not have been misled by him, for his translation appeared a year before the Frenchman's illustrations.

'In effort vain he must repentance seek' (Inf. XI.42) is a distortion which spoils the meaning. 'This one cometh not / Forc'd by thy sister's mastery' (Inf. XII.19-20) does violence both to mythology and to the meaning of 'ammaestrato'. 'Our need of small account he made' (Inf. XXIII.140) must surely have resulted from an over-hasty glance at 'mal contava la bisogna', and the same applies to 'Who may he be who bears this bitter look?' (Inf. XXVIII.93). Johnston has missed the point of the shadow in Purg. V.4-5: 'Lo, how the solar ray / From the left hand strikes him who is below.' Careless likewise is the rendering of Purg. XXVIII.68-9:

> And in her hands entwined were lovelier flowers
> Than this high region shows which needs no seed.

There is a bad slip in Par. XVII.118-20 which reverses the sense:

> And if I seem a timid friend to truth,
> 'Tis from the fear of losing fame with those
> Who shall call ancient this now passing time.

With the limitations indicated, Johnston's translation is quite a good one, much superior in metre and language to Pollock's, more readable, though much less useful, than Longfellow's. Though he often disappoints, he has many sustained passages that are pleasing and dignified, and two short ones are quoted by way of illustration.

> And then there came across the turbid wave
> The rushing of a sound so full of dread
> That the two shores with very trembling shook;
> Like was it to a fierce and mighty wind,
> Which, born impetuous of opposing heats,
> The forest strikes with pow'r disdaining check;
> It breaks the branches, tears them, flings them forth;
> Onward it rushes, dust compelling, proud;
> Wild beasts and shepherds flee before its rage. (Inf. IX.64-72)

> I saw a light which like a river flowed,
> Flashing with waves of glory, both its banks
> Rich with the wondrous livery of spring.
> Forth from this river issued living sparks,
> And these on every side dropped on the flowers,
> Like unto rubies which are set in gold.
> Then as if drunk with odours, these again
> Plunged in the body of the glorious stream,
> And as one entered, came another forth.   (Par. XXX.61-9)

The review of Johnston's translation in the *Athenaeum*, already mentioned, was brief but favourable. A valuable tribute came from W. M. Rossetti who, in his letter to *Notes and Queries* quoted above, says:

> The merit of the translation is certainly such as to qualify it for wider diffusion than circumstances give it at present.

In view of the fact that his own translation, made on the same principle and published three years earlier, had been coldly received, this spontaneous praise carries conviction. It is, indeed, a very fair comment on a good achievement.

BIBLIOGRAPHY TO CHAPTER V

POLLOCK

The Divine Comedy; or The Inferno, Purgatory, and Paradise, of Dante Alighieri, born MCCLXV, died MCCCXXI, rendered into English by Frederick Pollock, Esq. With fifty illustrations drawn by George Scharf, Junr. London: Chapman and Hall. 1854

ROSSETTI

The Comedy of Dante Allighieri [*sic*]. Part I – The Hell. Translated into blank verse by William Michael Rossetti, with introduction and notes. London and Cambridge: Macmillan and Co. 1865

LONGFELLOW

The Divine Comedy of Dante Alighieri, translated by Henry Wadsworth Longfellow. Boston: Ticknor and Fields. 1867, 3 vols. (quarto)

The Divine Comedy of Dante Alighieri, translated by Henry Wadsworth Longfellow. London: George Routledge & Sons. 1867 (octavo)

(There are numerous subsequent editions in many formats both in America and Europe.)

JOHNSTON

Translation of Dante's Inferno by David Johnston. Bath: Printed at the 'Chronicle' Office. 1867

Translation of Dante's Purgatorio, as above. 1867

Translation of Dante's Paradiso, as above. 1868

CHAPTER VI

MISCELLANEOUS

OF the four translators dealt with in this chapter, whose work is not readily classifiable elsewhere, three must be set down as eccentrics. Their translations are worthless from almost every point of view, and are recorded merely as curiosities. The other, Parsons, is a really interesting figure, and although his Dante has been long forgotten, we may be forgiven for dwelling on him at more length.

During the last twenty years of the nineteenth century we find quite a few versions of the Divine Comedy which might be described as 'experimental', and although none of these have achieved real success, their average quality is much higher than that of Bannerman, Whyte or Wilkie. They are discussed in Chapter IX.

THOMAS WILLIAM PARSONS (1819-92)

Parsons' father was an immigrant from Britain, who had graduated in medicine at Harvard, and practised as a doctor and dentist in Boston, where Thomas was born. The boy attended the Boston Latin School and, though he left without taking a degree, he was excellently grounded in the classics, as is evident from his writings and his occasional Latin verse. With his father he visited Europe in 1836-7, spending some time in Florence; on his return he studied medicine at Harvard, but did not complete the course. He was, however, styled Dr Parsons, and, like his father, practised in Boston. He visited Italy again in 1847, and paid a long visit to London in 1871-2; from the latter date to his death he devoted himself entirely to literature.

Parsons' was the first American translation of Dante to appear in print, and his work spread over a period of fifty years. As a New Englander he was a not unworthy forerunner of a line of gifted Dantists; although he was twelve years younger than Longfellow and not much older than Norton, he was in the field long before any of them. His experiments in metre, and his often expressed dissatisfaction with his own work, show him perpetually engaged in a poetic quest. Although his nature was reserved, he endeared himself to his circle of acquaintance, and what we know of him from others confirms the pleasant picture given of him as 'The Poet' in Longfellow's *Tales of a Wayside Inn* (1863):

> A Poet, too, was there, whose verse
> Was tender, musical, and terse;
> The inspiration, the delight,
> The gleam, the glory, the swift flight,
> Of thoughts so sudden, that they seem
> The revelations of a dream,
> All these were his; but with them came
> No envy of another's fame;
> He did not find his sleep less sweet
> For music in some neighbouring street,
> Nor rustling hear in every breeze
> The laurels of Miltiades.

Parsons began to memorise the Divine Comedy when he first visited Florence at the age of seventeen, and it remained the greatest single interest of his life. He published a few small volumes of verse; one of them, *The Shadow of the Obelisk*, appeared in London during his residence there in 1872. His poetry is now more or less forgotten, except for the well-known 'On a bust of Dante', prefixed to his first translation in 1843. This version contained cantos I-X of the Inferno, rendered in quatrains of ten-syllabled lines rhymed *a b a b*. He said that he had first tried terza rima, but had given it up, finding that 'the more exactly the measure of Dante was imitated, the ruder the verse'. Among the friendly critics of his earliest volume was Andrews Norton, father of the translator, who recalls, in his preface to the 1893 volume, listening to their discussions in his youth. Parsons was a notoriously slow worker; nothing further appeared till 1865, when he made a spurt and printed a version of Inf. I-XVII, with considerable revision of the earlier part, in time for the centenary. He went on to complete the Inferno and published it in 1867. Three years later he began to publish the Purgatorio, canto by canto, in the *Catholic World*; these instalments continued till 1872, when the second cantica was still incomplete. The first eight cantos were issued as The Ante-Purgatorio in 1875 (British edition 1876). All the cantos already published, together with some fragments of others, including four short extracts from the Paradiso, were collected in the volume issued under the auspices of Norton in 1893 after Parsons' death. A list of the passages translated is given in the Bibliography to this chapter.

Parsons was, as we have seen, on friendly terms with the Nortons when he was young; in later years he also enjoyed the friendship of Longfellow, Lowell and Holmes, and he was a valued member of the

Cambridge Dante Society from its formation. He held aloof, however, from the other New England literati. Kenneth MacKenzie in the *Dictionary of American Biography* speaks of him as 'reserved, sensitive and deeply religious', quoting a remark by T. B. Aldrich that Parsons 'carried his solitude with him into the street'. Louise Imogen Guiney, herself a poetess and occasional translator of Dante, who wrote a memorial sketch for the 1893 volume, has much to say of his extreme sensitiveness, carried sometimes to the point of affectation, and contributing to the slowness of his literary work.

> He worked with so real a religiousness that haste, or expediency, or compulsion never was allowed to touch him; merely a little passing mundane cloud, intruding on the medieval peace of his green-bowered desk at Wayland or Scituate, made him throw down his pen for the day.

In his preface of 1843 Parsons wrote:

> If the iron Alighieri himself confessed that his sacred song had made him lean, through many years, it may be acknowledged that, for ordinary faculties, simply to transmute the precious ore into a merchantable shape were no insignificant work. To render him properly requires, in short, somewhat of Dante's own moods; it needs time and toil. Fasting and solitude might not be amiss.

At the end of the 1867 volume he placed the colophon, 'Tantus labor non sit cassus', and Miss Guiney tells us that as he revised and polished the manuscript he would mark each 'baptised page' with the sign of the cross, and sometimes add the doleful rubric, 'Vae mihi! dies parum efficax'.

Parsons was a zealous Anglican, and his 1843 preface was aggressively Protestant. He had mellowed by 1870, when his first contribution to the *Catholic World* was published, but he felt that his position might seem ambiguous, and the tolerant editor allowed him to write an explanatory note which contained the sentences:

> The Romish doctrine of Purgatory may be combated as an article of faith, but it must be admitted as a true statement of the condition of mankind religiously considered. The wretched state of man living without God in the world, the self conviction of sin, the possibility of attaining through contrition and penance to the *peace which passeth understanding*, is the sum of the doctrine embodied in the Divina Commedia.

Dr La Piana gives a very full account of Parsons' work and of American judgments on it in D.A.P. pp. 76–89. Another useful compilation is *Letters of Thomas William Parsons* (Boston, 1940), edited by Zoltan Haraszti, with an essay on the subject's character and achievement by Austin Warren.

It was Parsons' original aim to make the Divine Comedy into what he called a 'popular' English poem; that is, he intended that it should be readable as poetry, and reflect rather than transliterate the original. Andrews Norton persuaded him to modify this aim, by keeping closer to the letter of Dante. Critics have differed, according to their views of the function of translation, about the wisdom of this course. To some the later cantos are pedestrian compared with the 1843 version. Charles Eliot Norton, on the other hand, although he gave high praise to Parsons' poetic qualities, felt that the first duty of a translator was to his original. Parsons himself seems eventually to have attempted a compromise between the two styles. For instance, Inf. III.77-8,

> quando noi fermerem li nostri passi
> su la trista riviera d'Acheronte,

was rendered in the 1843 edition as

> Soon as we slack awhile our painful pace
> On the sad margin of old Acheron.

In 1867 this became more literal:

> Soon as we stay our footsteps for a space
> Beside the dismal strand of Acheron,

but in 1893 the first version was almost entirely restored:

> Soon as we slack awhile our painful pace
> On the sad marge of ancient Acheron.

Parsons said in 1843 that, after various experiments, including 'defective' terza rima, he decided on 'the stately and solemn quatrain, the stanza of Gray and Dryden'. The decision was partly due to innate conservatism; he felt that the poetry of the past 'already had possession of the English ear'. Here is the opening of Inf. II as printed in the 1893 edition:

> Day was departing, and the dusky light
> Freed earthly creatures from their labor's load;
> I alone girt me to sustain the fight,
> (A strife no less with pity than my road),
> Which memory now shall paint in truth's own hue:
> O Muse, O soaring genius, help me here!
> O mind, recording all that met my view!
> Here shall thy native nobleness appear.

From the very beginning Parsons' four-line stanza was in perpetual conflict with the terzine which he was translating. In spite of his desire to make the Inferno into an English poem, he was far too conscious of the quality of the original to try, as one critic has alleged, to pad out three lines of Italian to four of English. Indeed he tends to compress; very often, as in the above example, he gets nine lines of Italian into eight of English; most of his cantos contain fewer lines than the original. In many cases he could not take any other course than that of using three lines of English to render three of Italian, which led to much awkwardness, and often meant that a terzina, divided between two quatrains, was dislocated and deprived of any rhyme linkage. He also had many difficulties at the end of cantos, where some extreme form of compression or padding had to be resorted to.

He started the Purgatorio in quatrains, but at the end of canto III he used a new expedient for the first time by departing from his normal rhyme scheme, the last fourteen lines rhyming *a b a b a c b d c d e f e f.* In canto IV he twice expands a quatrain to six lines rhymed *a b a b a b.* By canto V the introduction of variations is fully established, and throughout the remainder of the Purgatorio continuous quatrains are the exception rather than the rule. In a few places genuine terza rima is introduced and kept up for a few terzine. The longest such passage is at the conclusion of Purg. XX and reads:

> Like those old shepherds who first heard that lay
> We stood immovable and in suspense,
> Till the cry ceased, the trembling died away.
> Then did our holy journey recommence,
> Viewing the shades to their accustomed wail
> Turning, and grovelling in their penitence.
> Never did ignorance my mind assail
> With such a battle of desire to learn,
> (Unless herein my recollection fail)
> As seemed to make the soul within me yearn.
> I dared not slack our speed by asking aught,
> Nor of myself the cause could I discern:
> So timidly I went, and full of thought.

For the most part, however, the rhyme scheme in Purgatorio is quite irregular. Of the four fragments from the Paradiso the first is in 'defective' terza rima, and the other three are in quatrains with occasional variations.

The extent to which Parsons diverged from his original scheme seems to have gone largely unnoticed and unrecorded by critics. Toynbee (D.S. 1921) describes all the translation, with the exception of Par. I.1-36, as being in rhymed quatrains. But W. E. Gladstone may not have been so wide of the mark when (as recorded in Haraszti's edition of the Letters) he wrote to Parsons acknowledging a copy of the Ante-Purgatorio, 'I am glad you do not despair of or abandon the terza rima'. The remark has been taken to suggest that the learned statesman did not examine the volume with much care, but though there is no instance of sustained terza rima in these eight cantos, there is sufficient interlacing of rhymes to convey the impression of such a scheme.

Parsons' translation has many pleasant qualities. He keeps his vocabulary simple and vivid, avoiding long words, though now and again he uses such phrases as 'the sacerdotal sign' or 'adamantine cars' (the latter = 'quelle cose belle' in Inf. I.40). There are lines out of character like 'No sorrow paled their cheeks nor gladness flushed' (Inf. IV.84), and there is weakening like 'I knew my dreams false, but their truth observed' (Purg. XV.117). There is some clumsiness, and sometimes bad enjambement caused by the disparity between the terzine and the quatrains. On the other hand there are many good lines. Purg. XXX.92-3 has a fine ring:

> Listening their chant whose notes for evermore
> Repeat the rhythm of Heaven's eternal spheres.

There are neat renderings like 'Thine is cold flattery in this waste of Hell' (Inf. XXXII.96) or 'Lack land he may, but shall not lack disgrace' (Purg. XX.76), and an excellent Dantesque touch in Purg. XXVIII.63, 'like a gift she threw / On me her lifted eyes'.

It is almost equally easy to make a collection of pearls or husks from Parsons. The work was done over a long period of years, and varies considerably in quality. It puzzled the reviewers; the *Athenaeum*, dealing with the 1843 volume (23 Mar. 1844, pp. 267-8), agreed that Parsons had 'justified himself as a poet in his own right', but thought he was not so good as Dayman, whose Inferno was discussed in the same article. The same periodical was even less encouraging on the subject of the 1867 volume (22 Feb. 1868, pp. 286-7). Perhaps the best summing up is that of C. E. Norton in the *North American Review* (Vol. 102, 1866, pp. 509ff):

> The Divine Comedy in Parsons' translation remains at least a poem; but its tone is not that of Dante's poem; its merits are its own.

PATRICK BANNERMAN

This translator so far remains unidentified. His book contains no information about himself beyond his name. The publishers, William Blackwood and Sons Ltd., have kindly ascertained from their records that the entire cost of production was met by the translator; they printed 528 copies, and the book was priced at twelve shillings, but no sales are recorded. Probably the author disposed of most of them himself. He must have been a man of substance and also of some education; but his name cannot be found on the graduate roll of any Scottish University, nor in any of the directories of the period. The name is a common one in the north-east, where Patrick is often interchangeable with Peter; but no suitable candidate has been found. It is possible that the name was a pseudonym.

Bannerman is well in the running for the invidious distinction of having produced the worst English translation of the Divine Comedy. There are two contemporary verdicts on record. The *Athenaeum* (8 June 1850, p. 611) opined:

> A slight glance at this work is enough to satisfy the competent reader that the attempt is a failure. The version is rendered for the most part in couplets, – with an occasional triplet and unrhymed line, – and in no way represents the terza rima of the original. . . . In short a rendering so inelegant and faulty cannot be accepted as a fitting interpretation of the 'Divine' poem of the great Italian.

In the survey which appeared in the *Westminster Review* (Jan. 1861) Bannerman is dealt with at the end, along with Boyd, Hindley and O'Donnell:

> Of the few versions which remain to be considered, we scarcely know to which we ought to assign the bad pre-eminence of being the very worst of any. Mr Bannerman, if, as we presume, he is a Caledonian, has of course the same prescriptive right to be dull that a crow has to be black, or an adder deaf; but his nationality is no excuse at all for the presumption of undertaking to translate from a language of which he can really know nothing. His work, both as a translator and a poet, is as nearly worthless as anything we have seen.

The metrical form of Bannerman's translation has been variously described; Toynbee calls it 'heroic verse, irregularly rhymed', which is about as near as one can get. Some bibliographers have described it as being in heroic couplets, an impression that might be given by the first canto, beyond which probably few readers have persevered. This begins with seven couplets, followed by a triplet, another couplet, an unrhymed line, two more couplets, a triplet, a couplet, a triplet, and another unrhymed line; canto II opens with an assortment of couplets and triplets. But from that point onwards the general rule seems to be that each terzina is represented by an unrhymed line followed by a couplet. There are occasional alexandrines; oftener there are lines completely unscannable, if not indeed unreadable, like 'My sweet master said, who had me at's side' (Purg. X.47) or 'Why hast thou, my son, / Towards us, who are thy parents, thus done?' (Purg. XV.89-90). There are all kinds of oddities. In one place four consecutive lines are completely unrhymed; in another six successive lines rhyme with each other. The rhymes themselves are extraordinary; it is sometimes difficult to know which endings are really meant to rhyme. In Inf. XXII, for instance, we find the following series of line endings: 'hair – apart – depart – him – hair – otter – name – first – addressed – all – can – one – ascertain – ease – adversaries'. There are also such pairs as 'pray – Gomita', 'Pisistratus – gracious', 'Brigata – canto', 'utter – together'.

Metrical chaos apart, either regarded as a translation or as a piece of connected verse, Bannerman's attempt is almost entirely rubbish. He seldom manages to get more than fifty per cent of Dante's meaning; quite often he either obscures it completely, contradicts it, or says something totally different. How he arrived at these results is a mystery. By what process, for instance, did he turn Inf. II.3-6 into:

> And I alone was girding for the war,
> Both of the journey and of their piteous star
> Which he who pictures will not wander far?

In Inf. VI.109-10 we read: 'To perfect misery will not they attain / The accursed race'. Inf. XIV.52-4 is amusing:

> If Jupiter his workman wearied out,
> Struck with sharp thunderbolt before he fell
> (By such percussion, too, I came to hell) . . .

Many translators have made heavy going of Inf. XXX.139-41; Bannerman has:

> So 'twas with me, without the power to speak:
> The excuse I wished to make – something forbid
> Excusing, though I never thought I did.

Some terzine are chaotic, e.g. Purg. XVII.58-60:

> He acts with us as man does with himself –
> Face of entreaty, need though he espy,
> Sets himself ill-naturedly to deny.

Par. XXXI.16-18 reads:

> Descending down the flower, from bench to bench,
> They spoke of peace and ardour they acquired
> In voyage ventilating, the side untired.

At times one feels that Bannerman may be a disciple of Browning
in the matter of rhyming, e.g. Purg. XII.109-14:

> While turning round about our persons there,
> 'Blessed the poor in spirit', we hear men
> Sing, as if they said to us a sermon;
> But, ah! how different were those echoes from
> Th' infernal tones, notes that now approach us! –
> Here sweet song, and there laments ferocious.

Now and again one comes across a really good line, e.g. (Purg. VI.
125-6):

> a Marcellus seen again
> In every petty village partisan,

or 'The tremulous lustre of the morning star' (Purg. XII.90), or 'Behind
my ship, which, singing, cuts the waves' (Par. II.3). These appear,
however, to be entirely accidental, for there is no sign that Bannerman
made any effort to rise to the height of the more poetical passages.

BRUCE WHYTE

Little is known of this translator. In 1841 his *Histoire des langues
romanes et de leur littérature depuis leur origine jusqu'au XIVe siècle* was
published in Paris in three volumes. In the foreword he explains that
the book was originally written in English but the author, since 'lui et
sa famille résident en France depuis plusieurs années', had it turned
into French by M. Eichhoff, so that he could have the printing carried
out efficiently in Paris and under his personal supervision. The book
includes some translations from Dante, which remain in English. The
title page gives his name as M. A. Bruce Whyte, but the foreword is
signed A. Bruce Whyte, so the M. evidently stands for 'Monsieur'; in
one of the appendices he is referred to as Al. Bruce Whyte. In 1859
his translation of Dante's Inferno was published in London; the title
page describes him as Bruce Whyte, Advocate. There is a general
resemblance between the passages from the Comedy in the 1841 volume
and the version of 1859, but in the main the latter is greatly revised.
Whyte's name, and the use of the term 'Advocate', suggest Scottish
origin, but he cannot be traced in any of the existing records.

Whyte's rendering of Dante is one of the most peculiar perfor-
mances in the annals of translation. Its value, whether regarded as a
translation, a paraphrase, or a poem, was tersely stated by the *Athenaeum* reviewer (9 July 1859, pp. 44-5): 'The less that is said of it the
better.' He goes on in an ironic strain:

The author soars to a height almost unknown in the regions of poetry, and is lost to the sight of the humble observer, desirous to trace his course through indefinite space.

Spelling, punctuation and accuracy all receive adverse criticism. The *Westminster Review* in its article of 1861 said:

Mr Bruce Whyte's 'free translation' is readable in some parts, though perhaps scarcely worthy of being read. He has added and left out and spoiled a great portion of the original, so that the work is in pretty strict accordance with the title he has selected.

Whyte's long and involved Preliminary Discourse opens with a vigorous attack on the Italian commentators, especially Biagioli. Dante has been over-explained; 'it is high time therefore to allow him to speak for himself'. After discussing various extracts from the Comedy he continues:

We have said enough to convince the reader that we have no desire to disguise or slur over its defects. We frankly admit that its author is, at once, the most prolix and elliptical of Italian poets. Endued with unparalleled powers of description, he often indulges them to excess, regardless whether they are apposite or not; and, provided the object depicted starts palpably from the canvass, he frequently invests it with revolting, and occasionally with indecent accessories.

He bestows discerning praise on lines and passages, notably the episodes of Francesca, Farinata, Capaneus and Ugolino, and censures severely the descriptions of Thais, the impostors of canto XX, Malacoda's signal at the end of canto XXI, and Lucifer. In conclusion he says:

We beg, however, permission to say a word or two touching the translation, not with a view of disarming criticism, but to submit to competent judges the principles on which it has been conducted, and the omissions which cannot escape observation. We have considered it both as the privilege and duty of a translator to rectify any mistakes on point of fact; to explain palpable ellipses; to neglect or curtail passages of mere verbiage; and to omit altogether descriptions or allusions of an obscene or revolting nature.

He adds that he has cut out the catalogue of names in canto IV, curtailed the passage about the arsenal of Venice, 'admirable in itself but quite irrelative', in canto XXI, and abbreviated many of the transmutations in canto XXV which 'in prolixity and obscurity leave Ovid at an infinite distance behind them'.

Such principles as emerge from this dissertation are belied in the execution. Whyte does indeed omit lines 121-47 of canto IV; but lines 7-15 of canto XXI describing the arsenal are rendered in full, while the only omission in canto XXV is lines 115-7, presumably to avoid the supposed indecency of 'lo membro che l'uom cela'. Lines 136-9 of canto XXI are represented by:

> The fiends the signal gave
> And turning to the left pursued their way,

followed by two rows of dots. Strange confusion prevails in canto XXVIII, where we find, following line 24:

> 'Behold,' he cried, 'how Mahomet is rent!'
> His bowels 'twixt his thighs were evident:
> His heart was visible and all within.

Then come two rows of dots, followed by the first of the three lines above, then going on from line 32. There are other omissions which seem due to inadvertence or carelessness. Lines 91-3 of canto XXXIV, which could hardly be supposed offensive, are omitted altogether. Canto IX ends abruptly at line 123; canto X begins: 'The path thro' which we pass'd, as I have said . . . ', but this conveys nothing to the reader since it refers to the missing line 133 of the preceding canto; moreover there is no reference at all to the fact that this circle contains heretics.

As to the metre of this translation, Whyte's basic idea seems to have been to represent each pair of terzine by six lines rhymed *a b a b a b*. He gives no explanation, however, of this scheme, nor does he adhere to it with any regularity. If he can get the sense of Dante's six lines into five, then he just omits a rhyme; sometimes six lines are compressed to a quatrain; at other times he throws in an unrhymed line. Often, however, his six-line units are quite out of phase with the original. Alexandrines are freely mixed with the pentameters, and here and there we find lines of eight or nine syllables. Once or twice, perhaps by accident, a few lines reproduce Dante's rhyme scheme, but the only sustained example is one of nine terzine in canto XXX. The rhymes are very loose, e.g. 'musest – presumest', 'counterfeit – renegade – execrate'.

The translation itself is a labyrinth of confusion. Lines are transposed, emphases moved, similes changed, on no apparent principle and often to the detriment of sense and significance. This produces some remarkable results, e.g. (X.28ff), part of a passage on which Whyte had bestowed admiration in his Introduction:

Sudden I heard these accents emanate
From one the nearest tomb. Trembling my chief I sought,
Who thus reprov'd me: 'Why dost hesitate?
What cause of fear? Art thou deceived in aught?
Lo! Farinata deigns to elevate
His head sublime; if courteously besought,
His bust he will display.' – Counsell'd, I gaz'd
With wonder on the shade, whose brow and breast
Seem'd to defy the demons they amaz'd.

while in lines 127-9 of the same canto we read:

'Thy reason, I perceive,
Is wilder'd by the evils he denounc'd.
Be not alarm'd; deceiv'd he may deceive!'
And here he rais'd his finger and announc'd
Tidings of joy.

We may add to these curiosities part of Dante's address to Pope Nicolas III in canto XIX, lines 88ff, which is changed to dialogue:

I ask'd the ghost,
(Too confident, perhaps,) what sum of gold
Did holy Peter's sacred office cost?
Did Christ bestow the keys, or were they sold?
'It cost him not a doit. Christ only said
"Follow me!".' 'When good Matthias was enroll'd
To fill the void caus'd by the renegade,
The traitor Judas, what did they require?'
'Nothing!' 'Then bide! Thy crimes are well repaid.'

There are also some very odd lines and phrases, e.g. (I.29-30):

I strove to pace
Up the steep mountain's brow, one foot in air,
And one behind.

VIII.113 is rendered somewhat inconsequently: 'Long time he tarried not, an hour or so'. Geryon is represented as leaving the poets very abruptly at the end of canto XVII because 'no recompense he gets'. On the other hand there is often a profusion of unwanted ornament, as in Whyte's strange complication of the simile in XXX.136-41:

As he who dreams he nods on an abyss,
And fain would hope 'tis nothing but a dream,
Yet shudders at the fancied precipice;
So fain was I my chief's reproof to deem,
So strove in vain my terror to dismiss.

In the midst of all these departures from the text, it is difficult to judge Whyte's knowledge of the original; but he has a good many direct mistranslations which suggest that it was somewhat shaky. There is a ludicrous one at XXIII.41-2, which is rendered:

> Caring alone for him, the rest she leaves,
> With but one shift to veil their nudity,

which has to be read more than once to see that 'their' does not refer to 'the rest'. Some renderings are merely bizarre like VIII.115, 'barr'd the gates against their deadliest foe', or XXXIII.157, 'Whilst his vile body yet is glorified'.

Whyte has only three footnotes, and these merely serve to increase the general confusion. One, for instance, purports to explain the 'enigma' of XXVI.10-12 which Whyte had translated:

> Since come it must, would I might witness here
> Its full accomplishment, ere Time subdue
> My sense of wrong, and finish my career.

His literal rendering in the note and the remarks which follow it fail to convey what point he is trying to make, but he concludes by calling Dante's words 'an ebullition of spite'.

WILLIAM PATRICK WILKIE (1829-72)

Wilkie was a native of Edinburgh, eldest son of Captain William Wilkie. He adopted the law as a profession, and was admitted to the Faculty of Advocates in 1851. In 1862 he published an unrhymed translation of the Inferno, and a revised edition in 1866; in each case the very brief preface is dated from Greenhill (Edinburgh). We shall deal with the 1862 volume first and then say something of the changes made in 1866.

Wilkie's Inferno is merely a curiosity. There is no indication of his motive in producing it. His 1862 preface consists of one sentence:

> The text generally followed in this translation is that of Fraticelli (Florence, 1860); but I have occasionally taken a view of Dante's meaning for which none of his editors are responsible.

Fraticelli's Comedy was originally published in 1852, the edition of 1860 being the second. That he used Fraticelli is evident from the fact that a few extracts from the latter's commentary have found their way into Wilkie's English text; but his renderings of some lines are so entirely unconnected with the Italian that one certainly could not hold any editor responsible for them.

To deal first with metre, Wilkie's version contains the same number of lines as Dante's poem and keeps each group of three as a unit, although it is printed continuously in paragraphs. Its only resemblance to blank verse is the absence of rhyme, though even that creeps in occasionally. The lines are of irregular length, the variation being apparently quite arbitrary. By way of illustration we quote II.28-42.

'The Chosen Vessel, too, among the disembodied went,
to gather confirmation of that faith
which leadeth to salvation's way.
   'But I, why should I go? and who permitteth me?
Eneas I am not, nor am I Paul.
Unworthy I appear,
and, venturing to go,
most foolish I shall be:
Wiser art thou and rightly wilt discern.'
   As one unwilling what he lately willed,
reversing all his plans as novel thoughts arise,
swerves wholly from his first design,
thus, on that gloomy shore, my purpose ebbed away,
mid doubt and fears deterring from
that enterprise, so suddenly embraced.

It will be seen that the lines here vary from six to fourteen syllables; elsewhere we have many of four, and at least one of two, with some of sixteen syllables at the other extreme. Sometimes long passages consist almost entirely of either long or short lines; in canto III there are 103 lines of eight syllables or less.

One's first thought is that Wilkie simply used for each line the number of English syllables he needed to render the Italian, but a brief inspection disposes of this possibility. He omits or inserts words and phrases at random, e.g. in line 28 above 'among the disembodied' is his own addition, whereas in line 33 he has only translated half of 'me degno a ciò nè io nè altri crede'. Nor is the sense kept on a line-for-line basis, for phrases are continually transferred from one line to another. Sometimes a whole passage is reconstructed, e.g. XIV.37-42:

And, 'neath those burning and eternal showers,
full constant was the dance
of miserable hands
in whisking off the sparks, unceasingly replaced;
while, like to tinder when the flint is struck,
the sands ignited, doubling thus the torturings.

Nor can Wilkie be seen as a pioneer of free rhythm. There is no sign of any pattern in his irregularity, still less of poetic consciousness. He is thoroughly prosaic, and but for the inversions much of his trans-lation would pass for prose, e.g. (I.114-7):

> that I may lead thee through a place eternal, where / upon thine ear shall fall the shriekings of despair, / and thou shalt see the agony of ancient spirits, who / the second death implore.

Wilkie's inaccuracies, which are numerous, are mainly due to the liberties he takes with the text, rather than to misunderstanding. He is fond of introducing glosses, especially from Fraticelli's notes, into the translation, e.g. (X.97-9):

> You spirits seem to have prevision of
> things unevolved by time, yet Cavalcante is
> unwitting of his Guido's actual state.

His method involves much weakening, but occasionally he has a good line like 'O cumbrous garb for never-ending time' (XXIII.67), or such ingenious substitutions as (XXXI.22-4):

> 'So long the space of gloom,' replied my Guide,
> 'the searching glance must travel through,
> impatient fancy buildeth castles in the air.'

In canto XXI he embarks on a frolicsome style which, with inter-missions, lasts till the end of canto XXX. The episode of the barrators is treated with verve, e.g. (XXI.101-2):

> 'What if I prick him in the hinder parts?'
> 'Nay, stick him in the ribs,' was pleasantly rejoined.

'Ha, babe! didst think me no logician, eh?' cries the black cherub to Guido at XXVII.123, and four lines later Minos announces: 'Another blockhead for the thievish fire.'

The second edition of the Inferno in 1866 curiously omits the trans-lator's name from the title page, though it still appears at the end of the preface, which is even briefer than the first:

> This Translation was originally published towards the end of 1862. Several Cantos, which appeared ineffective or not sufficiently literal, have been carefully re-written.

The revision is entirely confined to the first eight cantos; the remainder is exactly as in the 1862 edition, except that a few very short footnotes are added. The general effect of this revision is to reduce the number of short lines, and to eliminate some of the more drastic departures from the original. It is not, however, carried out consistently, nor can

one see much sign of method. It looks as though Wilkie had got tired
of the process himself, since he left unchanged the bulk of the poem
which contains many oddities as great as those which he toned down.
By way of illustration both versions of VI.1-12 are reproduced below:

> Revived the mental life that failed
> when pity for that kindred pair
> with grief my wonted powers subdued,
> new torments, new tormented souls
> around I see, each way I move,
> each way I turn and gaze, for I
> in the third circle am: that of the showers
> ceaseless, accurs'd, heavy and cold,
> ever in course and quality the same:
> hailstones and snow with turbid water blent,
> pouring forever through the midnight gloom:
> whence putrid smells the soaking ground emits.   (1862)

> Revived the mental life which closed itself
> before the sufferings of that kindred pair
> whose keen distress my powers subdued,
> new torments, new tormented souls
> around I see, each way I move,
> each way I turn and gaze.
> In the third circle I am now, that of the rain
> ceaseless, accurst, heavy and cold
> ever in course and quality the same.
> Large hail and snow with turbid water blent
> pour through the lightless air; –
> stinketh the ground receiving this.   (1866)

The *Athenaeum* (4 Apr. 1863, pp. 452-3) dealt curtly and caustically
with Wilkie's translation, remarking: 'We suspect the manner of the
translation is as original as the matter of it.' Wilkie's motivation, both
in the translation and the revision, remains a puzzle; the work itself is
almost completely valueless.

BIBLIOGRAPHY TO CHAPTER VI

PARSONS

The first ten cantos of the Inferno of Dante Alighieri newly translated into English
    Verse. Boston: William D. Tickner. 1843
The First Canticle (Inferno) of the Divine Comedy of Dante Alighieri. Translated
    by Thomas William Parsons. Boston: De Vries, Ibarra and Company. 1867
The Ante-Purgatorio of Dante Alighieri. Translated by T. W. Parsons. Cam-
    bridge [Mass.]: J. Wilson and Son. 1875

The Ante-Purgatorio of Dante Alighieri. Translated by T. W. Parsons. London: Hatchards. 1876

The Divine Comedy of Dante Alighieri. Translated into English Verse by Thomas William Parsons. With a Preface by Charles Eliot Norton and a Memorial Sketch by Louisa Imogen Guiney. Boston and New York: Houghton Mifflin and Company. 1893. This volume includes:
Inferno, complete
Purgatorio I-XXII, XXIV, XXV.118-39, XXVI.1-40, XXVII, XXVIII.34-110, XXX, XXXI.1-90, XXXIII.1-33 and 64-135
Paradiso I.1-36, III.109-23, V.73-8, XI.43-84.

BANNERMAN

The Comedy of Dante Alighieri. Translated by Patrick Bannerman, Esq. Printed for the Author by William Blackwood and Sons, Edinburgh. 1850

WHYTE

A Free Translation, in verse, of the 'Inferno' of Dante, with a Preliminary Discourse and Notes by Bruce Whyte, Advocate, Author of 'A History of the Romance Tongues and their Literature'. London: Wright & Co. and Simpkin, Marshall & Co. 1859

WILKIE

Dante's Divina Commedia. The Inferno. Translated by W. P. Wilkie, Advocate. Edinburgh: Edmonston and Douglas. 1862

Dante's Inferno. Translated line for line. Second Edition. Edinburgh: Edmonston and Douglas. 1866. (Wilkie's name is missing from the title page but appears at the end of the Preface.)

CHAPTER VII

A SURFEIT OF TRIPLE RHYME

URING the second half of the nineteenth century the trickle of Dante translations in terza rima had increased to a veritable flood. In the forty years between Cayley's last volume and Urquhart's Inferno six complete Comedies and five versions of the first cantica in triple rhyme found their way into print. In vain did the reviewers multiply their warnings that the attempt was doomed to disaster; in vain did they pillory the authors by quoting and making fun of their absurdities. Volume after volume appeared, and although more than once a new translator was foolhardy enough to criticise his predecessors, very few could be described as much better than Dayman, and several were decidedly worse. These eleven translators were all British; three were lawyers, three clergymen, and the others belonged to the professional or independent classes. To them might be added the work of another clergyman, Auchmuty, but since his Purgatorio, although in triple rhyme, is couched in octosyllables, we have preferred to consider it among the experimental versions dealt with in Chapter IX.

Apart from the industry required to turn thousands of intricately rhymed verses into English, further energy was expended on the provision of notes and explanatory matter, sometimes of voluminous extent, and often the fruit of long labour. In addition to that several of the translators were obliged to subsidise their work heavily in order to secure publication. The motives which actuate translators are discussed elsewhere, but it is evident from the prefaces and forewords to these books that throughout the period the authors saw Dante mainly as a teacher and moralist, with a 'message' for contemporary society which it was their duty to convey. Although the beauties of Dante's poetry are mentioned and occasionally discussed, neither the actual performance nor the annotations suggest any high level of poetic appreciation.

Before dealing with the major translations we may mention some minor ones belonging to the same period. None of these are of much importance, but they contribute something to the overall picture.

Thomas Wade (1805-75) was a minor poet and journalist, a disciple

94

of Shelley, with an occasional touch of his master; his sonnets were commended by Saintsbury. He was also a dramatist, but the failure of his *Jew of Arragon* ended his ambitions in that direction. His fame rests mainly on a now rare volume of poems with the daunting title *Mundi et Cordis: de Rebus Sempiternis et Temporariis: Carmina* (1835). Harry Buxton Forman reprinted fifty of his sonnets in *Literary Anecdotes of the Nineteenth Century* (Vol. 1, 1895, pp. 48ff), and stated that he was in possession of a manuscript translation of Dante's Inferno by Wade, in terza rima, written in 1845-6. Forman thought well of the translation, but he reproduced only thirteen lines, viz. Inf. XXXIV. 127-39:

> Remote from Beelzebub, there is a place
> As far as downward doth the Tomb extend,
> Which not by vision, but by sound hath trace
> Of a small brook, that hither doth descend
> Along a hollowed rock which it hath worn
> In its winding course, that gently doth impend.
> My guide and I upon that way forlorn
> Entered to greet again the world sublime;
> And, holding all repose but as in scorn,
> He first, I following, did we upward climb,
> Until I saw the gracious heaven unfold
> Its beautiful things, thro' a round opening dim:
> And thence we pass'd, the stars to re-behold.

A further 42 lines were printed in the *London Quarterly Review* (Vol. 48, pp. 120-1). Toynbee (D.S. p. 211) says that the manuscript passed into the Macauley Collection in the Library of the University of Pennsylvania; but the curator, who has kindly made a search, can find no record of its ever having been in that Collection. It would therefore appear to be lost.

John Payne (1842-1916) is credited by Toynbee (D.S. p. 222) with a translation of the Divine Comedy and the Canzoniere in 'verse' (form unspecified), the manuscript of which was destroyed by Payne himself. In a footnote he quotes in support of this claim an unnamed biography, which would appear to be *The Life of John Payne* (1919) by Thomas Wright of Olney. Payne had remarkable linguistic talents, and has left translations of Villon, the Arabian Nights, Omar Khayyam, Hafiz, Heine and Boccaccio, as well as original poetry. The latter is of a high order, and has been strangely neglected, although Wright, who first met Payne in 1904, did his best to build up his reputation. When Wright published the *Life* he was already in possession of the manuscript of Payne's own *Autobiography* which he eventually edited and printed privately in a limited edition of 225 copies in 1926. The statement regarding Payne's early feats of translation differs somewhat in the two books, but we may take that in the *Autobiography* as being the more authoritative, although we do not quite know what Wright's 'editing' amounted to.

> Between the years of 14 and 21 I translated into English verse the Divina Commedia of Dante, the second part of Goethe's *Faust*, the *Hermann and Dorothea*, Lessing's *Nathan der Weise*, Calderon's *Magico Prodigioso*, and countless short poems by Goethe, Schiller, Heine and other German poets, and many Spanish, Italian and Portuguese lyrics, besides unnumbered pieces by French poets of the fifteenth, sixteenth and nineteenth centuries. The translations from Heine and Goethe contained in Vol. II of the Collected Poems are survivals from this period . . . but the majority of those above mentioned were subsequently destroyed as inadequate.

Payne says that he learned a dozen or more languages at Mr Ebenezer J. Pearce's school at Westbourne Park, which he left when he was thirteen, and he supported himself during the succeeding years in situations so various as auctioneer's clerk, coachbuilder, architect and usher. That Payne could have made a good translation of Dante can hardly be doubted; but the claims made in the foregoing account are too vast to carry much conviction in the virtual absence of evidence to substantiate them.

Hugh Bent is listed by Toynbee in D.S. p. 225, under date 1862, as having 'printed but not published' a terza rima translation of the Inferno. It would seem, from his footnote, that the attribution is based on a letter by Jonathan Bouchier in *Notes and Queries* (5th ser., vol. 8, p. 366, 10 Nov. 1877) containing a list of English translations of Dante, which includes the entry: 'Hugh Bent (a *nom de plume*), Inferno, printed, not published, 1862', with an asterisk denoting that it is in terza rima. No subsequent contributor to the correspondence which ensued mentioned Hugh Bent, and no trace has been found of the translation. It may have existed, however, for in 1856 an English version of Tasso's *Jerusalem Delivered* by Hugh Bent was published by Bell and Daldy. The name was a pseudonym adopted by George Atty, but if he ever printed his version of the Inferno it seems to have vanished completely.

An anonymous manuscript in the Bodleian (Toynbee d. 16), tentatively dated by him 1875, contains terza rima versions of nineteen passages varying from ten lines to two complete cantos (Inf. II and XXXIII), some 1250 lines in all. There are also fragments of a rhymed translation of the Walpurgis Night scene from Goethe's *Faust*, Part I, and two pages of trigonometrical equations. It bears a note from Edward Moore:

> These fragments sent to me by Rev. M. Lamert, June 1905. The translation is very uneven, *some* very happy turns but sometimes very commonplace.

This is followed by a note in Toynbee's writing: 'This came to me from Dr Moore. Sept. 1918.' The manuscript is very difficult to read, being full of erasures and cancellations, with alternatives interlined, and sometimes as many as three uncancelled versions to choose from. An examination indicated that the 'happy turns' must be few and far between.

Margaret Oliphant Oliphant (née Wilson; 1828-97) duplicated her middle name by marrying her cousin; she belonged to Midlothian. She possessed remarkable talent and versatility; her novels were widely successful, and *Salem Chapel* has retained its reputation. She had a long association with Blackwood's and was a contributor to their celebrated Magazine. At their request she became editor of their series, 'Foreign Classics for English Readers', for which she wrote the volumes on Dante and Cervantes and collaborated in the one on Molière. With Dante she was somewhat out of her depth, and her attempted popularisation of the Divine Comedy in a book of some 200 pages merely demonstrated her inability to cope with either Dante's thought or his poetry. Edward Moore, usually one of the most courteous of reviewers, stigmatised her volume in the *Academy* (25 Dec. 1886, pp. 419-20) as 'a shallow piece of popular book-making disfigured in the translations by the most grotesque blunders in rudimentary Italian grammar'. Commercially, however, it was a success; originally published in 1877, it was still being reprinted in the early years of the present century. Fragments of terza rima translation amounting to a few hundred lines, not particularly well chosen, are strewn throughout; they contain a sufficient number of mistranslations to justify Moore's condemnation, and are for the most part somewhat insipid paraphrases. One extract will suffice (Par. XXX.19-33) in which it will be noted that the terzine have got 'out of phase':

> The beauty that I gazed upon excels
>   Not only thought of ours, but well I deem
>   That in no other than her Maker dwells
> Power to enjoy so pure and full a beam
>   Of loveliness. I own me all outdone,
>   As never yet was player by his theme,

> Be it or gay or tragic, overcome;
>   For as the sun, that dazzles trembling eyes,
>   So all myself melts from my memory, won
> When but the thoughts of such a smile arise.
>   From the first day when I beheld her face,
>   Ne'er has my song forsook the high emprize
> To celebrate and laud my lady's grace.
>   Now must the singing cease: I may not run
>   This fair course further, having reached the place
> Where artists all must pause, their skill outdone.

In 1878 a slim volume was printed privately by the Formans, the edition being limited to 25 copies, bearing the title *The Metre of Dante's Comedy discussed and exemplified*. It contains translations in terza rima of Inf. I and III, Purg. I and Par. I by Alfred Forman; these had originally appeared in the *Civil Service Review* during 1874. The rhymes are feminine throughout; and in order to combine such an exacting metrical scheme with a reasonable poetic standard, great liberties are taken with the sense. The accompanying discussion, by Harry Buxton Forman, makes a plea for the preservation of the Italian hendecasyllable, frankly admitting that it can only be done by a trans-formation rather than a translation. With all their ingenuity, the Formans failed to make a convincing case, though one cannot but admire their virtuosity. Inf. III.1-9 reads:

> By me you reach the City of all sorrow –
>   By me the seat of unabandoned weeping –
>   By me the tribes that hope not in tomorrow:
> Justice had my great maker in her keeping;
>   Almighty might of God was my inventor,
>   Wisdom, and Love that lived when all was sleeping;
> Ere me no matter drew to any centre
>   Unless eternal, and I last for ever; –
>   Leave every hope behind you, ye who enter.

Even this standard cannot be kept up for four cantos; Purg. I.16-18 is almost unrecognisable:

> Joy found me, like a summer-hunting swallow,
>   Soon as I issued from the deadly places
>   Where all was sad that eye or ear could follow.

Still stranger expedients are resorted to at times, e.g. Par. I.82-4:

> The novel sound and large light made me shiver
>   With speed to know their cause – all old desire
>   Seemed now by this less sharp, and fugitiver.

It is true that some of the renderings are apologised for, after a fashion, in the discussion, which is certainly interesting in its approach, although the result is not likely to commend the method to future translators. In Germany the flow of terza rima versions continued unabated. Between Graul's Inferno (1843) already mentioned and the end of the century, eight translations of one or more cantiche in triple rhyme were published, and there were several in other kinds of rhyme. In France, where the classical rhymed measures were somewhat unsuitable for the reproduction of Dante's terzine, there were numerous versions in couplets or quatrains, although prose continued to be the most successful medium. In Spain the important and influential terza rima rendering of the complete Comedy by Juan Manuel de la Pezuela, Conde de Cheste, appeared for the centenary of 1865; he also translated Tasso, Ariosto and Camoens into Spanish. His versions are conscientious rather than poetical: 'poco inspiradas, pero que se acercan al original' says one Spanish critic. There were two more complete Comedies in Spanish terza rima before the end of the century.

THOMAS BROOKSBANK (1824-1902)

Brooksbank was the son and namesake of a solicitor of Gray's Inn. He himself reached the bar in 1849 via Trinity College, Cambridge, and the Inner Temple; Forster describes him as an equity draughtsman and conveyancer. The introductory note to his Inferno is dated from Lincoln's Inn; the book, published in 1854, is dedicated to his father. The foreword states with some precision that he spent a year and three quarters on the task, and that he hopes in due course to complete the whole Comedy, but no more was ever published. He continues:

> My chief, almost my sole, object has been to make a translation which, preserving the form and pressure of the greatest Epic since the old classic days, may be intelligible and readable to an English reader unacquainted with Italian. . . . I have chosen the metre of the original for my version, . . . and I feel convinced that, though it will at first sound unusual . . . in the ears of many readers, few will fail to observe, if they persevere, how well it suits the subject. . . .
> I think it right to say, that in writing my own I have been assisted by no other translation than the excellent one of Mr Cary, which I have frequently consulted, and to which I am pleased to avow my obligation.

The *Athenaeum* (24 Mar. 1855, pp. 348-9) thought Brooksbank had

less predilection than Mr Cayley for antiquated and out-of-the-way expressions; but, at the same time, he is far less vigorous, and he is sometimes driven into curious straits by the exigencies of his metre.

The *North British Review* (1854, pp. 451ff), noticing a number of recent translations, said:

> Mr Brooksbank's will probably give pleasure to a greater number of readers than the others. That pleasure would perhaps have been greater had he not adopted the complicated structure of verse in which the original has been written.

Similar remarks occur in the long article on Dante translations in the *Westminster Review* (Jan. 1861, pp. 201ff); while the author of the long summary in *Blackwood's Magazine* (June 1867, pp. 736ff) coupled the versions of Ford and Brooksbank as being 'generally correct' and bearing 'the impress of a refined mind', but inadequate for Dante's 'loftier flights'.

Brooksbank's preliminary matter and notes give a pleasant impression; they suggest intelligence, enthusiasm and earnestness, and are modest, if at times naive, in tone. There is, however, no sign of any strong poetic faculty, nor even of competent versification, and his rendering is a pedestrian one, full of the forced rhymes and padding so common in nineteenth-century terza rima. Despite the remarks of the *Athenaeum* reviewer, there are far too many archaisms of the 'I ween' and 'yclept' variety, with such lines as: 'In all thy questions I am pleas'd, God wot' (XIV.133). None the less, Brooksbank often compares favourably with Dayman and Cayley, and there are some moderately respectable passages such as IX.64-72:

> For now above the turbid waves a roar
>   Of sound came rushing on us, full of dread,
>   And at its coming trembled either shore.
> Not other is the whirlwind current bred,
>   Impetuous by opposing heats intense,
>   Which smites the forest, and ungoverned
> Dashes the branches, rends and whirls them thence,
>   And scattering the herdsman and the brute,
>   Sweeps proudly on like sand in clouds immense.

The Ugolino episode in canto XXXIII opens well, but deteriorates, mainly owing to the struggle for rhyme, e.g. (lines 70-75):

> And on that spot he died – and one by one,
>   Even as you glare on me, I saw them drop
>   Between the fifth and sixth days; then begun,
> Blind as I was upon their forms to grope;
>   Three days upon the dead my cries resound –
>   Then grief no longer could with hunger cope.

At his worst Brooksbank produces some very lame lines, e.g. 'Since when for ever round his hairs I swim' (XXVII.117). Sometimes the emphasis is shifted and the effect spoiled as in I.118-9:

> And thou shalt witness those who have not lost
> All their contentment even in the fire.

Other passages tend to incoherence, like XXVIII.37-42:

> A devil is behind, whose ruthless goad
> Pursues us ever, and his trenchant sword,
> Each time that we have trod the dismal road,
> Replaces in their order all the horde;
> Yet ere a second time we pass him by,
> The gashes must be all to health restor'd.

There are a few mistranslations. He has misunderstood IV.20-21 which is rendered:

> The torments dire . . . have painted on my face
> Pity: in thee 'tis terror they inspire.

XV.10-12 also shows lack of comprehension:

> These in such fashion rise above the ground;
> But never master, be he who he would,
> To rear their like in height or breadth was found.

There are however only about a dozen such slips, and in this respect he compares favourably with his contemporaries.

Brooksbank's footnotes are interesting, but mainly in the sense that they tell us something about himself and his outlook. His first (I.2) says:

> The whole Poem is an allegory, and I think we shall not be far wrong if we give an allegorical meaning to every passage at all capable of bearing one.

Fortunately he does not pursue this proposal. At VII.110 he comments: 'What a fine moral . . . !' and at XI.45 'What a grand moral is in this verse!' He quotes Milton, and is evidently an admirer of Tennyson, whose 'Locksley Hall' is somewhat irrelevantly cited in a long footnote to VI.104, 'dopo la gran sentenza'. In this connexion he seems eager to grasp, however faintly, some 'larger hope'; while he was at work on the Inferno the controversy over F. D. Maurice's dismissal for heresy was raging, and it is not unlikely that Brooksbank was ready to second the Poet Laureate in his championship of the Universalist.

Although Brooksbank's translation must be relegated with others of the mid-century to the lumber room, there is none the less something refreshing about it in contrast to the diffuseness and polemical tendencies of many similar versions.

JOHN WESLEY THOMAS (1798-1872)

Thomas was born at Exeter, where his father was a Wesleyan preacher, and he himself spent his life in the Wesleyan ministry; he occupied various charges and died at Dumfries. Although largely self-educated, he amassed an enormous fund of knowledge and was something of a linguist. Throughout his life he was continuously engaged in literary activities. His earliest work was *An Apology for Don Juan*, partly appreciation and partly criticism of Byron, in ottava rima; his anthology *Lyra Britannica* (1850) contains some original poems; his version of the Divine Comedy was published between 1859 and 1866; a pamphlet on *The Christian Sabbath* appeared in 1865, a volume of poems in 1867, a satiric poem, *The War of the Surplice*, in 1871; the latter deals with the troubles of Bishop Philpots a generation earlier. *The Tower, the Temple, and the Minster* and *William the Silent* were published posthumously in 1873.

An essay headed 'On the title of this Translation' is prefixed to the 1859 edition of the Inferno, justifying the rejection of the conventional 'Divine Comedy' in favour of the somewhat cumbrous 'The Trilogy; or Dante's Three Visions'. This title was retained when the books were reprinted in 1910, but dropped in 1914. The original volumes were published by subscription; the Lords spiritual and temporal and the clergy are well represented in the lists given.

In the preface to the Inferno Thomas lays down two principles of translation: first, to give the sense correctly; and second, 'to unite with a version almost literal the *form*, the *beauty*, and the *spirit* of the original'. He then comments briefly on his predecessors. Boyd's version is dismissed contemptuously; Cary's and Pollock's, being in blank verse, 'can give the reader no idea of Dante's music'; Wright's fails through using the wrong rhyme scheme; Carlyle's is 'avowedly a mere prose version'. Dayman, Brooksbank and Cayley have 'their separate excellencies, as well as faults'. He concludes, in words which were later to provide his critics with ammunition:

> Yet notwithstanding the competing claims of these widely differing translations, the author of the present version found that his own had so little in common with any other, that he deems himself justified in presenting it to the public.

He draws particular attention to the copious notes, 'the result of many years' reading, observation, and reflection', and remarks that 'for want of such illustration, many parts of Dante have hitherto remained obscure'.

The translation is in terza rima, and on the whole the terzine correspond to those of the original. Thomas' rhymes however are somewhat careless; there are several places where lines have been remodelled without noticing that the process interfered with the rhyming word, e.g. in Inf. XXVI.74 the line should end with 'perchance' instead of 'discourse' so as to rhyme with 'consonance – advance'. Similarly Purg. XXIX.74, 'Leaving the air along their track so painted', should have had 'air' at the end to rhyme with 'were – fair'. The rhymes themselves are often approximate; but the most notable feature is the very frequent feminine rhymes, which grow more frequent as the poem proceeds, particularly in the Paradiso. Thomas' eccentricities in this direction far exceed those noticed in Cayley; for instance, Par. XV.82-7 reads:

> Hence as a mortal this disparity
> I feel, yet though for thanks my tongue no trope has,
> My heart shall own thy blest paternity.
> And now my earnest prayer to thee this scope has,
> Make me acquainted fully with thy name,
> Gem of this jewell'd cross, O living topaz!

In Par. XVI.36 we find 'My sainted mother's anguish temporary' (to rhyme with 'there he – Hail Mary'), and in line 71 'practically a' (to rhyme with 'Urbiagaglia – Sinigaglia'). Often, too, when Thomas has found one rhyming word which he particularly wants, he has no compunction in distorting the context to bring in rhymes for it, e.g. (Purg. II.40-5):

> But I bent downward and he came to shore
> In vessel swift and trim, which made a swoop,
> Nor gulp'd the wave she lightly bounded o'er,
> With her celestial pilot on the poop.
> His looks a blest one legibly proclaim.
> Within, more than a hundred spirits droop,

where 'swoop' and 'droop' are absurdly inappropriate.

Thomas mixes archaisms of all sorts with colloquial expressions, producing many strange effects, ranging from mere flatness to sheer absurdity, e.g. 'And feeling 'twas "all right", himself, he frees' (Inf. XVII.102); 'When Mary her son's flesh for breakfast used' (Purg.

XXIII.30); 'This day will pacify thy hungry maw' (Purg. XXVII.117).
He is also an inveterate padder, and rivals Boyd in extending 'Taccia
Lucano' (Inf. XXV.94) to 'Let Lucan rest in mute repose profound'.
Cacophony is frequent. There are ugly monosyllabic lines like 'And
then for ever plunged in such dire bath' (Inf. XII.51); awkward ones
like 'To hear it it was needful too to see' (Purg. XXXI.15); others
produced by the need to rhyme, e.g. (Purg. XIV.99) 'O Romagnese,
in bastardy how hardy' (following 'tardy – Mainardi'). One infers a
defective ear from Purg. XII.49-51:

> The hard pavement further yet made evident
> Alcmaeon, whose resentment made so dear
> His mother's lamentable ornament,

and a lack of poetic appreciation in his version of Manfred's speech
(Purg. III.121-3):

> My sins were horrible beyond all bounds,
> But Goodness Infinite an arm doth own
> So great, whoe'er turn to it it surrounds.

Almost the whole of Thomas' translation is made up of such taste-
less and prosaic lines; in justice to him we may add that occasionally
he produces a short passage which is quite respectable and stands out
from the dismal background. The La Pia episode (Purg. V.130-6) is
an example:

> 'When to the world returning thou art led,
> And hast reposed from this long voyaging,'
> Following the second the third spirit said,
> 'Me, who am Pia, to remembrance bring.
> Siena gave, Maremma took my life:
> He knows it, who with his own jewell'd ring,
> Erst on my finger placed, made me his wife.'

Thomas does not seem to have much in the way of actual mistranslation, although the slovenliness of his phrasing often obscures
the meaning, e.g. (Inf. XXXI.97-9):

> 'I wish, if possible,' to him I said,
> 'What of the immense Briareus can be
> May be the next before my eyes display'd.'

Purg. IV.130-1 seems like a misreading: 'First, round its outside,
heaven with motion slow / Must bear me.' The strange wording of
Purg. XXVIII.44, 'if I may trust the sighs' is likely to be a misprint
for 'these eyes'.

Thomas' voluminous preliminary matter and notes contribute little to the value of his work and have been wisely and ruthlessly abridged by later editors. His anti-Roman prejudices are very violent, and often crudely expressed. He desires to claim Dante as a 'morning star of the Reformation', and he tabulates twelve important resemblances between Dante and Wiclif; elsewhere he adduces parallels between Dante and Luther. As might be expected, the doctrines of Purgatory and of prayers for the dead cause him much concern, and he provides two preliminary essays to explain them away as far as possible. In his preface he promises numerous quotations, and these are almost bewildering in their variety, and often of doubtful relevance. Theological warfare is carried on unceasingly. In a long note on Inf. XXII. 128 we are given the following reassurance:

> There is no ground for believing that 'the devil and his angels' are to be the official punishers of sin in the future world. Wicked men will be *associated with* them in misery, not punished by them (Matt. xxv.41); although, in various ways, the evil may be *mutual* plagues to each other, in the world to come, as in this. But it is only by the *Holy Angels* that the finally impenitent are to be arrested and delivered over to punishment (Matt. xiii.41-2).

To Purg. V.101 is annexed a two-page note on Mariolatry, and such protests recur at intervals, culminating in an apology for St Bernard's prayer in Par. XXXIII. The tone of the note to Hugh Capet in Purg. XX.52 is typical of many others:

> The father, if a butcher, was in a smaller way of business than some of his descendants, who have carried on a wholesale trade in slaughter.

Against Inf. XV.12 are some speculations as to 'lo maestro', the conclusion being that 'for aught we know, the Great Architect may have employed in hell, as well as on earth, subordinate agents to accomplish his work'. A jubilant note to Par. XVIII.88 announces that Thomas has succeeded in reproducing 'Diligite justitiam' etc. by an English sentence, 'Love justice ye who on earth decide in doom', which contains the requisite thirty-five letters, a feat unattempted by any predecessor. It is doubtful if any modern reader would take the trouble to plough through these notes. The 1910 editor could not have read them very carefully, for he preserves some obvious misprints.

In spite of Thomas' brash confidence and the obvious inferiority of his translation, his flair for publicity seems to have gained him some success, and no doubt he exploited the value of his name. He was able to publish at the end of his Paradiso a formidable array of eulogies from the contemporary press, including several highly reputable periodicals, as well as extracts from letters of commendation written by well-known professional men. One feels inclined to suspect that some of the reviews must have been 'inspired'. The *Athenaeum*, far from sympathetic to other practitioners of terza rima, thought that Thomas' Inferno showed 'some poetic taste and feeling' and that 'the author has music in his soul' (9 July 1859, pp. 44-5). Of the Purgatorio it averred that it was 'a version with which those who cannot read Italian may be well content' (20 Sep. 1862, pp. 364-5). Praise of the Paradiso (23 June 1866, pp. 831-2) was also expressed, but rather more faintly. Fifty years later the editor of the 1910 edition of Thomas singled out the praise of the *Athenaeum* for mention in his introductory note, but this compliment drew only a very brief commendation (5 Mar. 1910, p. 275).

The attitude of the *Westminster Review* was even stranger. In 1859 it found that Thomas' Inferno 'may compare with the best' and 'is much superior to Wright's and Cayley's', and in 1862 that his Purgatorio was executed with 'unusual success'. Yet between these two dates, in a long article to which we have already referred on 'Dante and his English Translators' (Jan. 1861) it dealt unsparingly with Thomas' Inferno.

> Mr Thomas's translation, though by no means meritorious, is certainly better than either his notes or preface. He tells us that his aim has been 'to give the sense correctly, and, by uniting the form, beauty, and spirit of the original, to do justice to Dante'. This would be an arrogant assumption in the mouth of the most successful translator, and we think that Mr Thomas would have done well if he had asked some candid friend whether he was at all justified in making use of it. His comments, which he says represent the labour of a life, consist chiefly of imperfect and misplaced classical and biblical knowledge, the former part of which might have been, and probably was, derived from Lemprière's Dictionary.... Is Dante's genius so usual a gift that every versifier can soar with safety where Dante has been before him? Are great poems so common that it is a small offence to disgust men with the very greatest? or so rare that it is necessary to select the Divina Commedia for the travesty of incompetent translation?

In the first essay prefixed to his Purgatorio, Thomas made some disparaging remarks about this article, without actually naming the periodical concerned, and without any real attempt to answer the criticisms.

The *Saturday Review*, from which Thomas did not venture to quote in his advertisement, was less than complimentary, and its remarks are significant:

... from an amiable desire to prove that Dante was as good a Christian as himself, Mr Thomas insists on giving Dante the sentiments of a particular Baptist in germ; and, favoured by a happy ignorance of the critical history of the Middle Ages, has read to the end of the Paradiso without suspecting his mistake. There is a mass of undigested learning in the Notes ... but the translation may be read with pleasure by many of the large class who do not understand either the man Dante or his times.

The most serious indictment of Thomas appeared shortly after the publication of his Paradiso, in the article 'Dante in English terza rima' in *Blackwood's Magazine* of June 1867, already quoted on earlier pages. It found Thomas' rendering 'prosaically literal and vulgar', averred that 'the poetry has ... somehow evaporated during the process of translation', and concluded:

... Mr Thomas justifies the publication of his work, by remarking in his preface that it has 'little in common with any previous translations'. We give an unreserved and thankful assent to this proposition; but it does occur to us to wonder whether no faint suspicion has crossed Mr Thomas's mind of the nature and cause of this marked difference.

To complete the list of contradictions we quote from the D.N.B. article on Thomas:

... An able translation, with scholarly notes and appendices. Its merits have been generally admitted by English students of Dante.

How this came to be placed on record is a puzzle; no competent student of Dante could possibly express such an opinion, nor is there any record of it apart from the reviews and letters already mentioned.

An examination of the five original sonnets contained in the preliminary matter of the Dante volumes would set at rest any doubts as to Thomas' poetic gifts. In his *Lyra Britannica*, moreover, an anthology of 'select beauties', which includes poems by Wordsworth, Scott, Byron, Shelley, Keats, and others, chosen by Thomas, he remarks that 'a few original pieces have been inserted, the appearance of which in *such* company will not, it is hoped, be deemed altogether presumptuous'. It should suffice to quote the concluding stanza of a 'Sunday School hymn', which is by no means untypical of Thomas' average attainment:

> Then when the Archangel's trump shall sound,
>   And Christ the judge appear;
> May we at his right hand be found,
>   And meet our teachers there.

As a translation or interpretation of Dante, Thomas' volumes have little or nothing to commend them, and the fact that they met with some measure of success is probably best explained by the remark of the *Saturday Review* critic, that Thomas 'may be read with pleasure by many of the large class who do not understand either the man Dante or his times'. Thomas was, indeed, the first great vulgariser of Dante. The process was begun in a more restrained way by Wright, nor was Cayley entirely guiltless; unfortunately, as we shall see, Thomas has not lacked successors.

CLAUDIA HAMILTON RAMSAY

Nothing has been discovered regarding the identity of this translator. Besides her version of the Divine Comedy (1862-3) she published one other book, *A Summer in Spain* (1874) which bears only the name Mrs Ramsay on the title page. Her initials appear in the preface to the Inferno. Paget Toynbee was unable to obtain dates for her life. The Library of Congress Catalog gives the full Christian names quoted above; this information came to them some forty years ago from a relative, but the record is no longer extant. We must therefore be content to glean what information we can from her writings, which make it clear that she spent many years in Italy, and that in 1874 she was resident in Rome. The account of her journey through Spain, complicated by the Carlist insurrection, shows that she and her friend were used to travelling and could cope with the problems arising in an unsettled country. Mrs Ramsay has the distinction of being the first woman to make an English translation of any considerable portion of the Divine Comedy, nor did she have a successor for over fifty years.

Mrs Ramsay has little to say in her preface of the translation itself. Having remarked that a translator is often a traducer, she still feels that for those who cannot read the original a faithful translation is better than total ignorance. She goes on:

> . . . But the faithfulness of a translation consists, not merely in the sense, but likewise in the sound; and therefore I have preferred attempting the very difficult triple rhyme of the original, rather than the easier task of writing in blank verse. I have also, as far as possible, kept the same words, the same rhymes, as in the original, and even its occasionally almost grotesque peculiarities.

The contemporary reviewers were gallant if a trifle patronising. Dealing with the first two volumes the *Athenaeum* (4 Apr. 1863, pp. 452-3) complimented her on her achievement, and thought 'many passages might be quoted as the most successful and agreeable of all the attempts in triple rhyme version that we have read'; the only quotation given, however, was Inf. III.1-9. The Paradiso was less enthusiastically reviewed a year later (5 Mar. 1864, p. 332), but the notes received special commendation. The *Saturday Review* (14 Nov. 1863, pp. 652-4) allowed her 'much fidelity and a remarkable degree of elegance', adding with exaggerated condescension:

> ... That she should fall short of the nervousness and precision of the masculine style with which she has to cope could not but have been expected, especially as her studies of the poem have no solid classical or historical basis to rest upon; but we are bound to say that she has performed a work exceedingly creditable to her talent and character.

The author of the article of June 1867 in *Blackwood's Magazine* was much less favourable. His main target of attack was Thomas, but he dealt with Mrs Ramsay in passing, remarking that in reading the translations of Ford and Brooksbank

> we feel that we are listening to scholars and gentlemen. It is, in many things, a descent to pass from either of these two versions to those of Mr Thomas and Mrs Ramsay.

This damaging comment is amplified with reference to Purg. XXII.114 where, to suit the rhyme, Mrs Ramsay had padded out the mere mention of Thetis in the original by adding the words: 'with the sea-flowers in her hair'. The review says:

> For such interpolations she makes room by corresponding omissions. And we have vainly searched her Divina Commedia for even attempts to render many a characteristic touch of Dante's own, more precious in our eyes than sea-flowers by the bushel.

This diagnosis is an accurate one. Mrs Ramsay's failure is mainly due to her lack of poetic skill and perception, and not to deficiency in classical or historical knowledge as the *Saturday* reviewer suggests. Although she did not lard her notes with classical quotations to the extent that other translators did, she quoted Greek and Latin authors and ideas when necessary, and showed a very fair degree of acquaintance with medieval history, as well as familiarity with variant readings and interpretations of her author.

Mrs Ramsay's fault is that she entirely fails to equate her practice with the lofty aims set out in her preface. She provides neither a faithful translation of the sense nor a convincing imitation of the sound; she consistently violates the ternary structure, while the 'grotesque peculiarities' of Dante, and also those which are less grotesque, are notably absent. Mrs Ramsay is an inveterate user of padding, mostly of the conventional or pseudo-poetical kind, typical of the romantic aftermath. The Scottish reviewer's phrase, 'sea-flowers by the bushel', sums it up neatly.

Mrs Ramsay keeps more or less to a line-for-line rendering for about three cantos, but thereafter she is very often out of phase with the original, through using an extra line, and has to compress later to catch up; in six cantos she finishes up with three lines more than the Italian, and in two cantos with six lines more. Thus we often find a well-known terzina, e.g. 'O luce etterna che sola in te sidi' starting half-way through one of Mrs Ramsay's triplets.

In her preface Mrs Ramsay avers that one of the reasons for making a translation is to help those whose knowledge of Italian is hardly equal to coping with Dante unaided:

> In these cases a faithful translation is better than total ignorance, or even than spelling painfully through a poem, with the aid of grammar and dictionary.

But a perusal of even the first canto of the Inferno makes it clear that her version would be little use to such a reader. Lines 19-21 read:

> And then the thoughts which caused me dire affright
> Were hush'd within me, and I fear'd no more,
> As I had done in all that dreadful night.

Line 30 is weakened to 'I strove the mountain-summit to ascend'; line 60 similarly to 'Made me return to where the darkness lay'. Virgil in line 63 'from long silence spake in whispers low'. Line 132 is omitted altogether and replaced by 'Wouldst lead me forth from out this desert lone'. An examination of any other canto would give similar results.

There is no reason to doubt Mrs Ramsay's familiarity with the Italian language; her departures from the original are obviously deliberate. She makes no mention of the text she used, but all her apparent departures from the normal interpretation can be traced to inferior readings then current. She had, indeed, given some attention to doubtful passages, for once or twice in her notes she defends her own rendering.

Her main object seems to be the attainment of that 'remarkable degree of elegance' noticed by one reviewer. She does not hesitate to change an expression, omit or invent a phrase, insert a gloss or a piece of padding, and this gives her verse the 'agreeable' quality commented on by the *Athenaeum*. Although she is by no means free from awkwardness and inversion, her verse flows more easily than that of her contemporary translators, but unfortunately the changes by which she achieves this result are almost invariably for the worse.

The renderings are often loose and slipshod, e.g. Purg. III.121-3:

> In life my sins did God's great judgments brave;
> But yet his arms of tender love embrace
> All who return to him before the grave.

Purg. XIII.102 becomes 'As one on whom the sun hath never beam'd', the essential gesture of raising the chin being left out. Loss of such essential features is common, e.g. Par. XIV.49-51:

> Thus clearer gleams the vision of our peace,
> More holy ardour from its depths doth glow,
> And fairer rays thence shine withouten cease.

The 'sea-flowers' of unwanted ornament are liberally sprinkled throughout, e.g. Purg. XXVII.49-51:

> So fierce the fiery glow
> That seething, molten glass, compared with this,
> Were as a grot where crystal waters flow.

In the same canto lines 106-7 become:

> She sitteth, night and morn,
> With eye intent upon the holy rays
> That shine around the glories of God's throne.

Of the same kind are 'on the viewless air' (Purg. XIII.26); 'unto the perfect morn' (Purg. XXIX.20), while in Par. XXIII.108 Mary is to 'shed more radiance on the crystal sea'.

Stock archaisms are frequent and tastelessly used, e.g. eyne, hight, clept, even sain (=said); 'I ween' or 'I wot' are often used for the sake of the rhyme, giving such a wretchedly inferior rendering as (Par. XX.10-12):

> For, each living light in bliss,
> Yet shining more and more, began, the while,
> A song too sweet for memory, I wis.

There are some tolerable passages in the poem, although it is difficult to find one of any length which does not display the translator's typical faults. The following (Par. XXXI.79-90) is as favourable a specimen as can be quoted.

> Lady, in whom my hope doth bloom so well,
> And who for my salvation wast content
> To leave thy footprints on the shores of Hell,

> For all the wonders, 'mong which I have bent
> My steps, I here acknowledge in this hour
> The grace and virtue with thy goodness blent.
> Thou hast from servitude most sad and sore
> Brought me unto a land of liberty,
> By every means of which thou hadst the power.
> Thy marvellous gifts do thou preserve in me,
> That still my spirit, which thou hast made whole,
> Freed from the flesh be pleasing unto thee.

Mrs Ramsay's notes are well written and helpful; naturally some of them are out of date today. She omits altogether many explanations which a student might expect to find in a commentary occupying so many pages; sometimes she strays into anecdotes and irrelevancies. A feature of her last volume is that the extent of the notes is almost doubled, amounting to 130 pages. These contain some interesting matter, including what amount to short essays on Thomas Aquinas, Albertus Magnus, Sigier of Brabant, Saint Francis of Assisi, Buonaventura and Saint Dominic. Most of the spirits encountered in Paradise are adequately commented on, and there is valuable information about the Florentine references in the Cacciaguida cantos.

JAMES FORD (1797-1877)

Ford was the younger son of Sir Richard Ford, Chief Magistrate at Bow Street from 1800 till his premature death in 1806 at the age of 48. James was educated at Rugby and Oriel; after holding various curacies and chaplaincies he became a Prebendary of Exeter in 1849; later he retired and went to live in Bath. His own family and his wife's both had estates in Cornwall, and he was a member of the Royal Institution of that county. Ford published a number of books: *The Four Gospels*, *Twelve Sermons*, *Steps to the Sanctuary*, and a translation of Segneri's *Quaresimale*.

His Inferno was published in 1865 on the occasion of the Dante sexcentenary. The preface contains an apology both for adding to the numerous English translations, and for the inevitable shortcomings of such a work. The only individual translators referred to are Carlyle and Rossetti, both in complimentary terms. Ford knew them personally; he expresses gratitude for their help, and to Carlyle for permission to use his Italian text.

The preface to Ford's complete Comedy of 1870 repeats most of the foregoing, and also replies to those critics who had regretted the absence of notes in the Inferno. He justifies the continuation of this

policy, pointing out that the Divine Comedy had already produced a
a host of commentators and controversialists, and he continues:

> ... To consult and study the greater part of these is not only a weariness
> to the flesh, but labour spent without any adequate remuneration; it
> may be, with positive loss.... Let the Reader of the Commedia en-
> deavour, in the first place, to gain a clear and definite view of its main
> object and general outline. Let him be content for a season to remain
> ignorant of many things.... There seems to be a particular danger, in
> these days, of our informing the intellect, at the neglect of cultivating the
> taste and moral affections.

Ford had revised his Inferno for the 1870 edition, which contains
the English only. He does not say what text he used for the Purgatorio
and Paradiso, but it was a less reliable one than Carlyle's for the
Inferno, since inferior readings are numerous. Quotations below are
from the 1870 volume.

Ford's translation is not much different in quality from those of his
immediate predecessors and followers. He is on the whole evener than
Dayman, but the evenness is a pedestrian one, and his best is well
below Dayman's. His worst lapses are rather less frequent than those
of Minchin and Plumptre, but pervading everything is the perpetual
conflict of sense and rhyme, in which too often both are sacrificed in an
unsatisfactory compromise.

Ford takes the usual liberties with his rhymes, though he is less
extreme than some others. We find 'teeth' rhyming with 'earth',
'thought' with 'distort', 'true' with 'go' and 'brow', 'one' with 'renown'
and 'vision'. He also repeats the commoner rhymes at very short
intervals, a practice which he defends in the preface on the ground
of the limited choice available in English. Strange expressions are
often dragged in to complete a set of rhymes, or padding is inserted,
e.g. (Inf. XXXIV.112-5):

> Now art thou under what is the reverse
> Of that half-sphere, which the dry spacious land
> O'ercovers, and beneath whose top a curse
> Once died the Man, who ne'er with sin was stain'd.

Obscurity and awkwardness often result, as in Purg. VIII.49-61:

> Already was the air obscur'd and brown,
> Yet not so much, that 'tween our eyes thereby
> Might not be trac'd what was in distance thrown.

The expository passages are often very weak, the logic of the argument disappearing in the struggle for metre and rhyme, e.g. (Purg. IV.67-75):

> How this may be – ponder it well, I pray,
>   With thoughts retir'd: imagine Sion's height,
>   As if, on earth, it with this Mountain lay,
> And one horizon should to both bring light
>   The hemispheres apart; along the line,
>   Which Phaeton ill knew to keep aright,
> Thou wouldst behold the sun careering shine
>   On one, and then on th' other adverse side;
>   If clear thy ken discerneth things divine.

Ford also uses superfluous ornament which only serves to spoil the effect, e.g.

> O piteous she, who help'd me, when distress'd!
> Thou courteous, too, obsequious to obey
> The truthful mandates of her gentle breast!   (Inf. II.133-5)

> Yet Sacerdotal curse is not supreme
> Eternal Love's reversal sweet to stay,
> While yet fair hope can cast a verdant gleam. (Purg. III.133-5)

Some lines may raise an unwanted smile, e.g.: 'Yet know, in brief, that all were Clergymen' (Inf. XV.106); 'None can export them from their native place' (Par. X.72).

At times Ford fails to convey the meaning adequately, and this seems sometimes to be due to misunderstanding of the original. He translates 'figura' in Inf. XVIII.12 as 'imposing aspect'; he omits 'genitrice' in Purg. III.115, so that line 116 refers to 'figlia'. Practical metaphors are often obscure, e.g. (Par. III.95-6):

> Fain would I know what was the web, which she
> Left on the shuttle, ere the thread was spun.

Similarly 'As by its half and quarter ten is known' (Par. XXVII.117) or 'Be, as a sixth, which does the four contain' (Par. V.60). The sense of Par. XXII.94-6 is completely dislocated:

> Jordan, full sure, was forc'd to retrograde,
>   God speaking; back in terror fled the main –
>   Less marvels, than if here He granted aid.

One reviewer praised the simile of Purg. III.79-84, which probably represents Ford at his best:

> Forth from the fold as troop a flock of sheep,
>   By one, two, three; while th' others still stand by,
>   Timid, and low aground their faces keep,

> And, with the leader all at once comply;
> Stop, if she stops, quick huddling to her side,
> Simple, and still; nor know the reason why.

Another reviewer commended several passages which all contain flowers of rhetoric, so that the commendation is probably a reflection of the taste of the time.

The reception of Ford's translation was mixed. The *Athenaeum* (21 Jan. 1871, pp. 72-3) opined that he had produced 'a scholarly translation, in some respects a decided advance on the labours of his predecessors'. The *Saturday Review* (25 Mar. 1871) was less complimentary. Several wrong interpretations were pointed out, and the review concludes: 'he has some talent for the work he has undertaken, if he did not so disguise it with rash haste or slovenliness.' The *Academy* (15 Feb. 1871, pp. 126-8) carried a signed review by Henry Fanshawe Tozer. He also pointed out some errors, and then compared Ford's translation with Cayley's, which he seemed to regard as the best standard (he mentions no other rhymed versions):

> Ford has a greater command of rhyme than Cayley and generally his verse has a smoother and easier flow; but Mr Cayley, though somewhat the stiffer of the two, is more accurate and certainly more pointed.

The faint praise of the composite article in *Blackwood's Magazine* (June 1867) has already been quoted in the article on Brooksbank. Tomlinson, in his notorious preface (1877), makes disparaging mention of Ford's Inferno, but does not seem to know that the whole Comedy had been published in 1870. It is pleasanter to record a handsome tribute paid by W. M. Rossetti in a footnote to his own Inferno (XXIV.6), which appeared a few months before Ford's:

> A terza rima translation by the Rev. Prebendary Ford, of Exeter, shortly to be published . . . is of so distinguished a degree of merit that, had I seen it before my prefatory remarks were in print, I should have felt bound to modify the opinion there intimated that terza rima translation need scarcely be re-attempted after Mr Cayley's version. . . . Mr Ford's has convinced me that another experiment in terza rima was well worth making.

In spite of this, however, we can only say that while Ford maintained a standard which compared respectably with his contemporaries, he made no new contribution towards the rendering of Dante in English.

CHARLES TOMLINSON (1808-97)

Tomlinson was a native of London; his father died early, and he made a humble start to a brilliant academic career by studying at the London Mechanics Institute. He had a scientific bent, and while he assisted his brother Lewis, who held a curacy near Salisbury, with his school, and later when he founded a school of his own in that city, he studied and wrote on physics, contributing articles to the *Saturday Magazine*, publishing a manual of Natural Philosophy, and editing a new edition of Daniell's *Meteorology*. He returned to London, where he was appointed Lecturer in Experimental Science at King's College School. He did important original work on the theory of surface tension, became a member of the British Association, a Fellow of the Chemistry Society, and a Fellow of the Royal Society. In his later years his interests turned to literature; his wife, Sarah Windsor, was also an author in a small way. From 1878 to 1880 he was Dante lecturer at University College, London, and besides contributing to the *Encyclopædia Britannica* he published various books on literary subjects, including a volume on *The Sonnet* which contains many of his own versions from the Italian, especially Petrarch, and a discussion on the art of translation. Among his other works are *The Literary History of the Divine Comedy* (1879) and *Dante, Beatrice and the Divine Comedy* (1894). He also made a translation of Goethe's *Hermann und Dorothea* in hexameters, and published a *Critical Examination of Goethe's Sonnets*. Tomlinson was a man of great ability and energy, with practical and successful experience of scientific investigation.

To his translation of the Inferno, published in 1877, Tomlinson prefixed an essay, 'Dante and his Translators', containing nearly 15,000 words, and largely devoted to adverse criticism of all previous efforts to render the Divine Comedy in English. One after another his predecessors are weighed and found wanting, being dealt with both in general terms and by means of detailed examples, some of which involve points so fine as to make us feel that Tomlinson's own standard is incredibly lofty. He analyses not only the work of every major translator already mentioned in these pages (with the unimportant exceptions of Hume and O'Donnell), but also shorter passages such as those of Merivale and Hunt. Some of his judgments are shrewd; but he seems strangely blind to the existence of readings and interpretations other than his own, and several times censures as inaccuracies renderings which are quite legitimate. None of the translators satisfy him: 'there is no version in our language that represents this great

poem in the three essential properties of form, literalness, and spirit.'
He gives some praise to Rossetti, Longfellow and Carlyle for the
second of these properties, and to Cayley for the first and third,
adding: 'The other numerous versions seem to me to be inexact paraphrases, but ill adapted to represent the poem in our language.' He
goes on to opine that there is something lacking in the current system
of education when he finds educated men producing 'no better results
than those which I have cited in this Essay'. Finally he says that in his
own translation 'an attempt is made to combine the three essential
properties of literalness, form, and spirit, in which respects it differs
from all other translations'.

The claim is large and indiscreet. Cayley had already been accused
of bad taste because he criticised a few of his predecessors, but Tomlinson had gone far beyond that. He had attacked, and sometimes
ridiculed, almost every translator of Dante into English who had ever
set pen to paper, and then announced a practical demonstration of how
the task should be done. In the circumstances, only a superlative
performance could have saved him from condemnation; but actually
his version is one of the most dismal failures in the record of Dante
translation, remarkable for the absence rather than the presence of the
'three essential properties', ranking no higher than those of Thomas
and Minchin and on the whole inferior to those of Dayman and Cayley.

The *Athenaeum* was not slow to respond to Tomlinson's challenging
statements. The reviewer (19 Jan. 1878, pp. 83-4) said that Tomlinson's attempt was 'predestined to be a laborious failure, and there we
would have been content to leave it, but ...'. The 'but', of course,
refers to the preface, and the writer goes on to give the translator a
thorough trouncing. By quotations from the first canto alone he disposes of all Tomlinson's pretensions, showing that he was even more
vulnerable than the writers whom he had condemned, and in the very
respects for which he had censured them.

For a sonneteer with strict views on the subject, Tomlinson's
rhymes are very loose, e.g. 'sit – wait – smite', 'thou – do – so', 'be –
reply – see'. One might be prepared to overlook some liberties in so
difficult a medium as English triple rhyme if the result were to improve the verse in other ways. But Tomlinson is as much a slave to the
exigencies of rhyme as his forerunners, and seldom writes more than
a few lines without the intrusion of some awkward inversion or
padding. A few lines from the Ulysses episode (Inf. XXVI.91ff) will
probably suffice the reader as an example of Tomlinson's average
attainment:

From Circe I departed who concealed
Me, for above a year, Gaeta near,
Ere from Aeneas the name that place had held.
Not my son's sweetness, nor compassion there
For my old father, nor the love so due
Which to Penelope should have brought cheer,
Could in my breast the ardour yet subdue
In worldly knowledge all expert to be,
In human vices, human virtues too.
But I set out on the deep open sea,
With one sole ship, and with that little band
Which never never had deserted me.
As far as Spain's, far as Morocco's strand
Did I adventure; the isle of Sards I know,
And others, of which that sea doth bathe the sand.
I and my company were old and slow:
When we had come unto the narrow strait
Where Hercules his cautionings doth show
That no one further on adventure wait,
On my right hand 'twas Seville I passed by,
And on the other did from Ceuta get.
'Brothers,' I said, 'who have arrived hereby,
Mid a hundred thousand perils, to the west,
Ye surely are not willing to deny
To the short waking time that may invest
Your senses still, that ye experience win
Of the lone world that 'hind the sun doth rest.
Consider now what is your origin;
Ye were not made like to the beasts to live,
In virtue rather and in truth to shine.'
This my oration did such ardour give
To my companions for the voyage on,
Scarce to hold back would they commands receive.

We shall supplement this extract only with a few examples of passages
with which Tomlinson had found fault in other translators. He dis-
liked Cary's paraphrase of XXXII.1-6; his own version is:

Did I of sharp and clucking rhymes possess
A store adapted to this dismal seat,
Upon which all the other rocks do press,
I would express the juice of my conceit
With greater fulness, but I have them not,
Hence, not unfearing, I on talking get.

He pointed out Cary's wrong interpretation of XVIII.42 'già di veder
costui non son digiuno'; his own is 'I've not kept fast till I to him
could get'. He criticised Pollock's 'I gave sleep and all my life' in
XIII.63 (evidently unaware that the reading 'li sonni e' polsi' is well

authenticated) and himself produced 'That veins and pulses scarcely I discerned'. He objected to Longfellow's 'Expecteth it will there be more than here' (VI.111) and to Rossetti's 'As was the saying of them where I was' (IV.105) as discordant, but his own versions of these passages are very awkward:

> Yet for this cursed people this the sting,
>   Though they to true perfection ne'er attain,
>   Yet to be greater there than here they cling.

> Thus we went on up to the luminous land,
>   Speaking of things 'twere prudent not to proclaim,
>   As was their talk while with them I remained.

He is scornful of Wright's XV.85, 'How man may best immortalise his name', which he renders thus:

> For in my mind is fixed and touches me
>   At heart, that good paternal image dear
>   Of you, whom hour by hour in the world I see,
>   Teaching me how man gets immortal here

(which makes us wonder where 'here' is). A child, he says, would not ask, like Gladstone's Anselmuccio (XXXIII.51), 'What ails thee, Father? such thy look is grown'; but would he be any more likely to talk like Tomlinson's 'dear little Anselm' and ask: 'Father! how thou lookest, what hast thou?'?

Some apparent mistranslations may be misprints, since Tomlinson was a good Italian scholar. For instance X.21 reads 'And to such wish thou only now dost guide' which looks as though a negative were missing. XV.10-12 is puzzling:

> On such a model were these margins stayed,
>   Albeit not so high or broad they be,
>   Whoever made them, 'twas the Master made.

It is regrettable that an able scholar should have made such a poor job of his translation, in spite of the fact that he was so skilful in detecting the faults of others. One might imagine that his poetic sense was deficient, but some of his other translations, especially those of Petrarch's sonnets, are competent and at times excellent.

WARBURTON PIKE (1818-82)

This translator belonged to a well-known Dorset family, many of whose members bore the name Warburton; their interests in the clay deposits of Purbeck are perpetuated in the style of the still existing firm, Fayle and Pike. The Warburton we are concerned with was born at Church Knowle, Dorset, and was the youngest son of William Pike. He was educated at University College, London, thence he went to the Middle Temple, and he was certificated as a Special Pleader in 1840. The preface to his Inferno (1881) is dated from Parkstone, Dorset, where he had probably retired. He has been confused with a relative, Warburton Mayer Pike (1861-1915), who did not use his middle name on his title pages. This explains why Toynbee records the date of the translator's death as 1915 (D.S. p. 239), and the British Museum Catalogue attributes to him two books written by his younger namesake.

In 1879 Pike published *Translations from Dante, Petrarch, Michael Angelo and Vittoria Colonna*. This included about 1,800 lines from the Divine Comedy in terza rima, together with a translation of Par. XXXIII by a lady whom he mentions but does not name in his preface. The complete Inferno followed in 1881. The only changes in the text are occasional variations of rhymes required when linking up the original extracts. The preface to the 1881 volume begins by saying that some of the work was done 'during the last year' when 'precluded to a great extent from my ordinary pursuits'. He continues rather casually:

> Terza rima was adopted without consideration, and persevered in partly because it had been begun; but it is open to question whether the Divina Commedia is not best translated in blank verse. I have no right to complain of the difficulties . . .

and he goes on to enumerate some of these. He mentions that he used Scartazzini's edition and followed Witte's text, also that he used 'the excellent translations by Longfellow and Pollock to check my own, and I am indebted to them for a few expressions. . . . The rhymed translations were not used.' Pike seems to have been a man of wide reading and culture, who had studied the Italian poets at some length. He shows his familiarity with various editions, commentaries and translations (some then very recent), and in his notes he often gives several alternative lines or even terzine to replace those in the text if some different reading or interpretation is preferred. He does not seem to have had much poetic ability. His translations of Petrarch's sonnets are inferior to Tomlinson's. Pike 'borrowed a few expressions' as he says for his Inferno; one wonders if he did the same for his Petrarch, because quite a few lines are identical or almost so with Tomlinson's.

Pike's Inferno is a pedestrian piece of work, on much the same level as others of the period. It shows signs of haste and lack of revision, and there is quite a gulf between Pike at his best and worst. Loose rhymes are frequent, e.g. 'union – one – gone', 'hence – arguments – cleanse'. There are some very lame lines like 'So I became on listening to this utterance' (XVII.88, to rhyme with 'glance') or 'None with the Soldan taking Acre had been' (XXVII.89). Cacophony is regrettably common, often due to the piling up of monosyllables, e.g.

As one who hears some great trick told just played	(VIII.22)
Being through earthquakes or props failed thrown o'er	(XII.6)
To have due care for their bark's safety's sake	(XXII.21)
I being mule loved brute's life, not man's, well	(XXIV.124)
If thou weep'st not, for what dost weeping keep?	(XXXIII.42)

The tyranny of rhyme is ever present, involving clumsiness, distortion and padding. The Francesca episode begins well, but soon deteriorates, and we have (V.115-7):

> Then, turning to the pair, I said, 'My ears,
> Francesca, and seeing thine agonies,
> Have made me sad and tender, even to tears.'

Even when he is quite correct, Pike is often obscure at first reading, e.g. (XXX.136-41):

> As one who dreams he is unfortunate,
> And while he dreams, he would it were a dream,
> Craving what is, as though 'twere not his state;
> Like him did I, who stood there speechless, seem;
> Longing to excuse myself, I made excuse
> Meanwhile, and that I did it did not deem.

Perhaps his most extraordinary terzina is XXXIV.1-3:

> 'Since now "Vexilla regis prodeunt
> Inferni" us-ward try', my Guide said so,
> 'If thou seest him by looking on in front.'

Pike's slang and colloquialisms are often vigorous and effective, e.g. 'There coin, and here myself, I pocketed' (XIX.72). Bocca in XXXII.86 is left 'still cursing hard and in full flow'.

Two of the best terzine noted are:

> So down the over-fall we quickly strode,
> Making our way o'er stones, which oft my weight
> Set rolling through my body's novel load.   (XII.28-30)

> To truth that bears the semblance of a lie,
> A man should close his lips where'er he may
> For without fault some shame may come thereby.   (XVI.124-6)

Pike's standard of accuracy is generally satisfactory, and his few slips are hardly worth enumerating.

The *Athenaeum* reviewer (6 Aug. 1881, p. 168), doubtless with Tomlinson's preface still in mind, appreciated the modesty of Pike's. Remarking that the new version was better than Tomlinson's, he was obliged to add that Pike had 'undertaken a work beyond his powers' and 'has not the gift of melodious verse'. E. D. A. Morshead, himself a Dante translator, dealt with the book in the *Academy* (13 Aug. 1881, p. 114). He found Pike 'almost always overweighted with successive long syllables' but at times 'firm and rhythmic', summing him up as 'faulty but passable'.

JAMES ROMANES SIBBALD (1839-85)

Son of John Sibbald, tweed manufacturer of Galashiels, and Jane Romanes of Lauder, James was engaged in the family business for a short time, but he retired early, with an adequate competence, and devoted himself to literary pursuits; he spent some time in Italy. He was rather delicate, and he remained a bachelor. During the last few years of his life he lived with his sisters at Napier Road, Edinburgh, and the *Scotsman* in an obituary notice mentioned him as a frequent contributor. He is described as 'a good conversationalist and a genial companion' and as 'quiet in manner and straightforward in his dealings'. Although he had no university education, it is evident from Sibbald's writings that he was a man of genuine culture and scholarship, and some poetic ability as well. His translation of the Inferno was published in 1884, and he died eighteen months thereafter. Had he lived he might well have made the first tolerable rhymed translation of the whole Comedy.

The preface to his Inferno is very short; he asks to be 'excused from entering into explanations that would but too naturally take the form of apologies', and continues:

> I will only say that while I have striven to be as faithful as I could to the words as well as to the sense of my author, the following translation is not offered as being always closely literal. The kind of verse employed I believe to be that best fitted to give some idea, however faint, of the rigidly measured and yet easy strength of Dante's terza rima; but whoever chooses to adopt it with its constantly recurring demand for rhymes necessarily becomes in some degree its servant. Such students as wish to follow the poet word by word will always find what they need in Dr J. A. Carlyle's excellent prose version of the Inferno, a work to which I have to acknowledge my own indebtedness at many points. The matter

of the notes, it is needless to say, has been in very great part found ready to my hand in existing Commentaries.

The book also contains an essay of 90 pages on 'Florence and Dante' which is well written and gives an accurate account of the poet's life and times so far as the scholarship of that day could provide it. The translation is in terza rima, using only masculine rhymes, and corresponding in the main to the terzine of the original, though Sibbald uses enjambement quite freely, both to relieve the continuous end-stopping and to help him in finding rhymes. On the whole the rhymes are good, with occasional imperfect sets.

Although Sibbald's Inferno can hardly be called a complete success, it is well above the average of nineteenth-century versions in terza rima. On the whole, it seems to rank higher than Haselfoot's, who might be given the next place, being quite as accurate, and of rather better poetic quality. We do not know how long Sibbald took to make his translation, but it bears the marks of much care and thought. He shows considerable ingenuity in remodelling sentences in such a way as to preserve the meaning and keep the rhythm natural and the rhyme unforced. By way of illustration several terzine are given below in the versions of Sibbald, Plumptre and Haselfoot:

XIII.58-60

> For I am he who held both keys in ward
>   Of Frederick's heart, and turned them how I would,
>   And softly oped it, and as softly barred . . .   (Sibbald)

> None other I than he who held each key
>   Of Frederick's heart, and turned them to and fro,
>   Locking, unlocking with such subtlety . . .   (Plumptre)

> I am the one who had in charge both keys
>   To Frederick's heart, and he who turned them so,
>   By locking and unlocking with smooth ease . . .   (Haselfoot)

XXIII.94-6

> And I to them: 'I was both bred and born
>   In the great city by fair Arno's stream,
>   And wear the body I have always worn.'   (Sibbald)

> And I: 'I had my birth and found my home
>   In the great city hard by Arno fair,
>   And in my own true body here I roam.'   (Plumptre)

> 'Born was I and grew up,' was my reply,
>   'In the great city on fair Arno's stream;
>   And in the flesh I ever wore am I.'   (Haselfoot)

XXXI.16-18

> When by the dolorous rout was overcast
>   The sacred enterprise of Charlemagne
>   Roland blew not so terrible a blast.   (Sibbald)

> After that dolorous rout when Charlemagne
>   His hopes of high emprise dispersed did see,
>   Not half so dread Orlando's loud refrain.   (Plumptre)

> After the dolorous rout whereby the loss
>   Of Charlemagne's saintly warriors was wrought,
>   Orlando sounded not with such dread force.   (Haselfoot)

These examples make evident the inferiority of Plumptre to the others, as well as the poetic quality which distinguishes Sibbald, and his greater success in preserving Dante's effects.

To show the average quality of Sibbald's work two passages are quoted below. They exhibit both his good qualities and his failures.

> He who in knowledge is exalted high,
>   Framing all Heavens gave such as should them guide,
>   That so each part might shine to all; whereby
> Is equal light diffused on every side:
>   And likewise to one guide and governor,
>   Of worldly splendours did control confide,
> That she in turns should different people dower
>   With this vain good; from blood should make it pass
>   To blood, in spite of human wit. Hence, power,
> Some races failing, other some amass,
>   According to her absolute decree
>   Which hidden lurks, like serpent in the grass.
> Vain 'gainst her foresight yours must ever be.
>   She makes provision, judges, holds her reign,
>   As doth his power supreme each deity.
> Her permutations can no truce sustain;
>   Necessity compels her to be swift,
>   So swift they follow who their turn must gain.   (VII.73-90)

> Of iron colour, and composed of stone,
>   A place called Malebolge is in Hell,
>   Girt by a cliff of substance like its own.
> In that malignant region yawns a well
>   Right in the centre, ample and profound;
>   Of which I duly will the structure tell.
> The zone that lies between them, then, is round –
>   Between the well and precipice hard and high;
>   Into ten vales divided is the ground.
> As is the figure offered to the eye,
>   Where numerous moats a castle's towers enclose
>   That they the walls may better fortify;

> A like appearance was made here by those.
> And as, again, from threshold of such place
> Many a drawbridge to the outworks goes,
> So ridges from the precipice's base
> Cutting athwart the moats and barriers run,
> Till at the well join the extremities. (XVIII.1-18)

There are, however, many places where Sibbald is forced to adopt the shifts which we have so often deplored. The terzina recording 'il gran rifiuto' (III.58-60) is spoiled by padding:

> Some first I recognised, and then the shade
> I saw and knew of him, the search to close,
> Whose dastard soul the great refusal made.

In XI.42 'sanza pro si penta' becomes 'without avail ... are in repentance drowned', the latter word being much favoured by translators grasping for a rhyme to 'found'. Sibbald's XII.119-20:

> Saying: 'In God's house ran he weapon through
> The heart which still on Thames wins cult devout'

is as clumsy as any, and 'Since the way lost the wholeness of its prime' a poor circumlocution for 'che la via fu rotta' (XXI.114). The last line of canto XIII, 'In my own house I up a gibbet went', is merely ridiculous.

The frequent use of a mild form of paraphrase to avoid rhyming difficulties leads at times to weakening, e.g. 'Where all the vileness of the world is cast' for 'che 'l mal dell'universo tutto insacca' (VII.18), or 'This one already I have surely met' for 'Già di veder costui non son digiuno' (XVIII.42). Archaisms are used with commendable restraint, but as usual one or two rhyming words are overworked, 'bland' being one of the worst offenders.

Sibbald's standard of accuracy is good, and only a few slips were noticed. His notes are well put together and admirably proportioned. He has many shrewd and sensible comments to make; his relation of crimes and punishments is interesting and effective; and the whole is enlivened by touches of quiet humour. His note on XXIII.142 is worth quoting:

> Even in Inferno the Merry Friar must have his joke. He is a gentleman, but a bit of a scholar too; and the University of Bologna is to him what Marischal College was to Captain Dalgetty.

Sibbald had an excellent press. The *Scotsman* (19 Apr. 1884, p. 11) gave him a long article concluding: 'The merits of this volume are such as to make us hope the author will give us a translation of the whole of the Divine Comedy.' The *Athenaeum* (17 May 1884, p. 628) reverted to its usual theme of the impossibility of terza rima in English, but admitted that the new version was 'by no means one of the least successful', continuing:

> Mr Sibbald has taken endless pains. So far as we have observed he has escaped all the usual pitfalls. His version offends less than any with which we are acquainted by a resort to forced dislocations of the sentence or the use of far-fetched words and phrases. . . . On the whole the translation is remarkably faithful, the lines run readily, the words, as has been said, are very little contorted . . .

although it added, deploring the impossibility of using feminine endings in English, 'all the massive sonorousness has vanished'. The *Saturday Review* (10 May 1884, pp. 615-6) was very complimentary, and called the translation 'a thoroughly readable English poem'. Best of all was the authoritative article in the *Academy* (14 June 1884, pp. 414-5) by Edward Moore, which concludes:

> Mr Sibbald is certainly to be congratulated on having produced a translation which would probably give an English reader a better conception of the original poem . . . than any other English translation yet published.

JAMES INNES MINCHIN (1825-1903)

No information has been obtained regarding Minchin's family, but he was at Haileybury during 1841-2, when he edited the College magazine and rowed in the College eight. He went to India in 1844 and spent nearly thirty years in the service first of the East India Company, and then of the British Government; in 1873 he retired and returned to England. He continued both the active and literary pursuits of his youth, for he gained a reputation as a rider and a sportsman and was also known for his literary work. He was a keen chess-player and edited the volume dealing with the International Tournament of 1883. The *Times* obituary notice mentions that he was 'a Latin and Greek scholar in the widest sense'. The notice records neither marriage nor offspring, and the only reference to his domestic affairs is his own statement in the preface to his Dante that in 1857 his family was in England.

In his youth he published two small volumes of poetry, *Trafford* (1848) and *Sybil* (1849). Later he wrote a sonnet sequence on the Indian Mutiny, *Ex Oriente*. In the preface to *Sybil* Minchin says that one of the poems was written as a companion-piece to Miss Barrett's *Courtship of Lady Geraldine*, 'the reading of which poem produced on me a greater effect than that of the work of any other living author'. The *Times* obituary says that Minchin's translation of Dante 'was read in manuscript by Robert Browning – who was a friend – and highly commended by him'. Minchin left for India at the age of nineteen in the same year that *Lady Geraldine's Courtship* was published; he is hardly likely to have known the authoress or her future husband at that time. He does not seem to have returned till his first home leave in 1866, five years after Mrs Browning's death; it is probable, however, that a copy of *Sybil* would be sent to Elizabeth Barrett, and the acquaintance with Browning may have arisen in that way. No mention of it has been noticed in the Browning letters.

The early volumes of poetry are immature, although they suggest that Minchin was enthusiastic and that he had read widely. There is a lack of robustness, however, which indicates that he was perhaps wise to turn to translation, although one wonders why his choice should have fallen on Dante, the measure of whose poetic stature he seems never to have fully grasped.

In the preface to his translation of the Divine Comedy, dated 1884, Minchin states that he made his first attempt at translating Dante in 1856, and completed the Inferno early the following year. He tells us that during the Mutiny in 1857 he lived in security amidst a peaceful agricultural community and, having many hours of solitary leisure, he finished the whole Comedy in October. He spent 1858 in revising it, then put it aside until he returned to England on leave in 1866, when Professor Brewer of King's College read and criticised the manuscript, recommended him to revise it further and then publish it, and told him 'that he considered it the best translation of the Purgatory and the Paradise that had come under his notice'. Unfortunately there is no indication of what translations the Professor knew, nor why he expressly excluded the Inferno from his commendation. On his return to India, Minchin spent another year in revision; but although he retired in 1873, it was 1885 before the book appeared in print.

Minchin says that he is acquainted with only three translations of the Comedy: Cary's, Longfellow's and Wright's. To all these he gives high praise, but he feels that 'Dante cannot be fairly represented to the English reader without his triple rhyme'. He believes that some versions in terza rima exist, and that Cayley's is excellent, but he is unacquainted with any of them. Towards the end of the preface he says:

In my opinion, fidelity to the original is a translator's first duty, and that I have refused to sacrifice in any attempt at meretricious ornament. . . . I believe that the Italian student who will take the trouble to compare my version with Dante's poem, however slight his knowledge of the Italian language may be, will find no difficulty in following the original line by line; mere paraphrase of foreign poetry is easy, faithful reproduction is hard. My effort has been to reproduce with exactitude the thoughts and, where possible, the words of Dante in verse that may give the English reader some idea of the exquisite harmony of the original.

Minchin does not appear to have been a vain man; from what little is recorded of him, one judges him rather modest. Probably he penned the foregoing in good faith and simplicity, without realising what a tremendous claim he was making. It must, alas, be said right away that Minchin's Divine Comedy is neither literal, nor verse for verse, nor faithful to the original; it reproduces neither Dante's thoughts nor words with anything approaching exactitude, and of the exquisite harmony it conveys no idea whatsoever. Metrically and linguistically it might be placed on a level with Cayley or Plumptre, but it contains more inaccuracies and ineptitudes than either of these. Moreover, one has an uneasy feeling that Minchin's evident satisfaction with his performance springs not from any lack of modesty, but from a fundamental incapacity to realise the essential features of Dante's poetry.

A few lines from the beginning of the poem (Inf. I.13-27) will illustrate Minchin's method:

> But when the mountain's slope began to start,
>   There, where there ceased that valley of the night,
>   Which with its terror had so pierced my heart,
> I looked aloft, and saw its shoulders bright
>   Already mantled with that planet's rays,
>   Which wanderers in all pathways leads aright.
> That sight the terror of my heart allays,
>   Which in its depths till then no respite gave,
>   That night I past in such a sore amaze.
> And as one breathless from a watery grave,
>   When he has reached the shore from out the sea,
>   Turns and looks back upon the perilous wave:
> So did my soul, which even yet would flee,
>   Turn backwards to behold the pass again
>   From which with life none ever issued free.

It can be seen that the student with only a slight knowledge of Italian who took Minchin at his face value and endeavoured to follow the original line by line would encounter numerous puzzles. Minchin's failure to perform what he promises is even more striking in the lyrical passages, e.g. Inf. V.121-38:

And she to me: 'There is no greater grief
    Than to remember us of happy time
    In misery, and that thy bard's belief.
But since of all our love to know the prime
    And early root thou hast such yearning strong,
    I will tell all, though weeping all the time.
We read one day for pleasure, in the song
    Of Launcelot, how Love him captive made;
    We were alone without one thought of wrong.
Many and many a time our eyes delayed
    The reading, and our faces paled apart;
    One point alone it was that us betrayed.
In reading of that worshipt smile o' the heart,
    Kissed by such lover on her lips' red core,
    This one, who never more from me must part,
Kissed me upon the mouth, trembling all o'er;
    For us our Galeotto was that book;
    That day we did not read it any more.'

As one might imagine from the above, the more complicated portions become very obscure, e.g. (Purg. IV.61-75):

Whence he to me: 'If with that mirror bright
    Castor and Pollux were in company,
    Which up and down the sun leads with his light,
The Zodiac's ruddy portion thou wouldst see
    Whirling around yet closer to the Bear,
    If in its olden path it yet may be.
The cause of this, if thou wouldst think with care,
    Imagine Zion, giving all thy mind,
    That on its under earth this mount doth bear,
So that they both with one horizon bind
    Their different hemispheres: hence lies the way,
    Which Phaethon had not the skill to find.
Thou'lt see how on this side the solar ray
    Must take a different course to the other sphere,
    If thou but givest thy intellect fair play.'

A footnote to this passage paraphrases Virgil as saying: 'For you must remember we are exactly antipodal to Sion, the meridian of the other hemisphere', which hardly seems likely to help the bewildered student.

Occasionally one comes across a few tolerable terzine in Minchin, but it is impossible to read many lines without meeting the kind of thing just quoted. Moreover there are frequent mistranslations; some may be charitably ascribed to misprints or to the exigencies of metre, e.g. the following seems to be an example of the latter, though it is unlikely that anyone could infer from it the real meaning (Par. X.88-90):

> Who to thy thirst the wine of his flask to share
> Would fain deny, possesses such a power
> As water, that to ocean must repair.

On the other hand 'Bound on that hillside by a higher Will' (Purg. XXVII.87) or (Purg. XXIX.19-20):

> But since that lightning, as it comes, doth bide,
> And as it lasts, acquireth splendour more,

must be due to lack of comprehension.

In his preface Minchin had hoped that a 'fair critic' would forgive him if he found 'here and there a faulty rhyme which would be inadmissible in a sonnet'. He also mentioned that he had 'purposely made use of some archaic words in the reproduction of an Italian poem which is at least half a century older than the works of our Chaucer'. The archaisms, such as 'raught', 'dight', 'laidly', are somewhat out of place in Minchin's Victorian English; and worst of all is his repeated use of the word 'wonne', which performs a variety of duties: 'Like as the Romans for the hosts that wonne / Across their bridge' (Inf. XVIII. 28-9); 'In order that his words might nearer wonne' (Inf. XXVIII.129); 'Than if among them in the vale ye wonne' (Purg. VII.90); 'Where the sun seems least hurriedly to wonne' (Par. XXIII.12), and dozens of similar cocurrences. At the opposite extreme the word 'galore' is very frequent, especially in Paradise, where we find 'a doctor learned galore' (XII.85). Ordinary words are strangely misused, 'steer' for instance being used to denote any kind of motion, e.g. 'Holy souls, ye cannot further steer' (Purg. XXVII.10-11).

The rhymes, however, are the most astonishing part of Minchin's performance. He interprets 'here and there' very liberally, for loose, and sometimes objectionable rhymes are everywhere; since Minchin himself mentions the sonnet as his standard his perpetual use of rhymes like 'blood – glowed – stood', 'assailed – mild', 'trees – eyes' can hardly be condoned. Most remarkable of all, however, are his double rhymes, which are extremely frequent. We find continually such ingenuities as (Purg. XIX.70-75):

> As on the fifth ledge I my entrance won
> The people who were waiting there I see a-
> Lying on earth, with faces aye turned down.
> 'Adhaesit pavimento anima mea'
> I heard them saying with such deep-drawn sighs,
> That of the words one scarce could catch the idea.

In Par. VII.4-7 (to suit *tua* in line 2) we have:

> Returning thus unto his strain anew, a-
> Gain was that substance heard by me to sing
> O'er which the doubled glory double grew. A-
> While those fair spirits moved in mazy ring . . .

To suit 'Ruggieri' in Inf. XXXIII.14, line 16 becomes: 'That by the effect of his suggestions eerie'. Even where no proper names are involved we have such rhymes as 'scandal – band all', 'cloister – paternoster – lost here', 'vacant – fecant – complacent'.

Minchin has some brief and helpful notes. Unfortunately he does not say what text he used, but it contains quite a few inferior readings. His long introduction gives an account of Dante's life and an outline of the scheme of the Comedy. There is a short essay on 'The Obligations of Dante to Virgil' which deals mainly with Aeneid VI. Proofs have been well revised, although there are a few apparent misprints.

The *Athenaeum* does not appear to have noticed Minchin's translation, and the only review of any consequence found is in the *Spectator* (27 Feb. 1886, pp. 286-8) which was mildly favourable, but pointed out numerous defects and mistakes, so well distributed that the critic had evidently read the whole work with some attention. The article concludes with the strange remark that Minchin's 'experiment is, with the exception of one German experiment of the same nature, unique'. It is not clear what this refers to – presumably to the claim of having translated the Comedy faithfully, verse for verse. If so it is the claim, not the performance, which is unique.

EDWARD HAYES PLUMPTRE (1821-91)

This translator was the son of Edward Hallows Plumptre, a London solicitor whose brother, Charles John Plumptre, was well known in his day as an educationist. The younger Edward had a brilliant academic career at University College, Oxford, where in 1844 he gained a double first in mathematics and classics. He held a fellowship at Brasenose for three years; was ordained in 1846; then taught at King's College, London, becoming professor of pastoral theology in 1853 and of exegesis in 1864. Just after leaving Oxford he married Harriet, sister of Frederick Denison Maurice, and was considerably influenced by the latter, some of whose theological ideas he discarded later, but whose social aims remained with him throughout life. He took an interest in evening classes and in the education of women, and from 1875 to 1877 he was principal of Queen's College, which had been founded by

Maurice. Plumptre was appointed a prebendary of Saint Paul's in 1863; then in 1881 he became Dean of Wells, a post which he occupied with success and dignity for the remaining ten years of his life.

No biography of Plumptre has been published, but the tributes of friends and colleagues give the impression of an able and amiable man, possessed of wide scholarship, indefatigable industry and boundless enthusiasm. His literary output was enormous and varied, including numerous scriptural commentaries on both the Old and New Testaments, translations of Sophocles and Aeschylus, a *Life of Thomas Ken*, and many books of sermons and poems. In spite of these activities, he carried on his teaching and pastoral duties with unfailing diligence and success.

Plumptre's original verse was described by a sympathetic critic as 'refined and elegant but seldom really forcible'. His hymns are the only part of it that has survived; they are well written for their purpose, and still retain their place in most collections. It may be mentioned that in his hundreds of notes he has little to say of Dante as a poet, nor does his translation show much sign of effort to rise to the level of the finer passages. His ear seems to have been easily satisfied, and one cannot think that his faculty of literary appreciation was acute. His versions of the Greek dramas, in unrhymed verse, maintain a respectable but not an impressive level, and are certainly better than his Dante.

In his preface Plumptre tells us that he had translated portions of the Comedy as early as 1867, and he felt from the first that terza rima was essential. In 1883 he printed the first four cantos of the Inferno, along with the Francesca and Ugolino episodes, and sent them for criticism to such friends and acquaintances as Cardinal Newman, W. E. Gladstone, Dean Church, Archdeacon Farrar, J. A. Symonds, J. G. Whittier, Edward Moore, H. F. Tozer and A. J. Butler. The answers varied but he felt that 'there was a balance in favour of completing what I had begun'; and the work appeared in two bulky volumes in 1886 and 1887. The first contained a life of Dante running to 100 pages and the English of the Inferno and Purgatorio; in the second were the Paradiso and Canzoniere, and almost 200 pages of studies, estimates, etc. The footnotes, in six-point type, were almost equal to the text in extent. The *Spectator* (17 Mar. 1888, pp. 387-8) in a glowing review said:

> No book about Dante has been published in England that will stand comparison with Dean Plumptre's. The only fitting epithet we can find for it is 'noble'.

The translation is 'lucid, ingenious, not unfrequently felicitous', the notes are 'admirable', the Introduction 'excellent'. Before quoting some less flattering reviews we shall discuss the translation itself. A few lines from the Francesca episode (Inf. V.115-38) will sufficiently illustrate the average level of the Dean's attainment.

> Then I turned to them and began inquire,
>   'Francesca,' so I spake, 'thy miseries
>   A pitying grief that makes me weep inspire.
> But tell me, in the time of those sweet sighs,
>   The hour, the mode, in which love led you on
>   Doubtful desires to know with open eyes.'
> And she to me: 'A greater grief is none
>   Than to remember happier seasons past
>   In anguish; this thy Teacher well hath known:
> But if thou seek'st to learn what brought at last
>   Our love's first hidden root to open sight,
>   I'll tell, as one who speaks while tears flow fast.
> It chanced one day we read for our delight
>   How love held fast the soul of Lancelot;
>   Alone were we, nor deemed but all was right;
> Full many a time our eyes their glances shot,
>   As we read on; our cheeks now paled, now blushed;
>   But one short moment doomed us to our lot.
> When as we read how smile long sought for flushed
>   Fair face at kiss of lover so renowned,
>   He kissed me on my lips, as impulse rushed,
> All trembling; now with me for aye is bound.
>   Writer and book were Gallehault to our will:
>   No time for reading more that day we found.'

This is probably as bad a version of the passage as exists in the depressing annals of English terza rima. The perpetual straining after very unimaginative rhymes, with the ludicrous padding and distortion produced, suggest that the Dean either had no conception of why these lines have been so much admired, or else was a very poor judge of his own achievement.

There is throughout a deplorable surrender of sense and style to the needs of rhyme by means of inversion, padding and misuse of words. Ulysses' speech (Inf. XXVI.112-20) reads:

> 'O brothers,' then I said, 'who evermore
>   Through thousand toils have journeyed to the West,
>   To this short remnant of your life of yore,
> Still with the sense of watchful insight blest,
>   Deny ye not the great experiment
>   Of world unpeopled where the sunsets rest;

> Let your thoughts be on your high lineage bent:
> Ye were not born to live as lives the brute,
> But to seek good and wisdom's high intent.'

Here it would seem that the rhyme 'shore' in the previous terzina and the 'West' in line 113 had been allowed to dominate what followed. This concession to rhyme causes continually recurring awkwardness, e.g. 'Then going further on my gazing tour' (Inf. XVII.61); 'Repentance bars in life or death-hour's bourn' (Purg. XXII.48); 'So to the winds on leaves all borne astray / Was tost the speech in which the Sibyl dealt' (Par. XXXIII.65-6). Clumsiness and cacophony are also frequent. Lines like 'Where floods that shame the stormiest sea's boast flow' (Inf. II.108) or 'The sun's bright darts were speeding with quick bounds' (Purg. II.55) are common. The padding inserted is often insipid or out of character, e.g. 'Yet knew it not in that confusion weak' (Inf. XXX.141). There is also weakening of strong expressions such as 'As though in scorn Hell was by him appraised' (Inf. X.36). A remarkable combination of infelicities occurs in Inf. XXXIII.149-53:

> And I – I oped them not,
> For to cheat him was chivalrous and true.
> Ha! ha! Ye Genoese, ye strange bad lot,
> Ill-mannered, full of every purpose vile,
> Why doth the world not cast you out to rot?

Mixed metaphors creep in from time to time, like 'So that by restless eyes my lips were sealed' (Purg. XV.84).

Plumptre had studied the Comedy very diligently; his notes show that he had weighed carefully variant readings and interpretations. In spite of this there are many places where the distortion of the sense amounts to mistranslation. There are cases like Inf. IX.84, 'And with that anguish seemed his strength half-gone', followed up by lines 101-3:

> And spoke no word to us, but had the mien
> Of one in whom deep cares and carking dwell,
> All else before him slighted and unseen,

all of which gives a quite erroneous impression of Dante's angel. Others seem to be due to a careless turn of phrase, often proceeding from the need to rhyme, which gives such a line as 'The ill we love is in our neighbour found' (Purg. XVII.113), where the wording obscures the meaning. Purg. XXVIII.25-8 is certainly mistranslated:

> And lo! to bar my progress, I descry
> A river on the left, whose rippling stream
> Bent down the grass that to its banks grew nigh,

but it is so obviously wrong that again one is inclined to ascribe it to carelessness.

Probably, after working on his translation for so long, the Dean had not much enthusiasm left for reading proofs. There are far too many misprints, and a great number of wrongly placed quotation marks; these are by no means covered by the errata list included in the second volume. It is certainly strange that a first-class honours graduate in mathematics should have let the formula for the sum of a geometrical progression appear in the form it does in the note to Par. XXVIII.93; it is still wrong in the entirely different type of the 1899 edition.

Plumptre's notes are voluminous, and contain a great deal of useful information. Unfortunately there runs through them evidence of his weakness for mingling or confusing conjecture and fact. Although his research into Dante's life was thorough, competent and independent, his conclusions carry less weight than they might owing to his readiness to accept very doubtful possibilities first as probabilities and then as evidence to elevate other possibilities in the same way. If Dante so much as mentions a place, the Dean is already half convinced that he must have been there. His speculations on Dante having visited England are a good example; he himself frankly admitted that he had 'a strong personal interest' in the matter. In 1881 he had published an article in the *Contemporary Review* proving that Dante had been at Oxford. The line of argument can be pursued in the notes to his translation. The mention of Guy de Montfort, 'Guizzante e Bruggia' and 'Clugni' start the train of evidence; by the time we reach the essay on 'Dante as an Observer and Traveller' at the end of the second volume the 'mutual support' of these passages is complete. Dante travelled via Arles (Inf. IX.112-5), up the Rhone Valley (Par. VI.58-60), attended Sigier's lectures in Paris (Par. X.136-8), noted the beavers in the Moselle or the Rhine (Inf. XVII.19-22), visited Cologne (Inf. XXIII.60-63), thence 'we follow him through the Netherlands to Bruges' (Inf. XV.4-6), then from Wissant up the Thames to London. The fact that Dante knew of Roger Bacon's optical theories immediately extended his route to Oxford. After that it was simple, by using Dante's references to clocks, his knowledge of Arthurian legend, and the fact that the bankers of Florence had dealings in the fourteenth century with the Dean and Chapter of Wells, to suggest that 'Dante would have gone a long way round' for the sake of seeing Arthur's grave at Glastonbury and Peter Lightfoot's clock at Wells. A good deal of fun was poked at the Dean by reviewers concerning these ingenious and ingenuous pieces of reasoning, and they wondered, in view of his 'strong personal interest', whether he would have reached the same conclusions had he been a Cambridge man or Dean of some other Cathedral.

Apart from this, however, the notes, indexes and numerous essays appended to Plumptre's translation were an achievement for his time; the hundred pages which he devoted in 'Estimates, Contemporary and Later' to surveying the course of Dante study, criticism and translation in Europe and America were excellent pioneer work. Of his fellow translators he writes kindly and modestly, and his words are worth quoting:

> There can, I believe, be no worse introduction to a translator's work than that he should sit in judgment on the labours of his predecessors. . . . I have no doubt that each of these versions has, like my own, its special merits and defects. I hope and believe that each of the translators has found in his work, as I have found in mine, its own best reward.

We have already quoted the *Spectator*; other critics were more severe. Edward Moore reviewed each volume in turn in the *Academy* (25 Dec. 1886, pp. 419-20; 14 Jan. 1888, pp. 19-20). While doing full justice to the solid value of his friend's research, and bestowing 'ungrudging praise' on the notes, he gave the translation itself very limited approval, and pointed out some of the flaws in the Dean's logic. The *Athenaeum*, reviewing the first volume (15 Jan. 1887, pp. 90-1), was caustic:

> We have so often given our reasons for believing that this measure [terza rima] will never be satisfactorily adapted to English words that there is no need to say here more on that head, except that Dr Plumptre's version confirms us in the opinion. If he, a scholar and practised translator, not devoid of a gift for versifying, can make no more of it than he has done, it seems useless to expect that anyone will ever do it. . . . Towards the end of this volume he seems almost to have given up the struggle.

When the second volume appeared the same reviewer (14 Jan. 1888, p. 46) expressed joy at finding some of his suggestions adopted in the errata list, but declined to change his view as to the merit of the translation.

We are obliged to concur with the *Athenaeum's* verdict and place Plumptre's among the poorer versions. It achieved a reputation, which lingered for many years, and was probably partly due to the writer's personal prestige. The more reliable authorities detected its faults from the beginning, and it has long since disappeared from the market.

FREDERICK KNELLER HASELFOOT HASELFOOT
(1829-1905)

Haselfoot was the elder son of a London lawyer, Charles Frederick Cock, and owes his somewhat clumsy name to the fact that he changed his paternal to his maternal surname by deed poll. He graduated at University College, Oxford, joined the Inner Temple, and was called to the bar in 1855. He mentions in his preface that he began the study of Dante in 1860, and made his translation of the Divine Comedy between 1872 and 1887. In 1899 a greatly revised second edition appeared. Haselfoot does not seem to have published anything else, so his Dante probably represents the fruit of almost forty years' leisure.

In the Introduction to the first edition of 1887 (which is reprinted in the second) he has quite a lot to say about translating Dante, but he writes of his own and other translations in a pleasant and modest fashion. He explains that he had met Thomas W. Parsons in 1872, and had seen some of his Purgatorio in manuscript. Haselfoot felt that 'excellent as was Mr Parsons' version, I could not think that he had cast it in the right mould', and he set to work himself on the Purgatorio in terza rima. After completing it he proceeded no further for several years, then resumed and finished the other cantiche. Haselfoot evidently had a somewhat photographic memory, for he mentions that by 1865 he had memorised the entire Comedy in Italian.

Haselfoot defends vigorously his choice of terza rima, and anticipates some of the objections likely to be made against it. 'The form of the poem', he says, 'seems to me to be part of its very essence.' He claims to have been very particular in his selection of rhymes, adding: 'Indeed, I have taken less licence in this respect than Dante himself.' He has endeavoured, he says, to use Dante's own words wherever possible and 'while avoiding obscurity, to preserve the downright terse simplicity of his style'.

As to his predecessors, he says that Cary's and Longfellow's were the only two versions to which he referred while composing his own. He praises the former, though he finds his style far removed from Dante's, and remarks that Cary 'ever and anon selects the most appropriate word, for which I have been not seldom indebted to him'. Of Longfellow he says nothing beyond mentioning his name, and he has no remarks on any of the terza rima translators.

The Introduction goes on to deal with texts and commentaries, and with the interpretation of time references, which Haselfoot had worked out for himself before Moore's lectures were published. It is evident from the preliminary matter and notes that Haselfoot's scholarship was genuine and thorough. He had studied the original diligently, was familiar with its problems and cruxes, knew Dante's other works, appreciated his philosophic and scientific background, and was abreast of modern research. When he adopts an unusual reading he always mentions it in a note, showing acquaintance with the choices available and justifying his decision.

The first edition of 1887 was well if not enthusiastically received. The *Athenaeum* (9 July 1887, pp. 48-9) said that Haselfoot's was 'the least unsuccessful rendering in terza rima which has yet been printed'. The *Saturday Review* (7 May 1887, p. 669) found the rhymes unimpeachably correct, the notes brief but sufficient, but deplored the frequent insertion of padding. The *Spectator* (21 May 1887, p. 603) took a rather poorer view, noticing 'a certain triviality in the notes, a ludicrous line in some of the noblest passages'. Edward Moore, reviewing the book in the *Academy* (25 June 1887, pp. 443-4) was non-committal; he bestowed praise on the preliminary matter and the notes, but criticised several lines and passages in the translation. Azeglio Valgimigli, in a general article on English versions of the Comedy (*Giornale dantesco*, Vol. IV N.S., p. 1) said:

> ... La versione di Haselfoot (in terza rima) è quella che più d'ogni altra richiama all' orrechio l'originale. Mi ha fatto questo effetto, leggendone vari canti.

In Butler's version of Scartazzini's *Handbuch* (*A Companion to Dante*, 1893), Haselfoot's translation is referred to as excellent; this testimonial is not, of course, in the original German. But the opinion that seems to have impressed the translator most was a private letter from Cardinal Manning, dated 3 Nov. 1889, which Haselfoot printed at the beginning of the 1899 volume, remarking:

> ... His approbation was the more gratifying to me because he was a finished Italian scholar, my acquaintance with him was but slight, and I was not a member of his Communion.

The Archbishop says that hitherto he had not believed that a rhymed translation of the Comedy was possible, then:

> You have reproduced the abruptness and energy of the original in a high degree, and also the literalness of the translation [*sic*]. Long passages throughout, nevertheless, read off like an original poem of great beauty. ... One other excellence is in the purity and simplicity of the English. Cary is latinistic: but your diction is monosyllabic English.

Haselfoot, thus encouraged, set to work to revise his translation very thoroughly, obviously determined to profit by the criticisms to which it had been subjected. In almost every instance where a line or passage had been adversely commented on, he rewrote it, some cantos were entirely remodelled, and the notes were revised and augmented. Incidentally the second edition, printed in Edinburgh, though similar to the first in style and format, was much better produced and is a pleasure to handle. Unfortunately none of the literary reviews which had criticised the first edition took any notice of the second, which was a pity, seeing that the translator had taken their strictures so much to heart. The extracts in this article are from the 1899 version.

Haselfoot's translation, although it exhibits many of the faults we have noticed in his contemporaries, is definitely the best nineteenth-century effort in terza rima, with the possible exception of Sibbald's Inferno. Despite his industry and ability, however, the reader is continually conscious of the struggle to fit meaning and metre, and the result, if respectable, is pedestrian. Cardinal Manning's view that part of it read 'like an original poem of great beauty' is not at all borne out by perusal. Perhaps the Cardinal was relieved to find that it was not so bad as others which had been shown to him; moreover his 'assumption of omniscience' was well known. Anyhow, if Haselfoot shines at all it is by comparison, and the *Athenaeum's* 'least unsuccessful' is the best adjective that can be applied to his work.

The *Athenaeum* reviewer quoted and commended the following passage (Par. XI.121-32):

> And this is he who was our patriarch;
>   Whence whoso follows what he bids him do,
>   Lades merchandise, thou see'st, of goodly mark.
> But his flock hungers now for viands new,
>   So strongly, that it needs must take concern
>   In seeking for strange brakes to scatter through.
> And as his sheep for paths remoter yearn,
>   And wander further from his guiding call,
>   More void of milk they to the fold return.
> Some, truly, fearing harm that may befall,
>   Cleave to the shepherd; but so few we find,
>   That scant cloth furnishes the cloaks of all.

This might be said to represent Haselfoot at his best; indeed it is seldom that one comes across so many lines without some more serious defect. The following (Inf.V.115-38) is more typical of his ordinary level.

Then turning to them I began again
   And spoke: 'Francesca, these thy agonies
   Make me for sad and piteous weeping fain.
But tell me, in the time of your sweet sighs
   By what and how did love concede you this,
   To learn what gave your dubious longings rise?'
And she to me: 'No greater grief there is,
   As knows thy Teacher, than to let the heart
   Recall, in misery, the time of bliss.
But if in such a longing mood thou art
   To know the root whence first our love took spray,
   I will enact a tearful speaker's part.
We for delight were reading on a day
   Of Lancelot, how Love of him made prize.
   Alone we were, suspicion far away.
For many times that reading tranced our eyes
   And made the colour from our faces flee;
   But one sole instant took us by surprise.
When we read how the smile he yearned to see
   Was by the kiss of such a lover sought,
   This one, who never shall be torn from me,
His own kiss to my lips all-trembling brought.
   With Galeot both the book and writer vied:
   That day we read not further in it aught.'

It can be seen that this passage is a decided improvement on Minchin and Plumptre, but it also shows the perpetual conflict of sense and sound, and acceptance of some inadequate equivalent for the sake of metre and rhyme. At its worst this produces all too often clumsiness, cacophony, weakening, obscurity and inaccuracy. There are distortions like (Purg. XXV.64-6):

   Whence in his doctrine severance was done
   Between the soul and possible intellect,
   Since organ by the last used he saw none.

Sometimes, as the *Spectator* remarked, the result is merely ludicrous, e.g. (Inf. XXIII.40-42):

   Snatches her boy and flees, nor tarrying makes,
   Since care for him o'er thought of self must rank,
   So long as putting but a shift on takes.

There is both weakening and inaccuracy in this rendering of a strong terzina (Purg. XV.70-72):

   It as much ardour as it finds imparts;
   So that as far as charity extends
   Eternal worth spreads over loving hearts.

The need for a rhyme to 'soul' in the previous terzina produces (Purg. XIII.94-6):

> O brother mine, on one true city's roll
> We all are entered; but thou fain wouldst say
> Did any one through life as pilgrim stroll
> In Italy?

A poor choice of words or phrases gives lines like: 'If they cull Heaven's sweets or Hell's poison taste' (Inf. VI.84); 'To set thy heart to peace's waters free' (Purg. XV.131); 'Where those grow sleek who 'scape from vain things' hold' (Par. X.96).

Though Haselfoot uses a sprinkling of archaisms like 'hight', 'dight', 'wot', etc. he is more sparing of them than many of his contemporaries. He is also less given to the more outrageous forms of padding, though from time to time he brings in an unsuitable phrase, e.g. 'Whose stroke closed my last day in deathful gloom' (Inf. XIV.54) or 'His blows on each repassing in parade' (Inf. XXVIII.42).

The standard of accuracy is good and there are no serious mistranslations, although in a number of places the sense is inaccurately rendered owing to the demands of rhyme and metre, e.g. 'When saying "I was there," will joy recall' (Inf. XVI.84) is, when looked at carefully, not what is meant at all. Similarly Purg. XIX.16-18:

> When speech in her had thus obtained a vent,
> She so began to sing that I was nigh
> Constrained to keep attention on her bent

will not bear close scrutiny.

The best terzina noticed in reading the poem was Par. XXIII.49-51:

> I was as one in whom remains behind
> Some trace of a forgotten dream, and who
> Attempts in vain to bring it back to mind.

There are other pleasing lines and passages, but they are not numerous. Haselfoot, as the last of the nineteenth-century users of terza rima, deserves the credit of the highest place among them by reason of his patience and perseverance, but that place is not in itself high.

ROBERT URQUHART

Nothing has been found out regarding the identity of this translator. His Inferno was privately printed in 1895 and is very scarce. The only copy traced was one in the Bodleian; there is not one in the British Museum. There has come into the writer's hands, however, what appears to be a press proof, roughly sewn and bound in plain paper boards, and bearing the stamp of the printers (Richard Clay & Sons Ltd., Bungay, 21 Sep. 94) on the first page of each signature. It is identical with the final print except for a few corrections marked on it, and that the title page bears the imprint of Macmillan and Co. and the date 1894. The name and address are struck out and the words 'privately printed' written above; this, with the date changed to 1895, appears on the copy in the Bodleian. Evidently Macmillan arranged for the production of the book but decided not to publish it; although they have been kind enough to search their records no information could be found.

Perhaps, however, the writer is as well left unidentified, for his translation is one of the worst in the long series of terza rima which filled the second half of the nineteenth century. It strikes one as having been hurriedly and roughly put together by forcing the sense of successive terzine into the metrical mould and using every kind of licence to preserve the rhyme scheme. Padding of the wildest kind is inserted, words are used in wrong senses, all sorts of awkwardness, obscurity and cacophony are permitted, numerous archaisms are resorted to, and some are even invented. Incidentally there are no marks of quotation throughout, which is very confusing, since the translation is by no means so lucid as to be self-explanatory.

The rendering of the simile at II.127-32 illustrates Urquhart's general level of performance:

> As flowers, which cold nocturnal dews begem,
>   Declined and shut, when by the sun's ray tinged,
>   Erect themselves all open on their stem;
> So came my faculties and powers unhinged,
>   And in my heart I felt such courage move
>   That I commenced, as one no fear had twinged.

Extreme awkwardness is frequent, e.g. (XXI.25-8):

> Then round I turned as one it long has irked
>   To have sight of that which he to shun must strive,
>   And who lets not, with sudden terror worked,
> Such looking him of his escape deprive.

Urquhart goes to very strange shifts to secure a rhyme, as a part of the Ulysses passage will show (Inf. XXVI.100-26):

> I took the high and open seas alert
>   Sole, with one ship, and with that little train,
>   Companions who would never me desert.

This shore and that I saw as far as Spain,
  Morocco, and Sardinia's island goth,
  And all the others watered by that main.
I and my mariners were old and loth
  When we attained that narrow ocean throat
  Where Hercules inscribed his barriers both,
That never man beyond should steer his boat:
  On my right hand I left fair Seville thence,
  And on the other now saw Ceuta float.
O brothers, who thro' many and immense
  Dangers have reached the far west, I begun,
  To that short watch and vigil of your sense,
Your human senses, which is yet to run,
  Do not the experience deny and bar
  Of the unpeopled world behind the sun.
Consider whence ye spring, and what ye are:
  Ye were not made to live like brutes in rest,
  But virtue and knowledge to pursue afar.
This little speech which I to them addrest,
  So eager for the voyage made my troop,
  That scarcely then I could have them represt:
So to the dawning having turned our poop,
  Winging our foolish flight with oars that stole
  Still winning to the southward, on we swoop.

The faults noticeable in this passage are liberally strewn throughout,
and it is not worth quoting further examples of them.

Such a system of translation introduces, as can readily be seen, many
inaccuracies, but these do not seem to be due to any lack of comprehension, for it is evident that Urquhart understood his text well, and
there are also indications that he appreciated its poetic qualities. Occasional passages are well executed, e.g. (XXIV.112-7):

As one who falls in strange and frensied mood,
  Cast down by demon, or the dread surprise
  Of cold obstruction that besets man's blood,
When risen, around him wildly rolls his eyes,
  All by the mighty agony amazed
  Which he has suffered, and beholding sighs.

Some of his additions too have a Dantesque quality, e.g. 'By the new
roots of this my self-sown tree' (XIII.73) or 'As if this shower no fruit
in him could breed' (XIV.48).

Urquhart, however, left his book without a word of explanatory
matter except a solitary footnote to XV.99, 'He hearkens well, who
heedeth her', which reads 'i.e. Fortune. *Vide* Canto VII.61-96'. This

shows that he was aware of the various efforts to explain this line, and had at least some acquaintance with the commentators.

No reviews have been found of Urquhart's book, and its scarcity indicates a very limited circulation.

BIBLIOGRAPHY TO CHAPTER VII

BROOKSBANK

Dante's Divine Comedy. The First Part. Hell. Translated in the Metre of the Original with Notes. By Thomas Brooksbank, M.A. Camb. London: John Parker and Son. 1854

THOMAS

The Trilogy; or Dante's Three Visions, translated into English, in the metre and triple rhyme of the original; with notes and illustrations, by the Rev. John Wesley Thomas. London: Henry G. Bohn. 3 vols. (Part I. Inferno, or The Vision of Hell, 1859; Part II. Purgatorio, or The Vision of Purgatory, 1862; Part III. Paradiso, or The Vision of Paradise, 1866). (There have been two reprints of this translation: in 'The Finsbury Library', edited John Telford, published Robert Culley, London, 1910; and in the 'Every Age Library', published Charles H. Kelly, London, 1914; both in 3 vols, and both with preliminary matter and footnotes greatly abridged.)

RAMSAY

Dante's Divina Commedia. Translated into English, in the metre and triple rhyme of the original. With Notes. By Mrs Ramsay. London: Tinsley Brothers. 3 vols. (I, Inferno, 1862; II, Purgatorio, 1862; III, Paradiso, 1863)

FORD

*The Inferno of Dante. Translated in the metre of the original. By James Ford, A.M. London: Smith, Elder & Co. 1865

The Divina Commedia of Dante. Translated into English verse by James Ford, A.M. London: Smith, Elder & Co. 1870

TOMLINSON

A Vision of Hell: the Inferno of Dante, translated into English tierce rhyme; with an Introductory Essay on Dante and his Translators. By Charles Tomlinson, F.R.S. London: S. W. Partridge and Co. 1877

PIKE

Translations from Dante, Petrarch, Michael Angelo and Vittoria Colonna. London: C. Kegan Paul & Co. 1879

The Divine Comedy of Dante Alighieri. Inferno. Translated by Warburton Pike. London: C. Kegan Paul & Co. 1881

SIBBALD

The Inferno. A Translation with notes and an introductory essay by James Romanes Sibbald. Edinburgh: published by David Douglas. 1884

* includes Italian text

MINCHIN

The Divine Comedy of Dante Alighieri. Translated verse for verse from the original into terza rima by James Innes Minchin. London: Longmans Green & Co. 1885

PLUMPTRE

The Commedia and Canzoniere of Dante Alighieri. A New Translation, with Notes, Essays and a Biographical Introduction, by E. H. Plumptre, D.D., Dean of Wells. London: Wm. Isbister Limited. 2 vols (1886, 1887). (This translation has been twice reprinted: in the above form in 1890, and in five volumes, foolscap octavo, in 1899, by the same publisher. The translation is unrevised. Plumptre's 'Life of Dante' was edited by A. J. Butler and published as a sixth volume uniform with above in 1900.

HASELFOOT

The Divina Commedia of Dante Alighieri, translated line for line in the terza rima of the original, with notes, by Frederick K. H. Haselfoot, M.A. London: Kegan Paul, Trench & Co. 1887

The Divina Commedia of Dante Alighieri, translated line for line in the terza rima of the original, with notes, by Frederick K. H. Haselfoot, M.A. Second edition, revised, corrected, and further annotated. London: Duckworth & Co. 1899

URQUHART

Dante's Divine Comedy. The Inferno. Translated in the terza rima of the original by Robert Urquhart. Privately printed. 1895

CHAPTER VIII

PROSE AND SCHOLARSHIP

OF the sixteen prose translations in English of one or more cantiche of the Divine Comedy six were published during the years 1880-1899 and four more between 1901 and 1905. This concentration is obviously connected with the development of Dante scholarship during the period. The Germans had been at it for some time; now British writers joined in these academic activities with some success. Perhaps the most notable name is that of Paget Jackson Toynbee (1855-1932), so often referred to in these pages, whose work as editor, bibliographer and critic was voluminous. The study of Dante is, moreover, under a great and lasting obligation to him for his magnificent bequests of books and manuscripts to the Bodleian and the British Museum. Another scholar of deservedly high repute was Edward Moore (1835-1916), Principal of St Edmund Hall, Oxford, for fifty years, whose *Contributions to the Textual Criticism of the 'Divina Commedia'* (1889) was a monument of erudition, and who also edited the Oxford Dante. Of the six translators in prose now to be discussed, four were scholars of some standing, and the other two were gifted amateurs.

As has been mentioned, four further translations in prose appeared during the first few years of the new century; then there was a long blank, and it was not until 1939 that the next prose version appeared. In 1880 with only two prose versions in existence there was scope for all kinds of experiment, ranging from a 'crib' to a highly stylised rendering; there was also the opportunity of incorporating the results of recent scholarship and research. By 1905 all these had been tried, and the market seemed saturated.

Before discussing the six prose translations of 1880-99, one interesting but unpublished version made during the period may be briefly described. Toynbee records both in D.S. and B.T.D., under date 1880, a prose translation of the Paradiso by James MacGregor, with a note to the effect that it is unpublished, being written in the margins of a printed copy of the Commedia, formerly in his possession, now in the Bodleian. MacGregor (1832-1910) was a native of Perthshire; he was ordained to the ministry of the Church of Scotland in 1855, and after holding various charges came to St Cuthbert's, Edinburgh, in 1873. While there he lost his first wife, sought comfort in overwork, and had a nervous breakdown. On his return from a holiday abroad, while still convalescent, he spent a few weeks cruising among the islands on the west coast of Scotland in a yacht belonging to his friend the Duke of Montrose. It was on board the *Columba* in August 1879 that he began the translation of Dante. It is written in a fine clear hand, partly in pencil, partly in ink, on the margins of an edition of the Comedy in Italian published by C. S. Arnold, London, in 1827. The book itself measures only 5½ by 3¼ in., and is printed in small type with fairly narrow margins. These are literally crammed with Mac-Gregor's English rendering, interspersed with notes, and a magnifying glass is often necessary to decipher it. The translation includes not only the whole of the Paradiso, as recorded by Toynbee, but the Purgatorio from the beginning to X.78, together with extracts from the Inferno and the later cantos of the Purgatorio. The notes in the book show that MacGregor had begun to use it in 1877, that most of the translation was done during the ten months to June 1880, and that after his second marriage in 1892 he began to read the Inferno with his wife. Odd references occur to intermediate dates; one is S.S. *Sardinian* 17/6/81, when MacGregor sailed to Canada as chaplain to the Governor-General. The last date noted is 1896. There are also observations about the weather and entries recording funerals. At the end of the Paradiso are the words:

11 Cumin Place. 22.6.80. Finished at Canto VI the translation of the Paradiso. It has been a source of pure pleasure.

The following short specimen (Purg. III.118-35) is typical; the various alternatives are printed as written.

After that my person was broken by two mortal thrusts I rendered myself weeping up to Him who freely pardons – willingly – Horrible were my sins, but the Infinite Goodness has an arm so great that it receives whatever turns back to it. If the shepherd of Cosenza who was sent by Clement to the hunt of me – chase – had then read this page – text – in God – God's book – the bones of my body had been still at the bridge end nigh to Benevento under the guard of the great mound of stones. Now the rain bathes them and the wind moves them outside my Kingdom near to the Verde whither he transported them with lights extinguished. By their malediction Eternal Love is not so lost that it cannot return while hope retains the smallest flower of green.

Dante seems to have been a private and domestic recreation for Mac-Gregor, who is not recorded as ever having written or preached on the subject. There is no mention of Dante in Frances Balfour's *Life and Letters of James MacGregor* (1912) where some of the correspondence of the period concerned is reproduced. Toynbee records that he found and bought the book at a sale, and doubtless its writer would have been surprised to know that his work had become the subject of an entry in Dante bibliographies.

ARTHUR JOHN BUTLER (1844-1910)

Butler was born at Putney, the eldest son of a Church of England clergyman who later became Dean of Lincoln. He was educated at Eton and Trinity College, Cambridge; he had a brilliant academic career, being eighth classic and a Junior Optime in mathematics. He received a fellowship at Trinity in 1869, and retained a lifelong interest in the affairs of the College. After holding a post as Board of Education examiner from 1870-87 he spent some years in the publishing business. In 1894 he returned to his former profession as Assistant Commissioner on Secondary Education; then from 1899 till his death he held an appointment in the Public Records Office. He was a proficient linguist and published translations from various languages; he was also a regular contributor and reviewer in literary periodicals. Well known as a mountaineer, he edited the *Alpine Journal* from 1890 to 1893. His natural modesty, courtesy and kindliness are attested by many of his fellow scholars.

The study of Dante was Butler's chief leisure occupation, and besides his prose translation of the Divine Comedy (1880-92) he published a useful introduction, *Dante: His Times and his Work* (1895); also, in the same year, an English version of Scartazzini's *Dante-Handbuch* (*A Companion to Dante*). His classical knowledge stood him in good stead, for he was thoroughly familiar with Aristotle and well acquainted with patristic and scholastic literature. He was also a pioneer of textual criticism, having himself examined and compared various manuscripts of the Comedy. The Purgatorio appeared first, in 1880, followed by the Paradiso in 1885; a revised edition of the latter was published in 1891, then a revised Purgatorio and the first and only Inferno in 1892. The revisions are not very extensive; quotations in this article are from the latest edition in each case.

When Butler published his first volume in 1880, his only serious predecessor as a prose translator was Carlyle, whose Inferno had appeared thirty years earlier. Butler, having learned from Carlyle that he did not intend to carry his translation further, began the Purgatorio with the idea that it would form a continuation of Carlyle's, which he considered admirable. He enunciates his principles briefly and clearly in his 1880 preface:

> Verse-translations of course we have, many and good; but no verse-translation can be a wholly satisfactory 'crib'; and it is at the production of a 'crib', pure and simple, that I have aimed.... I may perhaps remark here, that where a question has arisen between a literal and an elegant rendering, I have preferred the former; my object being, as I have said, not to attempt an addition to English literature, but to aid beginners in understanding that of Italy. Also, wherever it seemed possible to render an Italian word or idiom by a *cognate* form in English, I have not scrupled to do so, even at the cost of an occasional archaism.

Equally important, in Butler's view, was the establishment and elucidation of the text. He had familiarised himself with the source-literature and the work of the commentators, was keenly interested in textual and linguistic problems, and fascinated by Blanc's *Vocabulario*, Diez's *Wörterbuch* and Moore's projected critical text. Not only, therefore, did he supplement his translation with a full and exact body of notes, but he collated his text (Bianchi's edition of 1863) with the four early Italian editions reprinted by Vernon, the Naples edition of 1477 (as recorded by Barlow), the Aldine, Cassino and Witte's, and the Cambridge manuscript which Moore named C, and he printed the variants between the Italian text and the footnotes on each page.

Unfortunately Butler did not insert in his preliminary matter any systematic explanation of this collation, thereby detracting somewhat from its value. In one part of the preface to the 1880 volume he mentions the text used and some others; in another part he explains that he uses the numbers 1 to 5 to denote Foligno, Jesi, Mantua, del Tuppo and Naples (1477), and Gg for the Cambridge MS. To make matters worse, in the revision of the preface for the 1892 edition, this final paragraph was, no doubt inadvertently, omitted altogether. In the preface to both editions of Paradiso he mentions the texts used, but gives no explanation of the numerals 1 to 5 which appear in the variants. In the Inferno of 1892 the original paragraph from the 1880 preface is inserted. Had he only devoted a page to a list of abbreviations and symbols he would have saved much puzzlement to readers.

Even when one has disclaimed all thought of providing anything more than a 'crib', a literal prose translation is by no means so simple an undertaking as it sounds. Butler, like Carlyle, wavers between reproducing Italian constructions and replacing them with English idioms, inclining on the whole to the former. He also tends to translate literally the Italian particles and conjunctions, so that we get 'after that' for 'poi che' and 'poscia che', e.g. 'After that I had recognised some there' (Inf. III.58). Similarly 'mentre che' becomes 'while that' and 'prima che' 'before that', and we have circumlocutions like 'we left not our going, for that he talked' (Inf. IV.64); 'He who laments for that here one dies' (Par. XIV.25). 'Là dove' is often (not always) 'there where'. Unexpected prepositions are found, e.g. 'stung of gadflies' (Inf. III.65); 'the child that yields at the apple' (Purg. XXVII.45); 'to his body he would no other bier' (Par. XI.117). Stairs seem to give trouble: 'down and up over another's stairs' (Par. XVII.60); 'through the stairs of the eternal palace' (Par. XXI.7); 'up over that ladder' (Par. XXII.101). We get such phrases as 'the which' instead of the simple relative; and such pseudo-archaisms as 'who may He soon lead them on high' (Purg. XXI.72); 'dear my origin' (Par. XVI.22); 'before I could do it to ask' (Par. I.87). Unnecessary reflexives are preserved as in Inf. XII.139, 'and passed him back over the ford'.

The article is a prolific source of awkwardness; its use where not normal in English often seems unfortunate, as in 'you taught me how the man becomes eternal' (Inf. XV.85) or 'of his eyes he made ever gates to the heaven' (Purg. XV.111). At other times it is surprisingly omitted or changed, e.g. 'that vibration which a tongue had given' ('la lingua', Inf. XXVII.17-18).

The combination of these features with a word order which follows the original as nearly as possible gives at times very clumsy results. A notable instance is the line 'e detto l'ho perchè doler ti debbia!' (Inf. XXIV.151) which becomes 'And I have told it thee to the end that thou mayest need to grieve therefore'. One or two other similar examples are:

Love, who excuses no loved one from loving, seized me for his joy in me so mightily that, as thou seest, it leaves me not yet. (Inf. V.103-5)

For all the gold that is beneath the moon and that ever was, of these wearied souls could never make one of them rest. (Inf. VII.64-6)

Not otherwise is stupefied and confused, and gazing grows dumb the mountaineer, when rough and savage he enters a city, than each shade did in its appearance; but after they were discharged of their astonishment, the which in lofty hearts is soon at rest . . . (Purg. XXVI.67-72)

He was not yet very far from his rising when he began to make the earth feel some strengthening from his great virtue, since for such lady's sake a youth he ran upon his father's enmity, that to her, as to death, none unlocks the gate of pleasure. (Par. XI.55-60)

On the other hand there are many passages where, with an occasional lapse, Butler is free from these mannerisms and expresses Dante's meaning firmly and clearly, e.g.

> And as is he who falls, and does not know how, by force of a demon which drags him to earth, or of other obstruction which binds the man, when he rises and looks around him, all bewildered with the great anguish which he has undergone, and as he gazes, sighs . . . (Inf. XXIV.112-7)

> Then, like a clock, which calls us at the hour when the bride of God arises to sing matins to her spouse, that he may love her, where the one part draws and drives the other, sounding 'ting ting' with so sweet a note, that the spirit well-disposed swells with love, so saw I the glorious wheel move itself, and return voice to voice in harmony and in sweetness that cannot be known save in that place where joy is everlasting. (Par. X.139-48)

Although in general Butler's translation is accurate, and he was obviously at great pains to ascertain the exact meaning of words and phrases, there are quite a few mistranslations. Some of these were corrected in the revised editions, and in his preface to the Purgatorio of 1892 Butler acknowledged the help of Paget Toynbee, who had called his attention to some errors. That eminent Dantist had, however, by no means completed the task, for in one of his last contributions to the *Modern Language Review* (Vol. 24, 1929, pp. 55ff) he gave a list of mistranslations of Dante from various sources, in which Butler figures as the chief culprit. Although, says Toynbee, Butler claimed no more for his version than that it was 'a crib pure and simple', 'As a "crib", however, it is at times decidedly misleading'. He draws attention in particular to the rendering of 'terra' as 'land' where it should be 'city'; but although Butler certainly seems to have gone wrong in some cases he was not, as Toynbee rather unnecessarily adds, 'in blissful ignorance', for he comments on the matter in a footnote to Inf. XXXI.21. Another common slip of Butler's, not mentioned by Toynbee, is to translate 'assai' as 'enough' or 'sufficient' where it has the sense of 'much' or 'very'. There are one or two other such slips, but none of real importance.

As an aid to the serious student, Butler's translation was far ahead of anything that had hitherto been published in English. He certainly made no attempt to cope with the Comedy as a poem, but he stated his intentions clearly and on the whole fulfilled them. His notes are valuable, relevant and authoritative for their time, though admittedly sometimes rather heavy going. Some reviewers took him to task for giving so many long classical quotations in the original, without a translation, and certainly to come on a solid page of Aristotle, as at the end of Purg. XV, would daunt many readers.

The reception of Butler's volumes by the reviewers was a varied one. Edward Moore wrote long articles in the *Academy* on Paradiso (23 June 1886, pp. 52-3) and on Inferno (4 June 1892, pp. 535-6). He finds the translation 'close, literal and accurate' and the language 'plain, vigorous and unaffected', but he does not think it on the whole as good as Carlyle's. The first two volumes were well received by the *Athenaeum* (8 May 1880, pp. 594-5):

> ... if we were to say that it is, within its limits, the most scholarly specimen of Dantesque literature extant in the English language, we should hardly be praising it beyond its deserts.

Later (9 Jan. 1886, pp. 62-3) the Paradiso is found to be 'scholarly, perspicuous and satisfying'. The review of the Inferno (16 Apr. 1892, pp. 494-5) is less enthusiastic:

> We do not think Butler's own translation is quite so good as either Carlyle's or Norton's; it does not as a whole read so well and it shows a certain inclination for taking the less natural and straightforward view of a phrase, when one or other course is at the translator's option.

The *Saturday Review*, while praising the Italian text, the essays and the notes, took a very poor view of the translation of Purgatorio (5 June 1880, pp. 732-3), calling it a 'mere tessellation of words – a clumsy mosaic' and 'an ill-cemented conglomerate'. Later (6 Feb. 1886, pp. 196-7) it found the Paradiso 'much superior to his Purgatorio and may be read with pleasure'. An even kinder verdict was passed on the Inferno, reviewed along with Norton's Purgatorio (19 Mar. 1892, pp. 336-7). Butler's style is described as being midway between Carlyle and Norton, 'not so vigorous . . . as the first', 'very superior . . . to the second'. The difference must be ascribed to a change of reviewer, or else to a change in his ideas, because little variation is perceptible in Butler's style throughout. Some further notes on Butler's version will be found in the section of this chapter dealing with Norton.

WILLIAM STRATFORD DUGDALE (1828-82)

Dugdale was an elder son of a well-known Staffordshire family, and his father's namesake. He entered Balliol College, Oxford, in 1846, became a barrister-at-law of Lincoln's Inn in 1859, and was appointed High Sheriff of Stafford in 1876. Among other interests he inherited a family colliery at Baxterley, near Atherstone, and he lost his life while taking part in a rescue attempt following a disaster there on 2 May 1882, which was ultimately responsible for thirty-one fatalities.

Some time earlier Dugdale had undertaken a translation of the Purgatorio for Bohn's Libraries, intended as a companion volume to Carlyle's Inferno. Only three days before the disaster he had finished the manuscript, which was seen through the press by his widow, a daughter of Sir Charles Trevelyan, assisted by G. H. Bianchi. In considering this translation we must bear in mind that Dugdale had no opportunity of revising his work, and it cannot be doubted that had he done so some of the slips would have been rectified.

It can be assumed that Dugdale's general plan was to follow Carlyle's method by translating as literally as possible, thereby providing assistance to the student. The volume is printed uniformly with Carlyle's, having the translation, the Italian text and the footnotes in that order on each page. Dugdale's style is rather more modern than Carlyle's, with fewer inversions and eccentricities, and the language is less reminiscent of the Authorised Version of the Bible. At times he is wordy, as when he renders II.12 as 'that travel with their minds, though their bodies are standing still'; or III.78 as 'for to lose time is more displeasing, the more one knows its value'. He sometimes inserts what amounts to a gloss, e.g. 'the one already borne down with calamity, the other with apprehensions of it' (VI.108). Occasionally his verbosity gets beyond control, e.g. (VII.79-81):

> Nature had not been content with lavishing her multifarious hues, but with the sweetness of a thousand perfumes had produced there an indescribably delicious fragrance.

In places words are piled up to produce clumsiness and obscurity, e.g. (XXX.34-9):

> And my spirit, which now for a long time had not been as formerly, crushed trembling down with wonder at her presence, even before I had more knowledge of her with my eyes, through some hidden virtue emanating from her, felt the mighty power of old love.

There are some odd inversions, e.g. (XII.68-9):

> He that saw the reality did not see better than I the forms which I bending towards the ground trod on.

At times the wording is a trifle stilted, e.g. (VII.67-9):

> Thither . . . will we go where the mountain side forms a cavity within its bosom, and there we shall await the nascent day.

Dante's direct succinctness is here and there lost in such stock phrases as 'that will waft you to heaven after your hearts' desire' (XI.39).

We have seen that Carlyle hesitated between translating Dante's bolder verses literally and paraphrasing them. Unfortunately Dugdale almost invariably paraphrases, with consequent weakening, e.g. 'who shall be thy light, to guide thy intellect to the truth' (VI.45) or 'while still remains a feeble shade of hope' (III.135). Dugdale is sparing in the use of archaisms, which makes the occasional intrusion of 'withal', 'wot of', etc., all the more noticeable. He uses some ugly verbal forms like 'laidest', 'actedst', 'conductedst'. In one or two places anacoluthon is probably due to lack of revision; in others there are obvious slips or misprints.

With these reservations Dugdale's translation reads well; one extract must serve as an example of his average style (XV.67-75):

> That infinite and ineffable good, that lives above, so runs to love, as a ray darts upon a shining body. It gives itself in proportion to the love it finds; so that how far soever charity extends, the eternal glory extends above it. So that the more people know each other on high, the more there are to love truly, and the more love each other, and like a mirror, one reflects the other.

Dugdale, like Butler, used Bianchi's text, of which there were many editions in the middle of the century from 1844 onwards. It is generally reliable, though it contains some readings now recognised as inferior. Dugdale adheres to it in general, but is occasionally dissatisfied, citing possible alternatives in his notes. Unfortunately, however, he has neglected some of Bianchi's annotations, which would have saved him from mistranslating some passages, almost all of which are correctly explained in the Italian's commentary. Although the original text of II.94-7 is correctly punctuated, and although Bianchi paraphrases it in prose, Dugdale translates:

> No outrage has been done to me; if he who takes when and whom he pleases, has many times refused me this passage, he does it of his own most just will.

Similarly 'I never saw fiery vapours at nightfall or August clouds at sunset cleave the clear sky so rapidly' (V.37-9) is obviously wrong, though again Bianchi explains it correctly. By translating 'consorto divieto' by 'undivided possession' at XIV.87, Dugdale fails to make it link up with XV.45, which he renders 'when he spoke of refusal and companionship'. There are a dozen or more such slips, some of which would doubtless have been corrected in revision. Rather strangely, at XXI.65, where Dugdale prints Bianchi's 'contra voglia', his translation is evidently made from a text with the reading 'con tal voglia', which was common at the time.

The volume was favourably and sympathetically received by the reviewers. The *Saturday Review* (27 Oct. 1883, p. 545) thought it 'correct' and 'presented in good readable English'. The *Athenaeum* (20 Oct. 1883, p. 495) described it as 'creditably executed . . . agreeable . . . once or twice rather pedestrian'. Paget Toynbee paid it a belated compliment when reviewing Norton's Purgatorio in the *Academy* (23 July 1892, p. 64). He quoted a passage from both versions and, having averred that Dugdale's was the better of the two, he added:

> We may take the occasion to remark that Dugdale's translation is not so well known as it deserves to be, for, as may be gathered from the above specimen, it is both spirited and rhythmical, and on the whole it is correct.

WILLIAM WARREN VERNON (1834-1919)

William John Borlase-Warren-Venables-Vernon was the second son of George John, fifth Baron Vernon, and Isabella Caroline Ellison; he adopted for general use the simpler style of name which forms the heading above. Part of his childhood was spent in Italy; then he was educated at Eton and Christ Church, Oxford. He inherited his father's love of Italy and likewise his munificence in making available books which could not be published unless heavily subsidised. The elder Vernon was already editing the Commentary of Benvenuto da Imola when he died; his heir, the sixth Baron, in company with Sir James Lacaita, continued the work. On the death of the former in 1883 William and Sir James carried it to a conclusion, and it was published in Florence (5 vols., 1887). By this time Vernon had conceived the idea of an English commentary, based on Benvenuto's but not restricted to it, which would make the best thought on the Divine Comedy available to a wider public. Vernon himself had spent much time in Italy, and he was familiar with the leading Dantists of his day both at home and abroad. In his preface he tells of attending the private weekly 'readings' given in Florence by the Duke of Sermoneta, and how he set to work on his own 'Readings' without at first having publication in mind. He completed the Purgatorio first and it was published in 1889 with an Introduction by Dean Church. The Inferno followed in 1894 and the Paradiso in 1900. Each consisted of two bulky volumes, which were further enlarged for revised editions (1897-1909), the Inferno and Purgatorio being entirely rewritten and the Paradiso extensively revised. Vernon also published one or two smaller books on Dante, and shortly before his death an autobiography, *Reflec-*

tions of Seventy-two Years (1917). He left his collection of Dante books and papers to the library of the Athenaeum.

Vernon's work is included here because it contains a complete prose translation of the entire Comedy, not printed continuously, but in successive sections, each preceded by the Italian text, and followed by a commentary and also by voluminous footnotes. The translation includes numerous explanatory parentheses; in the first edition of the Purgatorio it was set in the same size of type and to the same measure as the commentary, and therefore was not easily isolated. A clearer style of typography was adopted for the later volumes, the translation being in smaller type and set to a narrower measure.

The translation is thus really intended as an aid to study and comprehension; it aims only at making quite clear the meaning of the Italian. Having no literary pretensions it can hardly be examined or criticised in the same way as other translations. It would lose by being transferred from its fragmentary form to continuous print, because the phrasing and the explanatory parentheses are closely linked to the commentary and notes and intended to be read in conjunction with them. A single terzina (Purg. XXI.64-6) will show Vernon's method:

> At first (before it is purified) it has indeed the wish (to ascend to Heaven), but that inclination (*talento*) does not allow it, which (inclination to be purified) Divine Justice imposes as a chastisement in opposition to the wish (to ascend) just as, (in life, there was in it the desire to ascend) contrary to the inclination to sin.

There are a few passages where Vernon writes directly and without parentheses, of which Par. XXX.61-9 will serve as an example.

> And I saw light in the shape of a river, blazing with radiance, streaming between two banks enamelled with a marvellous wealth of flowers. Out of that river issued vivid sparks, and settled themselves in the flowers on every side even as rubies in a chasing of gold. Then, as it were intoxicated by the perfumes, they plunged again into that wondrous flood, and if one entered in, another issued forth.

At the time when the Readings first appeared, the minutiae of Dante scholarship had attained such importance that the reviewers dealt at considerable length with each pair of Vernon's volumes as they appeared. The *Athenaeum* was courteous and kindly and in the three articles (5 Apr. 1890, pp. 431-2; 5 May 1894, pp. 570-1; 5 Jan. 1901, p. 10) was content with pointing out a few minor errors and complaining (as nearly every critic did) of the noble writer's tendency to verbosity. The *Saturday Review* (18 Jan. 1890, pp. 80-81) complimented Vernon on his prose translation of the Purgatorio which it found 'both clear and accurate'. The writer pointed out a number of mistakes, most of which were corrected in the next edition. The *Saturday* was also laudatory in later articles on Inferno and Paradiso.

War broke out, however, between Vernon and the *Academy* over Purgatorio and Paradiso. Rather strangely, between these two incidents, Vernon's Inferno was reviewed in the same paper (28 Apr. 1894, pp. 343-4) by a personal friend, Linda Villari, in eulogistic terms. On 8 Feb. 1890, pp. 92-3, Paget Toynbee dealt with Vernon's Readings on the Purgatorio at great length. He must have worked fast, for his list of complaints indicates that he had been through the 900 pages with considerable care. He thought the translation 'generally faithful and lucid' although Vernon 'occasionally misrepresents his author'. Then he gave a list of alleged mistranslations and 'missed points', and suggested that Vernon's erudition was 'not quite up-to-date', following this with an attack on the proof-reading, enumerating a host of misprints, remarking on Vernon's 'slipshod English', and concluding:

> These numerous blemishes . . . detract seriously from the value of what is in other respects an excellent book; for the plan of the work is well conceived, and for the most part well carried out.

Toynbee had, unfortunately, some justification for his animadversions in the matter of misprints: a line left out of an extract from the Convito; a verse from Milton strangely misquoted; and a terribly mangled quotation from Homer which, said Toynbee,

> may be said to eclipse even the performance of the daily papers on the occasion when a certain enlightened lord mayor delivered himself of a Greek quotation in a Mansion House speech.

Vernon replied to Toynbee's strictures in spirited fashion when he issued his revised edition of the Purgatorio. Toynbee had accused him of missing the point by rendering 'che si stavano' in Purg. IV.104 as 'were lying', arguing that they were all standing except Belacqua. Vernon changed 'lying' to 'reclining', but devoted a full page of footnote to the confutation of his (unnamed) critic, whom he rebuked thus:

> I would venture to point out that in rendering Italian words we English should be very careful to ascertain how such words are understood and used by Italians themselves, and should wholly disregard any conventional use by English writers.

From his intimate knowledge of Tuscan, Vernon was able to prove his point, and subsequent scholars have supported him. Another full page footnote was devoted to the question of La Pia's identity in Purg. V, where Vernon had enlisted the help of Scartazzini to refute Toynbee's charge that he was 'out of date' and 'unaware' of recent discoveries. When Vernon's Paradiso appeared, the *Academy* review (18 May 1901, pp. 420-1) was unsigned, but no less aggressive. The anonymous critic was very scornful of Vernon's rendering of 'risplende' in Par. I.2 by 'shines':

> *Risplendere* should be translated by to re-shine, to re-glow, to reflect, and not a little of Dante's philosophy is missed if his fundamental conception of Nature . . . is not borne in mind by the translator throughout the whole poem.

Vernon replied, evidently in scathing terms, but the *Academy* would not publish his letter, and as a result its contents were incorporated in the revised edition of Paradiso. In a very long footnote he refers to the 'utter absurdity' of the reviewer's contention, and cites the specific support of Professors Villari of Florence, D'Ovidio of Naples and Scherillo of Milan, also the emphatic agreement of Edward Moore. In a further short footnote on the following page he says:

> Professor D'Ovidio advises me to leave 'shines', and to ignore the criticism of the *Academy* reviewer. Professor Villari the same.

These passages of arms are typical of the passion for meticulous detail which resulted from the painstaking scholarship of the period. Vernon himself was dragged into the argument against his will. The *Times* obituary notice described him as a 'somewhat blind admirer of Scartazzini', but the garrulity which he shared with Benvenuto often delights and amuses, while his personal anecdotes of Italian speech and customs provide many pleasant oases among the arid tracts of learning.

CHARLES ELIOT NORTON (1827-1908)

Norton was born at Cambridge, Massachusetts, being the fifth child of Andrews Norton, a descendant of the earliest immigrants, then a professor at the Harvard Divinity School. The elder Norton was himself something of a Dante scholar, and he published a translation of Manzoni's *I Promessi Sposi* (1834). His wife also had literary interests and knew Italian. Charles was educated at Harvard, where he graduated in 1846. He spent some years in business, interspersed with European travel, then in 1855 he decided to devote himself to independent literary work. For two years he lived in Rome; in 1859 he printed privately a translation of Dante's Vita Nuova, which was not published till 1867.

His literary acquaintanceships were wide and numerous. That with Longfellow was the most important, but three others are of special interest. Norton's first meeting with Ruskin in 1856, on a paddle steamer between Vevey and Geneva, is described in *Praeterita*, Vol. III, ch. ii, and the next chapter tells of the progress of their friendship. Norton's association with James Russell Lowell was a long one, involving contributions to the *Atlantic Monthly* and later co-editorship of the *North American Review*. Norton met Thomas Carlyle in 1869 when the sage was seventy-four, an event which led to the former's criticism of Froude's version of Mrs Carlyle's letters, and to his editing Carlyle's correspondence (11 vols., 1883-91) at the request of the family. Among much other miscellaneous literary work Norton edited Donne, Mrs Bradstreet, and the *Orations and Addresses* of his lifelong friend George William Curtis. He also published a book entitled *Travel and Study in Italy* (1869).

In 1875 Norton was appointed Professor of the History of Art at Harvard, and in 1877, when Lowell became Minister to Spain, Norton took over his Dante course. Norton had long been a Dante enthusiast, as we have already seen in the article on Longfellow. He was perhaps the most potent influence of the century in furthering the study of Dante in America, less because of his scholarship than through his enthusiasm and his ability to communicate it. The various glimpses we have of Norton, from his youthful travels in Europe to his venerable retirement at Shady Hill, convey a pleasant picture of his character. When Ruskin first met him he thought he had 'the sweetest quiet smile I ever saw on any face', and he spoke of 'the bright eyes, the melodious voice, the perfect manner'. He noticed that Charles, while 'a man of the highest natural gifts,' was 'observant and critical rather than imaginative, but with an all-pervading sympathy and sensibility, absolutely free from envy, ambition, or covetousness; a scholar from his cradle'. Norton was an admirer of Turner and of *Modern Painters*, though he did not scruple to criticise some of Ruskin's ideas, while the latter deplored that 'only about the thirtieth or fortieth part of Charles Norton's effective contents and capacity are beneficially spent in the dilution of the hot lava, and fructification of the hot ashes, of American character'. We have a later picture of Norton lecturing on Dante by William Roscoe Thayer:

> To read Dante with Norton was almost an act of worship. There was in his voice something wonderfully stirring and wholly incommunicable. As he reached a favourite passage his face became radiant and his tones more tender. He explained fully from every side, – verbal, textual,

literary, spiritual. . . . He could compass the whole circle of the experience and the ideals of that world of which the Divine Comedy is the
supreme expression in language.

Norton was also active as one of the founders of the Cambridge Dante
Society; on Lowell's death he became its second president, retaining
this post and his interest in its affairs till his death.

Norton's version of the Vita Nuova, which in its original form was
a kind of paraphrase, was recast as a literal prose rendering, with the
sonnets rhymed and the longer poems in blank verse, and published
as a companion volume to Longfellow's Comedy. The prose has an
archaic flavour which divided the critics, but W. D. Howells approved
the choice, commending Norton as 'literal with a difference'. The
phrase might also be applied to his version of the Comedy.

Nearly a quarter of a century had elapsed since the publication of
Longfellow's Dante when Norton published his own prose version
(1891-2). The first volume, dedicated to Lowell, omits all reference
to Longfellow. It is evident from the Introduction that Norton's ideas
on the translation of Dante had changed. While admitting that a prose
rendering 'is at best as the dull plaster cast to the living marble or the
breathing bronze', he feels that it is still the best means of communi-
cating the substance of a poem which has 'such worth that it deserves
to be known by readers who must read it in their own tongue or not
at all'.

> In this case the aim of the translator should be to render the substance
> fully, exactly, and with as close a correspondence to the tone and style of
> the original as is possible between prose and poetry.

He praises the prose versions of Carlyle, Dugdale and Butler, and
acknowledges his indebtedness to the latter, although 'through what
seems to me occasional excess of literal fidelity his English is now and
then somewhat crabbed'. Then he defines his own principles.

> I have tried to be as literal in my translation as was consistent with good
> English, and to render Dante's own words in words as nearly corres-
> pondent to them as the difference in the languages would permit. But it
> is to be remembered that the familiar uses and subtle associations which
> give to words their full meaning are never absolutely the same in two
> languages. . . . Even the most felicitous prose translation must fail
> therefore at times to afford the entire and precise meaning of the original.

In the prefatory note to the revised edition of 1901 Norton remarks:

> In the work of revision, as originally in that of translation, I have sought
> assistance from the work of my predecessors in the same field, and I have

not hesitated to borrow a felicitous word or phrase wherever I might find it.

He makes specific mention of his indebtedness to 'my late friends Mr Longfellow and Sir Frederick Pollock', also to Vernon and Wicksteed as well as the others mentioned earlier. He concludes:

> In looking back over life I am not sorry to have devoted so much time to the study of Dante. It has been far more to me than merely an interesting literary occuapion. It is especially associated in remembrance with two dear masters and friends, Henry Wadsworth Longfellow and James Russell Lowell, and to their memory I dedicate these volumes.

Contemporary opinions of Norton's work were varied. In America W. R. Thayer, writing at length in two consecutive numbers of the *Nation*, found Norton's not only the best prose translation in English, but also superior to the verse renderings of Cary and Longfellow. He thought him 'invariably more concise, more exact, and no less lucid' than Carlyle; in short Norton 'has style and an extraordinary felicity of expression'. W. M. Payne, in the *Dial*, while he thought Norton 'at once accurate and elegant', was progressively less enthusiastic as each part appeared, and summed up by preferring Butler as 'more useful'. In Britain the *Athenaeum* reviewed each volume in turn (19 Dec. 1891, pp. 831-2; 13 Feb. 1892, pp. 212-3; 2 July 1892, p. 34), describing the translation as 'excellent', 'remarkable', with a 'literary flavour and balance superior to Carlyle's'. The *Saturday Review* (19 Mar. 1892, pp. 336-7) thought Norton 'correct, scholarly, nowise incompetent', but 'he still sticks somewhat in the letter', and is on the whole inferior to Butler. The newly inaugurated T.L.S. was mildly favourable when it reviewed the revised edition (29 Aug. 1902).

Norton's first edition was reviewed in the *Academy* by Paget Toynbee. In dealing with the Inferno (13 Feb. 1892, pp. 151-2) he was very complimentary, finding that Norton had 'succeeded admirably' and was better than Carlyle. When, however, he dealt with the Purgatorio (23 July 1892, p. 64), his second thoughts were different:

> We must confess to having read this second instalment of Mr Norton's prose version of the Divine Comedy with a certain feeling of disappointment.

Then, referring to Norton's remarks on Butler's version, he goes on:

> We are bound to say, since Mr Norton challenges the comparison, that we find Mr Butler's 'crib', taken as a whole, at least as readable as Mr Norton's present volume.... In his translation of the Inferno ... Mr Norton undoubtedly at times reaches a high pitch of excellence. We are

sorry to be unable to say the same of his version of the Purgatorio. It seems to us to be lacking in ease and rhythm, and to err, strangely enough, not unfrequently in being too literal, and, hence, awkward.

This was followed by a comparison of Norton's rendering of Purg. VI.76-90 with Dugdale's, to the latter's advantage. Toynbee concludes by remarking that Norton's translation 'besides being strictly accurate, has a special value of its own', namely that the writer has been able to use a better text through having the advantage of recent research. This last point is indeed well taken; Norton, who made specific acknowledgment to Moore's *Textual Criticism*, although he does not discuss textual problems or variant readings, corrected nearly all the inferior interpretations found in Longfellow and (though Toynbee does not say so) is free from the lapses which occur in Butler.

So far as style is concerned, Toynbee's comparison of the passages from Norton and Dugdale is unconvincing. One sentence which he criticises may serve as an illustration. Norton wrote 'that gentle soul was so ready, only at the sweet sound of his native land'; Dugdale 'that gentle spirit was so prompt, at the mere name of his dear native land'; and Butler 'that noble soul was thus ready, only for the sweet sound of its own country' (Purg. VI.79-80). Dante's 'dolce suon della sua terra' implies the 'sound of the name', and Toynbee's contention that 'name' alone is better than 'sound' is hardly a valid one, especially if literal translation is aimed at. Moreover Toynbee, despite his knowledge and prestige, cannot be accounted an authority on style.

All the contemporary reviewers, in their anxiety to compare Norton's with other prose versions, seem to have missed its central feature, which is devotion to the method and manner of Longfellow. This was natural in the circumstances. Norton had been one of the poet's most ardent disciples, and a member of the small band who worked at the revision of his translation. These lines, which he had helped to forge, must have been permanently lodged in his mind and when, twenty years later, he set to work on his own version he must have instinctively adopted many of them. That he conned the text with great care is evident; that he consulted other translations and did not hesitate to borrow from them is clear from internal evidence as well as from his own statement. But he is never far from Longfellow; sometimes indeed too near, for often the rhythm of blank verse persists to the detriment of the translation as clear prose. In the Inferno where, by his own admission, Norton made considerable use of Carlyle, he is less reminiscent of Longfellow. For purposes of comparison, and to illustrate the later development of the New England tradition, passages

from Longfellow and Norton will be reproduced in the second volume
of this work when dealing with their successors, Johnson and Langdon.
Something more on the subject of Longfellow's influence and its per-
petuation by Norton will also be said there.

It is indeed the fact that Norton is a sharer in the New England
tradition that distinguishes his literalness from that of Butler. Like
the latter Norton often 'sticks in the letter' as his critic said. Thus
though 'to do their good, or to fly their harm' represents veritably
word for word 'a far lor pro o a fuggir lor danno' (Inf. II.110), it is
very dubious English. But when both translations are compared by
means of their sustained passages it is the presence of style, undefinable
perhaps yet all-pervading, which distinguishes Norton from the quite
deliberate 'stylelessness' of Butler. The following passage (Purg.
XXVIII.1-33) in both versions (in which it will be noticed that quite a
few phrases are identical) should show what Howells meant when he
described Norton as 'literal with a difference' and what Toynbee, perhaps too intent on the Italian, probably missed.

Fain now to search within and round about the divine forest dense and
living, which was tempering the new day to my eyes, without longer
waiting I left the bank, taking the level ground very slowly, over the soil
which on every side breathed fragrance. A sweet breeze that had no
variation in itself smote me on the brow, not with heavier stroke than a
soft wind; at which the branches, readily trembling, one and all were
bending toward the quarter where the holy mountain casts its first
shadow; yet not so swayed from their uprightness, that the little birds
among the tops had to leave the practice of their every art; but, singing
with full joy, they received the early breezes among the leaves, which
were keeping a burden to their rhymes, such as gathers from bough to
bough through the pine forest on the shore of Chiassi, when Aeolus lets
forth the Scirocco. Now had my slow steps carried me within the ancient
wood so far that I could not see back to where I had entered it: and lo,
a stream took from me further progress, which with its little waves was
bending toward the left the grass that sprang up on its bank. All the
waters, that are purest here on the earth, would seem to have some
mixture in them, compared with that which hides nothing, although it
moves along dusky under the perpetual shadow, which never lets the
sun or moon shine there. (Norton)

Already fain to search within and around the divine forest thick and
living, which to my eyes was tempering the new day, without waiting
more I left the bank, taking the level ground at gentle pace over the soil
which on all sides gave sweet odours. A soft breeze, without any change
in it, smote me on the forehead, with no heavier stroke than a gentle
wind; by reason of which the leaves, quickly trembling, were all bending
towards the quarter where the holy mount casts its earliest shade; not,

however, spread from their natural uprightness so much that the birds
through the tree-tops needed to leave setting all their arts in work: but
with full joy chanting they received the early shadows among the leaves,
which were keeping a ground-bass to their strains, such as collects itself
from branch to branch through the pinewood on the shore of Chiassi
when Aeolus is letting Scirocco forth. Already my slow steps had carried
me so far within the ancient wood that I could no longer see back to
where I entered, and lo a stream stayed my further going, which towards
the left with its little waves was bending the grass that sprang upon its
bank. All the waters that are in this world most pure had seemed to have
in them some admixture beside that which hides naught; albeit it moves
along all brown beneath the perpetual shade, which lets not sun nor moon
shine ever there. (Butler)

Norton's notes are brief, since it was no part of his plan to discuss
controversial subjects or textual problems like Butler. What he has
included is useful and well expressed. Extensive revisions and additions in the second edition bear testimony to the care with which he
composed them.

SIR EDWARD SULLIVAN (1852-1928)

Sullivan was the son of his namesake, the first baronet, who was one
of the most eminent of Irish Lord Chancellors, and of Bessie Josephine
Bailey. Born in Ireland, he was educated at the Portora Royal School,
Enniskillen, then at Trinity College, Dublin, where he took a first in
classics and was prizeman in Latin verse. He was admitted to King's
Inns, Dublin, as a barrister in 1879 and to the Middle Temple in 1888.
He was interested both in literature and in book production; his magnificent edition of the *Book of Kells* testifies to his skill as an amateur
bookbinder. He edited *Tales from Scott* and Buck Whaley's *Memoirs*,
and did other occasional writing.

The short preface to his prose translation of the Inferno (1893) is
dated from Dublin. It is evident that he set out to improve on existing
translations, for he writes:

The following rendering is an attempt to put Dante's immortal Comedy
before English readers in a form which – allowing for differences of idiom –
accurately represents the original, without entirely sacrificing the poetical
spirit which is so marked a characteristic of the work. The prose versions
which have hitherto been published – though few in number – seem to
have been framed rather as a help to students of the Italian text, than
with a view to give the English reader any insight of a connected kind into
Dante's poem. I know of no prose rendering in our language which is
throughout intelligible without the aid of the original text.

He considers Carlyle's by far the best of the prose versions, but none the less faulty; and he thinks all the rhymed versions fail completely. He goes on:

> I have endeavoured, as far as possible, to couch my translation in the simple and solemn language with which all readers of our Bible have been long familiar. Its archaic style would appear, for obvious reasons, to be peculiarly appropriate to the rendering of such a work as Dante's masterpiece; for, while prose in form, it seems to suggest, rather than to repel, the introduction of expressions of a poetical character.

Although elsewhere the preface suggests that this volume was intended as the first instalment of a complete Comedy, no more was published.

Sullivan seems to have aimed at making a version which should be accurate and at the same time reproduce some quality of the original which others had missed. Just what he means by 'insight of a connected kind into Dante's poem' is not too clear, and the preface does not develop his ideas. The language of the Authorised Version is evidently to be drawn on to assist in the result. Unfortunately, the ability to relish the flavour of Jacobean English by no means infers the skill to use it. The biblical reminiscences of Carlyle's version are a reflection of background rather than a deliberate attempt at imitation. Sullivan's idiom is a synthetic one, occasionally impressive, frequently clumsy, often conveying a faintly ridiculous sense of pastiche.

He is sedulous in his archaisms. The third person singular of the present tense ends in '-th' throughout, except that we are spared 'batheth'. Equally persistent is the use of the conjunctions 'when that', 'after that' and 'for that', which is irritating and unjustifiable. Expressions like 'or ever', 'erewhile' and 'an' (=if) occur repeatedly. There are also antiquated words like 'drave', 'wot', 'damosel'. There are quite a few direct quotations from the Bible, e.g. 'alle segrete cose' (III.21) is rendered 'the things man hath not seen'. There are quotations from other sources, such as 'to labour in her wreck' (XIX.57) where a footnote refers the reader to *Macbeth*. For the most part, however, the archaisms are of an artificial kind, written into the material without regard to the tone of the original, and they tend to produce verbosity or weakening, e.g 'that on high she softeneth to relenting the judgment that yieldeth not' (II.96) or 'for that I stole from out the sacristy its goodly garniture' (XXIV.137-8). Sometimes the style tends to fatuity as in 'As the rivulet cometh forth from Bulicame, which, as it cometh forth, the sinful women share amongst them' (XIV.79-80). At XIX.17 'mio bel San Giovanni' becomes 'my San Giovanni's stately dome'. Juxtaposition of old and new spoils the effect in 'unburden

DCEM

thee of all depression' (XXX.144) or 'I do believe that thou art fooling me' (XXXIII.139). Sometimes the passion for archaism outruns discretion and we get tautology like 'I would fain have gladly gone some other way' (XXXI.141); and what meaning are we to attach to Virgil's bidding, 'Look, and pass away' (III.51)?

The tendency to iambic rhythm is a danger in all stylised prose, and it is very marked in Sullivan. Sometimes as many as twelve or fifteen consecutive lines fall into blank verse, and there is seldom a portion of any length in which several such lines do not occur. There are examples also of stranger rhythms; it is difficult to avoid reading II.133-5 thus:

> O clothed with pity she, that came to succour me!
> And gracious thou, that didst give heed so speedily
> Unto the words of truth that she addressed to thee!

Sullivan's accuracy is spoiled by persistent over-elaboration which often obscures the original force and emphasis. There are also frequent departures from the text that seem to have no justification. There is an assortment of these in cantos IX and X. Line 18 of the former is rendered 'whose only punishment is hopeless hope', which occurs word for word in David Johnston's blank verse translation. Line 27 becomes 'to rescue thence a spirit from the circle of Judas', which raises unwanted questions. Lines 86-7, 'he made signal to me to stand unmoved, and bow myself before him' are ridiculous through a bad choice of word for 'queto'. In line 92 the angel 'crossed the loathsome threshold'. X.57 becomes 'but after that its suspicions were wholly set at rest', which is quite misleading.

The general effect may be gathered from a longer passage (V.121-38):

> No deeper sorrow is, than to recall a time of happiness, in misery's hour; and this thy Teacher knoweth. But if thou hast concern so great to learn our loves' first source, I shall do even as one that speaketh in his tears. We read one day, to while the hour, of Lancelot, how love enthralled him: we were alone, with never a thought of harm. And oft and oft that reading brought our eyes together and drave the colour to our cheeks; but one point, only one, it was that overcame us. When we came to read of how the smiling lips he loved were kissed by lover such as he, he that no more shall e'er be parted from me, kissed my mouth trembling through. Our Galahad was the book and he that penned it: that day we read in it no more.

It is hard to see what purpose the translation was intended to serve, or why it should be supposed to give an 'insight of a connected kind into Dante's poem'. Indeed, Carlyle's Inferno is a great deal more likely to convey what Sullivan refers to as 'a shadowy idea' of the original than his own, the language of which is even more misleading than Cary's as an indication of the kind of idiom in which Dante wrote. The *Spectator* (23 Dec. 1893, p. 219) thought that Sullivan's translation read well and had a 'dignified flow of well-balanced language'. The *Saturday Review* (6 Jan. 1894, p. 18) disapproved of Sullivan's references to his predecessors in his preface, and pointed out some stylistic defects, but concluded: 'taking the work on its own merits we are glad to give it a welcome'. The *Athenaeum* (1 July 1893, p. 33) detected the fallacy underlying Sullivan's method, remarking: 'Sir Edward's avowed endeavour is to use biblical language; we do not perceive that he has realised that endeavour in any marked degree', and summed up his effort as 'well-meant but the reverse of successful'. This seems a fair verdict. The version has no features that make it worthy of permanence, and has long been forgotten.

PHILIP HENRY WICKSTEED (1844-1927)

Philip Henry was the second son of the Rev. Charles Wicksteed, a Unitarian minister, who retired from a charge in Leeds in 1854 to Hafod-y-Coed. Here Philip acquired a love of the country which caused him likewise to choose rural surroundings for his own retirement. He was educated at Ruthin Grammar School, University College, London, and Manchester New College, where he was runner-up for the gold medal in classics. He then entered the Unitarian ministry and, after holding charges at Taunton and Dukinfield, he succeeded Martineau at Little Portland Street Chapel in London. He remained there till 1897, when he went to live near Wantage, which was his home for the rest of his life. His retirement from the ministry by no means ended his active life; his activities in writing and lecturing were arduous and continued for twenty years. At the age of twenty-three he had married Rebecca Solly, daughter of a Unitarian minister; their union lasted fifty-five years and they had eight children.

It is impossible here to do justice to Wicksteed's amazing intellectual grasp and tireless energy. Classical scholar, brilliant mathematician and economist, philosopher and linguist – he was all these, besides being a hard-working and devoted pastor, an earnest and impressive preacher, and an indefatigable missionary in the cause of culture. He was the associate of Mrs Humphrey Ward in the Hall of Liberal Theology. He was the champion of Ibsen when almost the whole British press was hysterically abusing *A Doll's House* and *Ghosts*. He mastered and developed Stanley Jevons' theory of value and converted, among others, George Bernard Shaw who, in a signed obituary notice in the *Times* (25 Mar. 1927) said that, having been 'put up by the British socialists as their champion' to repel Wicksteed's attack on Marx,

> the controversy ended in my education and conversion by my opponent, and the disappearance of the Marxian theory of value from the articles of faith of British Socialism.

Among Wicksteed's many friends, who included some of the most distinguished thinkers of the age, was C. H. Herford, who near the end of his own life wrote a biography, *Philip Henry Wicksteed: his Life and Work* (1931), to which the reader may be referred for fuller details of this remarkable man's activities.

Even to catalogue Wicksteed's contributions to the study of Dante would take up too much space here; Herford's complete and well-arranged bibliography gives a notion of its extent. His *Six Sermons* (1879, and frequently reprinted) were influential, and contained translations of many lines of the Comedy. In addition to his prose rendering of the Paradiso he also translated the Convivio and all but one of the Latin works, Witte's essays on Dante, parts of Villani's Chronicle, and some of the *Early Lives of Dante*. There are numerous other books of value to Dantists which we shall not mention here. It must be stressed however that in this department of his work as in all others Wicksteed was a thoroughly competent theologian and philosopher, abreast of the most recent developments, and capable of independent and constructive thought – not to be labelled, as Herford points out, as a mere 'populariser of Dante'.

None the less, from the days of *Six Sermons* onwards, the popularisation of Dante was an important and deliberate part of his work, for he wholeheartedly believed that Dante should be more widely known. He was therefore an enthusiastic collaborator with Hermann Oeslner and Thomas Okey, who joined with the then youthful publishing house of Dent to launch the 'Temple Classics' edition of Dante's works. These six pocket volumes contain the Italian text with a literal prose translation facing it, and also a wealth of explanatory matter, including maps, diagrams, genealogical tables, etc., which enable even the complete beginner to make his way intelligently through the medieval labyrinth. The series commended itself alike to scholars and general readers for its inexpensiveness, conciseness, comprehensiveness and reliability, and there have been many testimonials to its value. In recent years comparable editions of Dante have become more common, but throughout the early part of the present century the Temple Classics played a vital role in making Dante accessible.

So far as the Divine Comedy is concerned Wicksteed produced the Paradiso volume in its entirety, wrote the longer notes at the end of the other two cantiche, the arguments for the Purgatorio, and was responsible for most of the diagrams. Reference has already been made to the revision of Carlyle's Inferno for the Temple edition; Okey's Purgatorio will be dealt with in the second volume.

The Paradiso was the first of the three parts to appear in the series, and in his Editorial Note (at the end of the volume) Wicksteed set out his aims:

> The preceding translation of the Paradiso was undertaken for the sole purpose of enabling the publisher to bring out a cheap edition of the text, accompanied with an English version. It claims no merit except having accomplished this purpose. Still less does it claim any superiority over its predecessors, or wish to enter into rivalry with them. The translator has attempted first and foremost to satisfy himself as to the author's exact meaning, and then to express it (1) precisely, (2) with lucidity, (3) worthily, (4) with as close adherence to the vocabulary and syntax of the original as English idiom allows. He has consciously adopted a happy turn of expression in one passage from Mr Norton's translation, and in two cases he has borrowed words he had not himself been fortunate enough to hit upon from Mr Butler. The many other coincidences with these (and doubtless other) translations arose, to the best of his belief, independently.

In the matter of accuracy, Wicksteed's scholarship is a guarantee of fidelity. There are of course the odd cases where we may disagree with his reading or interpretation, but we can be sure that his decisions were never made lightly, and sometimes indeed phrases which appear odd at first have justified themselves and contributed to a fuller understanding of the original. It is otherwise, however, with the quest for lucidity. Wicksteed's fourth requirement of 'close adherence to the vocabulary and syntax of the original' necessarily involved numerous departures from normal English word order, and he superimposed on this, possibly to fulfil his third requirement of making the rendering 'worthy', a kind of artificial archaism so highly mannered as to become irritating when read continuously. Carlyle's Inferno, which had been selected for the Temple edition, has a slight flavour of biblical archaism, but Wicksteed's Paradiso is so highly stylised as to savour of pastiche. The inversions required by the effort to preserve the Italian word order are rendered more rather than less obscure by the introduction of what are often pseudo-sixteenth-century forms. It cannot be said that 'that John whichso thou please to take' sheds any special light on 'qual Giovanni, quel prender vuoli', nor that 'O father his, Felice in good sooth' is an illuminating rendering of 'O padre suo veramente Felice'. Moreover, the habit of archaism grows and produces peculiarities not in the original like 'to avert or weariness or peril' for 'per cessar fatica o rischio'. 'Devoutly as I most may' (= 'si devoto / quant' esser posso più') is merely awkward, and 'more far' for 'più avanti' hardly English. We can see, however, from Wicksteed's other renderings of Dante, and from the short extracts translated in *Six Sermons* twenty years earlier, that he was always inclined towards this kind of language for the purpose. The passages in *Six Sermons*, translated for a different context, are freer from inversion, but they show the same characteristics, and it seems clear that this was what Wicksteed considered a 'worthy' idiom to represent his original. His son, the Rev. Joseph Wicksteed, was kind enough many years ago to give the writer some recollections of his father in the days when he was working on this translation. He recalls on one occasion suggesting that in the interests of simplicity 'volume' might be changed to 'book' in one passage of the Paradiso. This suggestion did not meet with the translator's approval, but later he was 'gently amused' and admitted that he tended to regard his own version with almost as much reverence as the text. His son continues:

> What strikes you as over-stylisation in his translation of Dante's Paradiso was a deliberate attempt to capture not merely the subtle meaning but the not less subtle rhythm and cadence that pulsed for him in every line and stanza of the original. In reading poetry he made himself as it were the instrument upon which the music was played.

By the time he wrote his version of the Paradiso, Wicksteed had almost equated his chosen English idiom with the original, and he probably failed to realise that, although it gave him complete satisfaction, it might hardly fulfil the demand for lucidity which he himself had prescribed.

A brief quotation (Par. XXXIII.85-96) will show Wicksteed's style at its best in one of the more difficult passages.

> Within its depths I saw ingathered, bound by love in one volume, the scattered leaves of all the universe;
> substance and accidents and their relations, as though together fused, after such fashion that what I tell of is one simple flame.
> The universal form of this complex I think that I beheld, because more largely, as I say this, I feel that I rejoice.
> A single moment maketh a deeper lethargy for me than twenty and five centuries have wrought on the emprise that erst threw Neptune in amaze at Argo's shadow.

Another rather unfortunate feature of Wicksteed's translation is the tendency for his prose to fall into perfectly regular blank verse, and it is not uncommon to find a succession of terzine like the following (XXI.106-11):

> 'Twixt the two shores of Italy crags arise,
> and not far distant from thy fatherland,
> so high the thunders sound far lower down,
> and make a hump whose name is Catria,
> 'neath which a hermitage is consecrate,
> which erst was given only unto prayer.

None of the journals which normally reviewed each new version of Dante as it appeared seem to have noticed the Temple Classics at the time of their publication, although there have been many expressions of opinion, both favourable and adverse, since. There can be no doubt that Wicksteed's manner has antagonised some able judges; on the other hand many readers have testified to the value of his book as an introduction to the original and a guide to their studies, and for a serious student the vagaries of Wicksteed's English are not formidable obstacles. Moreover, Wicksteed's arguments, prefixed to each canto, and sometimes almost amounting to a short essay, are most valuable. As he himself said in a note at the end of the volume (unfortunately tucked away among the end matter where it may never be seen):

> The notes at the end of each Canto are to be taken in close connection with the Arguments which, when carefully read, will be found to contain, directly or by implication, many explanations that the reader may perhaps have looked for in vain in the notes.

These arguments are designed to set the whole scheme of the Paradiso in perspective, and if they are neglected, the notes in themselves may seem somewhat bald; this may explain why Melville Best Anderson thought they were 'often wanting in urbanity'.

Wicksteed had a notable posthumous triumph when Charles Hall Grandgent selected the Temple Classics translation for a new American edition of Dante in English for which he was responsible. He had previously praised Norton's rendering but in his Introduction to *The Carlyle-Wicksteed Translation*, published in New York in 1932, he opines that the latter is 'the most valuable prose version of Dante', 'clear, dignified and accurate, in simple idiomatic prose'. This decision had much to recommend it, although Grandgent somewhat overstates his case.

BIBLIOGRAPHY TO CHAPTER VIII

BUTLER

*The Purgatory of Dante Alighieri. Edited with translation and notes by Arthur John Butler, late Fellow of Trinity College, Cambridge. London: Macmillan and Co. 1880. (A second revised edition was issued by the same publishers in 1892.)

*The Paradise of Dante Alighieri (etc., as above). 1885. (A second revised edition was issued as above in 1891.)

*The Hell of Dante Alighieri (etc., as above). 1892

DUGDALE

*Dante's Divine Comedy: The Purgatorio. A Prose Translation by the late William Stratford Dugdale. London: George Bell & Sons. 1883.

VERNON

*Readings on the Inferno of Dante, by the Honble. William Warren Vernon, M.A., with an Introduction by the Rev. Edward Moore, D.D. London: Macmillan & Co. 1894, 2 vols. (A second edition, entirely rewritten, was published by Methuen & Co. Ltd. in 1906.)

*Readings on the Purgatorio of Dante, etc., with an Introduction by the Very Rev. the Dean of St. Paul's. London: Macmillan & Co. 1889, 2 vols. (A second edition, entirely rewritten, was published by Macmillan in 1897; a third edition, further revised, by Methuen in 1907.)

*Readings on the Paradiso of Dante, etc., with an Introduction by the Bishop of Ripon. London: Macmillan & Co. Ltd. 1900, 2 vols. (A second edition, extensively revised, was published by Methuen in 1909.)

NORTON

The Divine Comedy of Dante Alighieri. Translated by Charles Eliot Norton. Boston and New York: Houghton Mifflin and Company. 3 vols (1891, 1891, 1892) (Simultaneously with the above the three volumes were published in London with Macmillan & Co's imprint. A second edition, revised by the translator, was issued under the same imprints in 1902.)

SULLIVAN

The Comedy of Dante Alighieri rendered into English by Sir Edward Sullivan, Bart. Hell. London: Elliot Stock. 1893. (An identical reprint of the above volume, bound in paper covers, with the description 'Cheaper Edition' on title page, was issued by the same publishers in 1895.)

WICKSTEED

*The Paradiso of Dante Alighieri. London: J. M. Dent & Sons Ltd. 1899. (This is a volume in the Temple Classics series, and is now in the 21st edition.)

* includes Italian text

CHAPTER IX

EXPERIMENTS AND CURIOSITIES

W E have already noted a few attempts to translate Dante into some metrical form with no direct relation to that of the original: Boyd's six-line stanzas, for instance, and Parsons' quatrains. Such versions were, however, very much in the minority. The closing years of the century saw more frequent attempts at using new metres; perhaps partly because of continued dissatisfaction with the depressing results obtained in terza rima, and partly because some would-be translators reacted against the use of prose which was becoming popular. There had been some earlier efforts at diversity other than those already mentioned. In the section dealing with Musgrave, the only translator to produce a complete cantica in Spenserian stanzas, will be found particulars of fragments in the same metre by various other authors. In that dealing with Lee-Hamilton, included here as the first translator, and the only one before 1900, to attempt hendecasyllabic blank terzine in English, there are some remarks on this form, but the matter will be discussed more fully in dealing with his twentieth-century successors in the second volume.

Here we may describe briefly a translation of the complete Comedy which came into the hands of Paget Toynbee and was gifted by him to the British Museum (Addit. MS. Nos. 39170-1). It was made by a Church of Scotland missionary, William Charteris, who is known to have been stationed at Smyrna in 1880, and may earlier have been in Alexandria. The last folio bears the date 1876, and the work was probably undertaken to occupy leisure time. The translation is in irregularly rhymed decasyllables, with occasional passages in couplets, and a few Spenserian stanzas. Charteris' translation is of little value; it keeps for the most part at a pedestrian level, and contains much paraphrase and padding. The following, which represents Par. III. 79-87, will be as much as the reader wants; it includes one of the worst renderings ever made of 'E' n la sua volontade è nostra pace'.

> Nay 'tis clear we cannot swerve
> From will of God but keep within its line,
> For that our wills be one with the divine,
> Essential is in happiness to live!

Like pleasure then to all it well may give,
As it does to our King, who to his will
Us all suborns, that souls are made to fill
Step after step within this holy Heaven.
To do his will, us all this peace has given,
That will, the ocean whither all things flow
Which he creates or Nature makes us know!

On the continent, however, there had been numerous experimental versions, and some of these doubtless became known to British translators of Dante. Naturally many of the earlier French efforts were in the Alexandrine couplets of the classic age. In 1837 Ledreuille published an Inferno in quatrains; Aroux' Comedy (1842) is in irregularly rhymed Alexandrines. Perrodil's Inferno (1862) is in the same six-line stanza as Wilstach's, described below. By far the most successful of French rhymed translations, however, was that of Louis Ratisbonne, whose Comedy appeared between 1852 and 1860. He uses the same six-line stanza as Henry Boyd (*a a b c c b*), but keeps strictly to Dante's terzine, using one stanza to each pair, and introducing where necessary a seventh line rhyming with its predecessor at the end of a canto. A most interesting discussion of French translations of Dante is found in Hippolyte Topin's *Discours Préliminaire* to his Paradiso (1862). His own version, which includes some cantos from the Inferno and Purgatorio contains a great variety of styles: terza rima, *vers blancs*, *rimes plates*, *rimes croisées* and some still odder arrangements. He also quotes from numerous other translators in various languages. Unfortunately the book is rare, but it is worth looking for, since Topin's questing spirit led him into many byways of interest to the student of translation.

In German terza rima and blank terzine were by far the most popular forms, accounting for some nine tenths of the versions published. In 1853 Julius Braun published an Inferno mostly in rhymed quatrains with the sub-title 'für das deutsche Volk'. Josefa von Hoffinger, the first female German translator, used the same six-line stanza as I. C. Wright (*a b a c b c*) for her complete Comedy (1865), while Baron's Inferno (1870) is in rhymed hexameters. Scartazzini found Braun's version 'piuttosto una imitazione che una versione', but praised its poetic merits warmly, and expressed regret that 'il popolo tedesco si curò ben poco del libro destinatogli'. No other experimental version in German appeared during the rest of the century.

Of the five versions in English now to be discussed one is completely worthless and ranks merely as a curiosity. The only substantial translations by Americans during the century are those by Parsons, Longfellow, Wilstach and Norton, and it is distressing to record that the third of these, who comes within the scope of the present chapter, is abysmally below the standard of his fellow-countrymen. The other translators now to be dealt with are, however, of much greater interest, even if they must be written off as unsuccessful. Since they have all been almost totally forgotten it is worth while to record a few details of their lives, theories and achievements.

JOHN AUGUSTINE WILSTACH (1824-97)

Wilstach was born in Washington, D.C., educated at Cincinnati College, graduated as a lawyer, and began practice in 1850. He was Master in Chancery (1852-62) and Commissioner of Immigration for Indiana (1867-72). Thereafter he devoted himself mainly to literature. He published a translation of the complete works of Virgil in English verse in 1884, and in the same year appeared *The Virgilians*, a review of literature relating to Virgil. His translation of the Divine Comedy appeared in 1888, followed by *Dante, the Danteans, and Things Dantean* in 1889. His son, Joseph Walker Wilstach, was likewise both lawyer and author; his translation of the Odes of Horace was printed privately in 1883. The assistance of another son, Paul, is acknowledged in the preparation of the index for Wilstach's Comedy.

The first paragraph of Wilstach's short preface to his translation is the only part of it that relates to his method and principles, and it runs as follows:

> In attempting a rhymed translation into English of Dante's Divina Commedia, the author has been governed by the conviction that only thus can one hope to approximate to a reproduction of the effect created by the original; that the form is so inseparable from the soul of the work as to compel the translator to accept all the risks involved in the effort to represent it. The author is aware that he subjects himself, by this course, to severer criticism, but since in translation, especially in the translation of a great national work, so much that is characteristic of the original is sure to be lost, it is hoped that one may be pardoned for putting himself under bonds, and denying himself the freedom which inevitably leads to the expression of too much of the translator's personality. Fidelity to the Italian poet has therefore been the *jus et norma* of the translator's dealing with the text.

The argument is rather illogical, but the reader might be pardoned for supposing Wilstach to mean that he had used Dante's rhyme scheme. This, however, is not the case. The translation is, very strangely, printed in stanzas of nine lines, with space between each, but it really consists of six-line stanzas rhymed *a b b a c c*. Each successive pair of nine-line units, therefore, consists of three stanzas, the second occupying the last three lines of the first and the first three lines of the second. In practice Wilstach occasionally fails to rhyme one of his lines, and at other times repeats a rhyme so that three or four consecutive lines end in the same sound. He goes to some trouble to rearrange matters so that he can produce something approximating to the triple 'vidi' of Par. XXX.95-7-9, and the triple 'Cristo' which occurs several times; but he does not attempt the triple 'per ammenda' of Purg. XX. Each canto has the same number of lines as the original, so always ends with a broken stanza of either one, four or seven lines, the final line rhyming with the first line of the preceding one or two terzine. The rhymes are often loose, and we get such pairs as 'once – affronts', 'sense – intents', 'wilds – defiles', 'powers – bars'.

Lines of eight or twelve syllables are strewn throughout, suggesting lack of revision. There are numerous obvious misprints, and no doubt others less obvious, which may account for some of these variations. The typography of the volumes is unpleasant, in spite of the fact that Wilstach refers proudly in his preface to a special ligature which he has had cut for the letters 'eu' to represent the Greek diphthong in Capaneus, etc. He probably financed the production of his work, and the awkward lay-out and imposition of the pages may be due to him rather than to the printer. Each canto is preceded by a list of 'Persons speaking' and 'Persons appearing', by no means an easy thing to compile, and this, since it is done neither accurately nor consistently, would have been better omitted.

The translation itself is as near worthless as any English version of Dante ever made. Indeed Wilstach might be said to have ensured failure before he started by adopting such an extraordinary stanza form, unhappy enough for any purpose, but intolerable for the Divine Comedy. However, he was probably incapable of handling any kind of metre, for all he produces is a jumble of mostly ill-chosen words which scan and rhyme after a fashion but do not reproduce any aspect of the original. Besides being almost continuously awkward, inaccurate and obscure, they are often lame and cacophonous as well. Even when his matter is nearly right, his words seem to be thrown down at random, e.g. (Par. I.25-7):

> And thou me shalt unto thy favorite tree
> See come, and with those leaves me form a crown,
> And worthily treat the theme and thy renown.

The following lines (Inf. V.127-38) are typical of his methods:

> One day we read, 'mongst histories old and new,
>   Of Launcelot, how love held him in constraint;
>   We were alone, without suspicion's taint;
> At times the reading made our eyes to meet,
>   At times the color in our faces changed,
>   But one sole thing our fates all disarranged:
> When read we how, the queen's fond smile to greet,
>   He kissed the lady, him, whom from my side
>   No lapse of painful ages shall divide,
> Thus mine for aye, my mouth all trembling kissed.
>   Our Galahad thus the book and author proved;
>   That day we read no more.

His renderings are often fatuous, e.g. 'Through me those lost are never found again' in the inscription on the gate of hell (Inf. III.3), while Purg. III.117 has not only been misunderstood but very inconsequently rendered: 'and tell / The truth to her, whate'er ye tell as well'. At the other extreme there are ill-judged efforts at poetic effect like the concluding lines of Purg. XXXI:

> The peerless traits of thy transcendent worth,
>   As seen unveiled in bowers of Eden bright.

Wilstach has a flair for facetious sarcasm and abuse, and makes the most of his opportunities. So we have (Inf. XXII.94-6):

> And their great marshal spoke to Butterfly,
>   Who rolled his eyes to strike, this gentle word:
>   'Take thyself off, thou damned infernal bird!'

Sometimes this ability stands him in good stead, e.g. (Inf. XIX.70-2):

> A son, indeed, I was of the She-Bear,
>   And showered so much the little Bears with pelf
>   That pursed I wealth above and here myself.

Wilstach borrowed freely in his notes from other translators, both with and without acknowledgment, laying Longfellow under frequent contribution. He mentions Cary more than once, and it looks as though he had relied on Cary's version a good deal, particularly in the Purgatorio, where the coincidences in cases where the latter's phrases are not direct translations of the Italian are too striking to be accidental. Thus he has 'Christians and proud!' (X.121), 'Forth from his plastic hand' (XVI.85), 'Let thine heels spurn the earth' (XIX.61), 'upon a restless wing' (XX.39), 'a sea-sponge clinging to the rock' (XXV.56), 'the umbered flame' (XXVI.7), and many others.

In his preface Wilstach remarks that he 'has accumulated a large store of interesting and suggestive material', some of which he has put in his notes, the rest being reserved for the separate book already referred to. From the contents of his Virgil and Dante volumes one would say that Wilstach was inclined to treat his originals as a basis for the compilation of enormous scrap-books of miscellaneous information – historical, political, social, philosophic. He was an active and curious inquirer, and although probably many of his notes are borrowed, he was an indefatigable collector of odds and ends. His annotations to the Comedy are an accumulation of oddities. In a long comment on Inf. III.60, 'il gran rifiuto', he does his best to clear Celestine V of the popular imputation, citing, among other parallels, a recent instance, 'the resignation, based on considerations of health, of an American bishop, Grace, of Saint Paul', and even finding it appropriate to append his own version of 'sunt lachrymae rerum' which is: 'For tears all history weeps, and touch all hearts / Such tears'. A note of five pages to Inf. XIX.52-7 on Guelfs and Ghibellines, showing that these two parties troubled American politics also, tells the story of Roger Williams, 'the Dante of his time', whom 'his reverses made a Ghibelline'. At the end of Purg. I Wilstach gives a fanciful description of the Southern Cross, making it obvious that he had never seen it, or else that he had deliberately misrepresented it. He also identifies the three stars of Purg. VIII which are 'those of the first magnitude in the constellations of Euridanus [sic], Argo, and the Golden Fish'. A sketch map annexed to Purg. XXIX.12, showing Dante's route through the Earthly Paradise, makes it clear that Wilstach has misread the indications of direction in the text. His last note to the Purgatorio (XXXIII.124-6) is laconic: 'The jealous woman!' In a note to Par. VI he informs us that 'American annals have produced an American Camillus: Sitting Buffalo, usually called Sitting Bull, Tatonkaiyotonka, a chief of the Dakotas', on whose military genius he expatiates.

Wilstach's greatest discovery, on which he evidently prides himself, is that not only does each cantica end with the word 'stars', but the same word also occurs in Purg. XVII.72 which is the middle point of the Commedia. We shall see later that a more recent translator has made a similar discovery, but having used a different method of computation he locates the midpoint somewhat later in the canto.

The critics made short work of Wilstach. George Rice Carpenter in the Nation (21 Feb. 1889, pp. 163-4) called the translation so distinctly commonplace or worse, that it would not be worth while to speak of it at any length, had not certain reviews of it which have appeared as advertisements taken pains to praise it highly.... It bears sometimes so little resemblance to the original that one wonders if the author had ever read Dante in Italian.

The notes are alleged to be mainly from Longfellow and Butler, with the addition of 'a sort of cheap American wit, the wit that tries to be smart'. Edward Moore in the *Academy* (17 Aug. 1889, p. 99) said much the same, rather more politely; the translation 'cannot be pronounced successful either in form or execution'. The *Athenaeum* (23 Feb. 1889, pp. 241-2) was facetious. Remarking that Fay's Concordance, which had just been published, was 'among the useful results of the study of Dante' the writer goes on to say that Wilstach's translation 'must be ranked very low among the ornamental', and:

> As regards his notes, if Mr Wilstach were not obviously in earnest we should be inclined to suspect him of a joke at the expense of the Dean of Wells,

referring to the fun poked at Plumptre's notes by the same journal a short time before. Our summing up must be that in translating and annotating Dante, Wilstach was guilty of an impertinence the magnitude of which he was probably incapable of comprehending.

CHARLES LANCELOT SHADWELL (1840-1919)

Shadwell was born in London and educated at Westminster School and Christ Church, Oxford. He became a Fellow of Oriel in 1864, and there he spent the rest of his active life, as lecturer in jurisprudence, treasurer and finally Provost (1905-14). He made notable contributions towards the history of the Oxford colleges, and among his hobbies are recorded chess and chronograms. He remained unmarried, and one of the features of a studious life was his long and close friendship with Walter Pater, whose literary executor he became. Shadwell was popular and respected in Oxford; the Introductions to his Dante volumes, written by Pater, John Earle and J. W. Mackail, are a tribute to his standing. He published a translation of the *Quaestio de Aqua et Terra* in 1904. His first experiments in translating the Divine Comedy were made in 1882 with the Ulysses dassage in Inf. VIXX; these stanzas were published by Toynbee in his anthology, *In the Footprints of Dante* (1907).

Shadwell chose the sub-title 'An Experiment in Literal Verse Translation' for his renderings of Dante, which were published in three volumes: Purg. I-XXVII in 1892, Purg. XXVIII-XXXIII in 1899, and

Paradiso in 1915. The books are uniformly and handsomely designed, well printed and tastefully bound.

In a brief and modest preface to the first volume Shadwell explained and defended his unprecedented experiment. He began by pointing out the difficulties and limitations of the usual modes of translating Dante. Rhyme is, he thinks, essential, but he gives the familiar reasons for thinking that the obstacles to triple rhyme in English are insuperable. Then he announces:

> In the translation here published, the metre chosen is that used by Andrew Marvell in his well-known Horatian *Ode to Cromwell*.

There follows a justification of a choice which he realised would cause some astonishment, under four headings:

(1) It provides a sequence of stanzas, corresponding to the terzine of the original, which can at will be kept separate or run into each other.
(2) Its sense capacity, 28 English syllables against 33 Italian, is almost exactly right.
(3) The second couplet of the stanza is well adapted for introducing a parenthetic statement of any kind, which is a use to which Dante frequently puts the last line of a terzina (some examples are quoted).
(4) There is a resemblance between the language of the two poets, who both produce great effects by the use of very simple and homely words; and are also alike in that they employ, on occasion, expressions outside the ordinary poetical vocabulary, as well as images and ideas which belong to learning and science.

The preface ends with an explanation of the reason for terminating the translation at canto XXVII, since the last six cantos constitute, from various points of view, a distinct section of the poem.

At the end of the Introduction Pater, who had seen the translation 'from time to time during its growth', adds a few words of approval. He feels that the metre selected

> strikes the note of a dignified plain-song, capable however on demand of a high degree of expressiveness. . . . Nothing quite like this has yet been done for presenting Dante to English readers. . . . His translator, following him, with humble scholarly purpose, has really trod in his steps; rising and falling with him, if so it be. . . . His reproduction of a poem full certainly of 'the patience of genius' is itself a work of rare patience and scholarship, conspicuously free from 'the haste / By which all action is disgraced'.

In the preface to the 1899 volume Shadwell professed himself, in spite of adverse criticisms, still satisfied with his choice. In his introduction to the Paradiso Mackail says:

> The merits of this particular metrical form are great. It has now been

shown to bear surprisingly well the test of continuous work on a large scale; and with the skilful management that has been applied to it, it gives, in the judgment of the present writer, a striking approximation to the colour and movement of the original.

Even the most hostile critic, and there were many, admitted that Shadwell's version was a brilliant *tour de force*. It presented the paradox of a metrical choice, which would probably have been dismissed as ludicrous by most students of poetry at the first mention, and which seemed doomed to certain failure, achieving a reproduction of content at least, which attains an astonishing degree of success. The work must indeed have been one of 'rare patience', for in spite of inevitable weakening and a few lapses, Shadwell succeeded in fitting a genuinely literal rendering of Dante's terzine into his stanzas. He was, of course, helped by the fact that, although he had to find four rhymes to Dante's three, they were not a triplet, but two pairs; and, moreover, he could deal with each stanza separately, in the absence of a link rhyme. This last point is a great advantage, since in terza rima the translator is always dealing with two or three triplets at a time. In practice Shadwell's second and third reasons for his choice are of minor importance. His 28 syllables give him little advantage over iambic pentameters with 30; and his argument about the parenthetic statement is special pleading. In any case, he by no means always avails himself of this alleged convenience; indeed one of the examples given in his preface is the Italian of Purg. VIII.6, 'che paia il giorno pianger che si more', which he spoils in his rendering mainly through failure to use the couplet in such a way:

> Then, if he hear the distant bell,
> That seems the dying day to knell,
> Its sound hath power to move
> The new-bound pilgrim's love.

The unexpressed converse of this third proposition is regrettably true; where the roll or sweep of the terzina culminates majestically in the last line his couplet fails completely, and the contrast of the two cases is well illustrated by Purg. XV.67-72:

> The untold, unbounded good above
> Runs to combine itself with love,
> Even as the sunbeam's light
> Is drawn to bodies bright.
> It renders warmth for warmth, whereby
> The fervour of our charity
> Is to its fullest measure
> Increased from heavenly treasure.

In the former of these stanzas the second couplet deals adequately with 'com' a lucido corpo raggio vene', but in the latter the majestic climax of 'cresce sovr' essa l'etterno valore' has vanished.

Shadwell's fourth proposition as to the similarity in language between Dante and Marvell is likewise limited in its application. When neatness and precision are wanted, the Marvellian stanza can often supply it admirably, e.g. (Purg. XXXI.58-63):

> Thy part 'twas not to stoop thy wings,
> And court the breath of lightsome things,
>   The glance of girlish eye,
>   Or like brief vanity.
> The second onset and the third
> The nestling waits: for full-fledged bird
>   In vain the net is spread,
>   In vain the shaft is sped.

But later in the same canto, we find Shadwell's ingenuity defeated by the ecstasy of lines 139-45, even with three stanzas to reproduce them:

> O thou refulgent splendour bright
> Of living and eternal light,
>   Who, though Parnassus' shade
>   His cheek had pallid made,
> Yea, though he tasted of its stream,
> Would not with mind beclouded seem,
>   If he essayed to show
>   The fulness of thy glow,
> As in that place to me 'twas given,
> Set to the harmony of heaven,
>   When I beheld thee clear,
>   Loosed in the open air?

It is true that Marvell displays something akin to Dante's amazing versatility, and not infrequently gets his effects by a similar use of unconventional material, but in the Cromwell stanza the formal element is in command, and Marvell himself acknowledges this by the way in which he selects and disposes his matter.

As Professor Bickersteth points out in his pamphlet *On Translating Dante*, the short lines of Shadwell's (and Auchmuty's) translations simply do not afford room for the reproduction of Dante's effects. Pater rightly opined that Shadwell was 'not least successful in the speculative or philosophic passages'. As soon as the blend of sound and sense becomes vital, the defects of Shadwell's medium are obvious, e.g. (Purg. XIX.19-24):

'I am' she sang 'the Siren sweet,
Who on mid sea the mariners meet,
   And charm them with my measure,
   That fills them all with pleasure:
Ulysses from his wandering track
I drew: right seldom turns he back,
   Who once with me will dwell,
   So potent is my spell.'

The cadence has changed to a jingle, just as it does in Par. XIV.28-30:

The one and two and three that never
From three and two and one may sever,
   But all together stay,
   To live and reign for aye;
By limit ne'er may they be bounded,
Nor by aught other be surrounded:
   Yea but about they fall,
   And circumscribe it all.

The feminine rhymes tend to aggravate the jingle and deprive the verse of its dignity, e.g. (Par. XXXIII.70-2):

And send one sparkle of Thy glory,
To aid me tell the wondrous story;
   And yet leave some behind
   To those of after kind.

The necessity for using short words, owing to the cramped lines, produces awkward clusters of monosyllables like 'Whence the big air in rain came down' (Purg. V.118) and this, combined with the omission of small words for which there is no room increases the awkwardness, as in 'Then close, as in guides' track, I saw' (Purg. XXIX,64). A combination of these expedients gives such a disastrous stanza as (Par. VI.76-8):

Still Cleopatra sadly rues
His hot pursuit, which bade her choose
   In asp's embrace to meet
   Death hasty and unsweet.

As we have seen, Shadwell is sometimes forced to use two stanzas to represent one terzina. Very occasionally he spreads the sense of two terzine over three stanzas, but as a rule where expansion is required he makes three of Dante's lines into eight of his own, preserving the independence of what precedes and follows. About twenty of these instances occur in the Purgatorio, and about double that number in the Paradiso, canto IX containing as many as five. The end of a canto

invariably presents a difficulty since Shadwell must either get four of
Dante's lines into his own four shorter ones, or expand them to two
stanzas. On the whole he prefers compression, which often involves
baldness, e.g. (Purg. XIX.142-5):

> Alagia my good niece is still
> Yonder, so turn she not to ill
> After our evil line:
> And she is all of mine.

Expansion as a rule involves some padding, but he has one ending
where the additional lines are used to good effect, and the pun might
have raised a grim smile from Dante himself (Par. XVIII.133-6):

> Well mayst thou say 'To him I turn,
> For him my fervent longings burn,
>   Who sought the desert lone
>   And chose it for his own,
> Yea! and to martyrdom was sent,
> The dancer maiden to content:
>   Him I desire, that so
>   Fisher nor Pool I know.'

Shadwell's ingenuity enables him to do justice to the acrostic of
Purg. XII and the similar effects in Par. XIX and XX. He does not
attempt the 'Cristo' rhymes but, with something of a struggle, he
manages the triple 'per ammenda' and 'vidi'. Dante's macaronic passages do not daunt him, and indeed he goes one better, as it were, in
Par. XVIII.91-3 by providing a Latin rhyme of his own:

> *Diligite iustitiam*
> Were the first verb and noun that came,
>   *Qui iudicatis terram*
>   Was latest *ubi eram.*

He not only keeps Arnaut Daniel's speech (Purg. XXVI.140-7) in
Provençal, but coaxes it into Marvellian stanzas, the last of which runs:

> Vos prec per la valor, la quale
> Guida vos al som delle scale,
>   Sovenhavos ancor
>   A temps de ma dolor.

A remarkably large number of good stanzas could be culled from
Shadwell's translation, but it may suffice to give an example from the
difficult final canto (Par. XXXIII.58-66):

As one who dreams, and when 'tis o'er,
The dream returns to him no more,
  While still within his breast
  Remains the thought impressed,
So 'tis with me: that vision will,
Though all but spent, yet trickle still;
  Nor ever from my heart
  Its sweetness may depart.
'Tis thus the Sun unseals the snow;
Thus in the wind the light leaves blow;
  Thus was the Sibyl's lore
  Scattered for evermore.

The critics were divided. Some were obviously astonished to find such an apparently hopeless task carried out with such dignity. Arthur Galton in the *Academy* (25 Mar. 1893, pp. 258-9) praised the first volume, feeling that 'if the music be not precisely Dante's, yet Mr Shadwell has composed an English poem that is harmonious and solemn', and making a plea that it should not be judged hastily but read at length and pondered in detail. The *Saturday Review* (28 Jan. 1893, pp. 105-6) conceded that Shadwell was 'remarkably close, very intelligible and by no means inelegant', but even with 'a double portion of goodwill' found his metrical experiment an 'utter failure'. The *Athenaeum* (21 Jan. 1893, pp. 79-80) thought the attempt 'a singular instance of perversity in the field of translation', and repeated the opinion (27 May 1899, pp. 652-3) when the second volume appeared: 'The metre, indeed, becomes even less tolerable on further acquaintance.' When the Paradiso was published the *Athenaeum* reviewer (4 Sep. 1915, pp. 156-7), making no reference to the previous volumes, thought that Shadwell 'handles his metre with consummate skill'. An early issue of the T.L.S. (29 Aug. 1902) said of the Purgatorio:

> . . . the work of a ripe scholar with a subtle sense of language, though it may not give the flowing quality of the terza rima, yet reproduces with singular success the concise and austere simplicity and the felicity of phrase which are so characteristic of Dante's poem.

One cannot read Shadwell without admiring the ingenuity and perseverance which he put into his gallant but hopeless effort. Perhaps one who is familiar with the Italian can best appreciate its good qualities, but then such a person is not in need of a translation. Looking at the process in reverse, however, it cannot be contended for a moment that Shadwell's stanzas convey any adequate notion of Dante's manner, even though they reproduce an amazing amount of his matter, and they would form a very poor guide for the reader whose knowledge of the Comedy can be obtained only from an English translation.

GEORGE MUSGRAVE (1855-1932)

This translator was the third son of John Musgrave of Whitehaven, later of Wasdale Hall, Cumberland. From St John's College, Oxford, he went to the Middle Temple, was called to the bar in 1881, and is recorded by Foster as a practising barrister, although no further details of his legal career have been found. His translation of the Inferno in Spenserian stanzas was published in 1893; a revised edition appeared posthumously in 1933, with an editorial note by E. A. Parker who explains that the translator's original intention of completing the Comedy had to be abandoned owing to ill health, latterly aggravated by blindness. This also interrupted the final revision of the Inferno, which had only reached canto VI, but Parker corrected the remainder from the translator's notes and memoranda, embodying such changes as he felt to be an improvement. The extent of the revision was very considerable, almost every stanza in the poem showing alterations. Unless otherwise stated the quotations below are from the revised edition. It may be remarked that, apart altogether from the translation itself, the two books exemplify the changes in taste which forty years brought about. An irritating feature of the 1893 volume was the extraordinary and unnecessary array of different types; throughout the poem small capitals, full capitals, italics and even italic capitals are constantly used, while several lines, and in one place a whole stanza (III.1-9), are in Old English black letter. The battery of quotation marks produced by the antiquated habit of repeating them at the beginning of every line is further complicated by the strange, though not consistently employed, treatment of quotations within a speech, which are quoted both at the beginning and end of each line, in addition to being, in some cases, in italic. The printer seems to have had the idea of keeping the length of the lines as nearly equal as possible by varying the space between the words, which is sometimes over a quarter of an inch, with disastrous visual effect. The Oxford edition of 1933, on the other hand, is beautifully set and printed in Fournier type, and all the other defects of the earlier one are put right.

Although Musgrave makes no reference to earlier efforts, the idea of rendering the Divine Comedy in Spenserian stanzas was not new. As early as 1814 such a version of the Ugolino episode and other fragments appeared in an anonymous volume, *Poetical Epistles and Speci-*

mens of Translation, containing a variety of renderings ranging from portions of Klopstock's *Messiah* to some Petrarch sonnets and odes by Anacreon and Tyrtaeus. The author has since been identified as Robert Morehead (1777-1842), a native of Stirlingshire, who won an exhibition to Baliol, kept terms at the Temple, took Anglican orders, and was for some years Dean of Edinburgh. The passages from Dante are printed by Toynbee (D.E.L. 1, pp. 647-50); they are in the style of the preceding century, and of little value either as translation or poetry. Toynbee also prints (D.E.L. 2, pp. 474-6) versions in Spenserians of Purg. II.10-26 and Inf. IX.64-103, which were included, without any reference to their provenance, in an anonymous article on Milton and Dante in the *Quarterly Review* of June 1827. Nothing is known of the translator, and no other fragments are extant. The style has some eighteenth-century features, but is rather better than Morehead's.

An experiment on a larger scale was made by Edmund Doidge Anderson Morshead, known also as a translator of Sophocles. His *Dante: an Essay* (1875) contained the episodes of Francesca, Ulysses and Ugolino and Par. XXV.1-9 in Spenserians, as well as a passage from Inf. XXX in rhymed couplets. Later he published several Spenserian fragments in the *Oxford Magazine*: Purg. II.55-133 in 1884, Purg. III.91-145 in 1885 and, eventually, Purg. XXII.55-112 in 1904. Morshead's versification is skilful, but he has to struggle with the usual difficulties. Manfred's speech in Purg. III begins:

> I felt this double death-wound rend and rive
> My body, and with tears I renderèd
> My soul to Him who loveth to forgive;
> Deep were my sins and deadly was my dread,
> Yet wide were th' Everlasting Arms outspread,
> Me to enfold, and every penitent!
> Would that in God that writing he had read –
> Cosenza's prelate, who, by Clement sent,
> Doglike did hunt my corpse forth from its monument!

There was also a slightly later experiment than Musgrave's. Epiphanius Wilson (1845-1916), a native of England who spent most of his life in the United States as an Episcopalian clergyman, published an analysis of the Divine Comedy, *Dante Interpreted* (1899), which included 60 passages, comprising some 1,200 lines in all, rendered in Spenserian stanzas. An inventory of these is given by Toynbee (D.S. pp. 260-2). Wilson is probably the most successful of the translators who have tried this measure. He has, of course, the advantage of picking his passages, so that he does not have to perform a series of Procrustean operations on various parts of a complete canto; even so he has a good deal of awkwardness and padding. His version of Par. XXXIII.124-32 is as follows:

> O Light Eternal! in Thyself alone
> That dwellest, Who alone art comprehended
> By Thine Own Self, knowing Thyself and known
> To no one else, in love and smiles unended;
> That circle, in reflected light extended
> In Thee, as it appeared, when I surveyed,
> Seemed to contain, with its own colour blended,
> An outlined image on the light portrayed,
> Absorbing my fixed glance, in human pattern made.

In a short preface Musgrave says that he writes 'primarily for the many' but hopes also for 'the sanction of scholars'.

> His aim has been to convey a vivid impression: to make his version simple and readable; to maintain a sensitive fidelity to the spirit of the original, while avoiding all false literality or adherence to the mere letter.

Considering that terza rima cannot be naturalised in English, he justifies his adoption of Spenserians mainly on the ground that it is a characteristic English measure based on a multiple of three; Dante himself also writes 'in a surprising number of instances, in *triplets of triplets*'.

Musgrave's selection of a new vehicle to suit the Divine Comedy is, however, even less justifiable than Shadwell's. The latter at least succeeds in isolating the terzina, whereas the former complicates his task still further by substituting one intricate system of rhyme linkage for another, and also by imposing a highly artificial stanza pattern on what is in general continuous verse. The fact that nine is a multiple of three is a largely illusory advantage. Although the Comedy contains many sets of three terzine which form a sense-group, there is no certainty that these will occur in the right place for the translator to take advantage of the fact. Good luck sometimes plays into his hands; at other times by some manoeuvring he pads or compresses to get the stanza where he wants it; but oftener he has to take things as they come, with the division of the stanza dislocating the original pattern, and possibly an awkward enjambement as well. We can see this clearly in canto II, where in four places six of Dante's lines are expanded to a full stanza, in order that other stanzas may coincide with essential breaks in the sense, and this process invariably involves padding. Nor is it possible, even with such devices, to avoid the end of the stanza coming in the wrong place. Ulysses' address to his men begins with the last three lines of a stanza and has to be run on to the next without a stop: 'While somewhat yet remains, O be it not denied / Now, in the waning vigil of your sense' (XXVI.114-5). Worse expedients are resorted to at times, e.g. (XXIII.139-42) where a very awkward break again occurs at the end of the stanza:

> My Guide stood still, then let his head down droop
> And, after, said: 'False then the fiend did tell
> The way to us, who hooks the sinners there!' – 'Ah! well,
>
> Oft heard I in Bologna,' quoth the Friar, . . .

The end of a canto often necessitates some contrivance, since either expansion or compression is required to finish with a complete stanza. Thus the last thirteen lines of canto XIV have to be padded out to two full stanzas, the first of which, corresponding to six lines of Italian, is an example of the shifts to which the author is reduced:

> Still I importuned, asking yet again:
> 'Master, but where is Phlegethon? And where
> Does Lethe flow? Of one thou dost refrain
> From telling; while the other would appear
> Drawn from that old man's ever-dropping tear.'
> Whereat: 'In all thy questions,' he replied,
> 'Thou givest me indeed right happy cheer;
> And yet the boiling of the bloody tide
> Might, as to one at least, full answer have supplied.'

Indeed it can readily be seen that the translator has little or no chance to make use of any of the effects to be obtained from the Spenserian stanza, since he is too busy forcing the sense into the frame of metre and rhyme, so that many verses are a mere conglomeration of words, altogether lacking pattern. The concluding Alexandrine, for instance, so admirable when it can be employed to terminate the period with majesty or pathos as the case may be, becomes too often just another line with two unwanted syllables to be filled up, because it will rarely coincide with the opportunity of exploiting its possibilities. Moreover, having only three rhyming sounds to each nine lines, Musgrave is hard put to it to find suitable words. We get rhymes like 'through't – to't', 'infuriated (four syllables) – said', 'companion (four syllables) – upon', 'Ninus's (three syllables) – Semiramis'. Attempts to remedy some of the awkward rhymes are ineffective. In the first edition III.37-9 reads:

> And mixt with them are all those dastard elves,
> That band of Angels Base, who neither were
> *For* God, nor *'gainst*, but only for Themselves.

In the revised version this becomes:

> With whom's the sort that faith and duty shelves,
> As did that Angel Host who neither were
> For God nor against, but only for themselves.

Musgrave's use of feminine rhymes is also irritating, for they are mere concessions to his difficulties, with no poetic justification whatever, e.g. (II.43-51):

> Then answered unto me that Shade magnanimous:
> 'If right thy meaning I have comprehended,
> Thy soul is haunted by that pusillanimous
> And boggling fear that all too oft hath tended
> To fray men back from ventures high and splendid,
> As objects falsely seen full oft are scaring
> To ridden steeds that shy. But here be ended
> Thy doubts and dreads, while I am now declaring
> What things myself have heard and why I'm hither faring.

There is a certain amount of pseudo-poetry. Line 63 of canto I disappears entirely and is replaced by 'Through a long silent glade dim in the day nigh done', while in V.99 the Po descends 'From sounding heights afar in quest of quietude'. Spenserian language is for the most part wisely avoided; in one place the 'drowsihead' of the first edition becomes 'drowsiness' in the second. There are coinages like 'masterment', with an occasional 'wight' or 'antre', while conventional archaisms like 'wot', 'ween', 'whilome' are used mainly as rhyme words. Musgrave renders the Malebranche episode with some verve, renaming them Terrortail, Puppyface, Shockbeard, etc. An ingenious version of VII.19-21 occurs in the first edition:

> Justice of God – ah, God! who, who but Thou
> Could *hoard* for us such torments? And O why
> Do our own sins so *squander* us?

The conceit, emphasised by his own italics, disappears altogether in the revision.

Musgrave devoted much care and thought to his task, and so far as his accuracy is concerned, after making allowance for the effects of padding, there can be little complaint. He has many good stanzas, but space forbids quoting more than one (XVII.10-18) which has some Spenserian qualities:

> His face was like the face of a just man,
> So mild it seemed, and outwardly so fair;
> But all the rest into a reptile ran.

Two paws he had, to the arm-pits sleek with hair,
While breast and back and both his haunches were
Painted with nodes and circlets. Turk ne'er made,
Nor Tartar, of weaved silk, colours more rare,
Broidering in hues of subtly-varied shade;
Such webs upon her loom Arachnè never laid.

Musgrave's first edition had a good press. The *Athenaeum* (14 Oct. 1893, pp. 515-6) thought it a 'new, decidedly interesting attempt' and 'a good poem', but deplored the archaic tags and the padding. The *Spectator* (10 Feb. 1894, p. 206) said that the 'difficult metre' was 'handled with great success' and that 'the versification is of uncommon excellence'. The *Saturday Review* (6 Jan. 1894, p. 18) thought 'Spenserians not suitable', but the translation though 'somewhat rococo in taste' was 'not dull'. By the time the 1933 volume appeared tastes had changed. The T.L.S. (18 Jan. 1934, p. 36) granted that it was 'finely executed', but with no 'convincing fusion of the thought and the form'. The *New Statesman* (22 July 1933, pp. 110-11) was severe, finding 'the Spenserian stanza wholly unsuitable' and the result 'ridiculously remote from Dante'. It concluded with the very apt remark:

> Much literary skill has gone into the making of this version; poetry, however, does not derive from literary skill.

This is a very fair summing up of the matter.

An interesting feature of the 1933 edition is the 44 illustrations by John D. Batten who, like Musgrave, had died before the book was published. They were commissioned by the translator, and presented by him to Lady Margaret Hall, Oxford. E. A. Parker, who edited the book, tells us elsewhere that Musgrave 'could never satisfy himself that he had brought the text to a level of excellence worthy of the drawings – his most valued possessions'. The drawings are wood engravings, of varying relevance and interest, more likely to be admired for some degree of technical skill than for any light they shed on the poem, although R. A. Bell says that Batten's 'studious mind revelled in the preliminary labour of working out a thorough understanding of the complex geographical plan of the Inferno'.

ARTHUR COMPTON AUCHMUTY (1842-1917)

Auchmuty was of Irish extraction, grandson of Samuel Forbes Auchmuty of Ballymahon, County Longford, and son of a namesake who was in Anglican orders and resided at Blunsdon, Wilts. Arthur took a second in Greats at Lincoln College, Oxford, and also won the

Newdigate with a poem on 'Julian the Apostate' in heroic couplets. He was ordained by the Bishop of Peterborough, became Vicar of Lucton, Herefordshire, and headmaster of the Grammar School there, holding the former appointment till 1882 and the latter till 1905, when he retired and lived first in Birmingham and later in Liverpool. His quiet life was punctuated by occasional publications: a book of original verse in 1869, volumes of sermons in 1876 and 1887, a version of *Oedipus at Colonus* in irregular blank verse in 1894, Dante's Purgatorio in 1899, and he also acted as editor of some collections of poems. A pamphlet, *Four Sonnets for the Times*, issued in 1900, was a vigorous protest against the jingoism of the Boer War period, couched in a tone of invective that Dante might have relished.

Auchmuty's Purgatorio contains no introductory matter whatsoever; it renders Dante terzina by terzina, in lines of eight syllables, and in terza rima. The idea in his mind seems to have been that English decasyllables had a greater sense content than the original, and must be filled out by padding. Professor Bickersteth, in his pamphlet *On Translating Dante*, calls it, in spite of obvious defects, 'a remarkable achievement and well illustrates the natural terseness of the English tongue; for he omits nothing of the original'. While this is an exaggeration, it must be granted that Auchmuty leaves out very little, but he pays a heavy price for the supposed advantage of syllabic equivalence. Gallant, spirited and ingenious as his effort is, it would hardly be too severe to say that there are not three consecutive terzine in the poem from which the hopelessness of the attempt is not abundantly evident. Octosyllabic measures have been put to good use by writers as various as Butler, Swift, Prior and Scott for narrative, dramatic, satiric and other purposes, but as a vehicle for Dante's terzine they are impossible.

Not only is the recurrence of the triple rhymes at such short intervals intolerably irksome, but the difficulty of finding rhymes is greatly increased. One of the reasons why it has been possible at all to produce even a mediocre imitation of Dante's triple rhyme in English is that our decasyllable, with its slightly increased sense-content as compared with the Italian, gives the translator just sufficient space to work in a slight change of construction or vocabulary to suit the rhyme. Octosyllables allow no such freedom; again and again the right word is just a syllable too long, and the wrong one must be used instead. To take an instance, in Purg. XXVII.10-15 for the lines ending in 'presso – messo' the English 'said – laid' have been obvious enough to be adopted by over half-a-dozen of the terza rima translators; several others have used one of these words. No corresponding rhyme leaps to the mind for line 11; every one has adopted a different expedient, the best being Binyon's 'enter unafraid'. A larger number of translators have used other rhyming words, requiring modifications which sometimes might be described as gymnastic feats. For Auchmuty, however, there is no alternative; he has no room for recasting, so 'said – laid' is unavoidable. Here is what he produces:

> Then: 'Whom alone the Fire hath stung,
> Saint souls, goes further; in, then, wade,
> Nor deaf be to yon tuneful tongue.'
> When we were near him, thus he said,
> Whence I became, when that I learned,
> Like him who in the grave is laid.

Admittedly almost every particle of Dante's meaning is present, but the effect is merely ludicrous.

Apart from the rhyming difficulty, the use of short words is essential, producing staccato or cacophonous effects, completely at variance with the original, e.g. (III.121-3):

> Horrible the evils I had wrought:
> But Goodness Infinite so wide
> Hath arms, that nought turns there for nought.

Moreover, the necessity for compression causes the omission of articles, conjunctions, etc., and this, together with inversion, often throws a haze of obscurity over the meaning, e.g. (X.109-11):

> Not what its mode, but what ensues
> The torment, think on: think, but end
> At the great Doom no worst can choose,

where the sense is more likely to be obtained from the context than from the syntax. The expository passages are thus very difficult to follow. At other times we get such desperate expedients as (XX.88-90):

> Lo, once again the mock-bow'd knees!
> Again, the vinegar, the gall!
> The thieves, the death, the accursed trees!

Auchmuty doubtless had to cudgel his brains over this terzina at some length before wasting three precious syllables on 'accursed' which is not in the Italian, but the result is that the whole point of the satire is lost.

Professor Bickersteth comments that in the satiric passages Auchmuty 'smacks of Hudibras', and it is true that the result is often quite effective, e.g. (XIV.103-11):

> Marvel not, Tuscan, at my tears,
>   When Guy of Prata, Hugoline
>   Of Asso, I recall, our peers;
> Frederick Tignoso and his line;
>   The Travers' house, the Anástagni's,
>   Both sunk alike into decline:
> The dames, the knights, the toils, the ease,
>   Kindling to love and courtesy;
>   Where hearts all malice now one sees.

The *Athenaeum* reviewer (9 June 1900, p. 716) thought that Auchmuty's Purgatorio could 'pass muster as an eccentricity, but hardly as anything more'. This must, in spite of the author's ingenuity and accuracy, be the final verdict, and perhaps the best service he has rendered to the cause of Dante translation is to have left a concrete demonstration of the unsuitability of octosyllables for the purpose.

EUGENE JACOB LEE-HAMILTON (1845-1907)

Lee-Hamilton was born in London; after spending most of his childhood abroad, he studied French and German at Oriel College, Oxford, but left without taking a degree. In 1869 he received a minor diplomatic appointment as attaché with the Foreign Office; he was at the British embassy in Paris during the Franco-German War, and later held other diplomatic posts. Among his accomplishments were skating and dancing. In 1875 he was stricken by a nervous disease which incapacitated him from all physical activity, and kept him almost entirely recumbent, for fully twenty years. During most of that time he lived at Florence with his mother and his half-sister, Violet Paget (better known by her pen-name, Vernon Lee), and their home was a rendezvous for literary and artistic society, Henry James and Paul Bourget being among the frequent visitors. During this period Lee-Hamilton beguiled the time by writing verse, published half a dozen small volumes of poems at dates from 1878 to 1894, and achieved something of a reputation as a sonneteer; he was also the author of a tragedy in verse. In 1896 he recovered completely from his illness and resumed an active life. He visited Canada and the United States, and he married Annie E. Houldsworth, already known as a novelist, author of *The Years that the Locust hath eaten*. With her he settled between Florence and Fiesole and husband and wife collaborated in a volume of verse, *Forest Notes* (1899). He published two novels, and a book of sonnets commemorating the death of his infant daughter in 1904, a blow from which he did not completely recover. He had published his translation of the Inferno in 1898, and later completed the Purgatorio in manuscript; but he sank into a depression which ended in death by a paralytic stroke in 1907. A selection of his poems appeared in the Canterbury Poets series in 1903; the introduction, by William Sharp, contains a very full memoir of the subject's life up to that date and an appreciation of his work. Further biographical information will be found in Peter Gunn's recent *Vernon Lee* (1964). Lee-Hamilton's reputation did not long survive him. He did not find his way into the anthologies and his books, published in limited editions, had little circulation. He was a deft handler of words, especially within the limited compass of the sonnet, but his genius was imitative rather than original; Swinburne and Baudelaire were among the most obvious influences.

Lee-Hamilton was the first translator in English to attempt to re-produce the Divine Comedy in hendecasyllabic blank terzine, on the principle used by Philalethes more than half a century earlier, as recorded in Chapter V above. Although the German version won much applause on the continent, it had also numerous critics. Scartazzini, although one of Philalethes' admirers, confessed that he found the uninterrupted succession of feminine endings 'noioso e stanchevole, essendo il genio della lingua tutto diverso da quello dell' italiana'. Even in German, where feminine endings are available in greater variety than in English, the difficulty of finding a suitable word for the end of the line often led to the kind of awkwardness found in Philalethes' version of Par. III.82-7:

> Drum wie wir durch dies Reich von Grad zu Grad sind,
> Gefällt's dem ganzen Reich und dessen König,
> Der uns an seinem Wollen Lust läßt finden.
> Und unser Friede ist sein Wille; er ist
> Das Meer, zu dem sich alles hinbeweget,
> Was er erschafft und was Natur hervorbringt.

As will be seen this difficulty proved a serious one so far as Lee-Hamilton was concerned, and his translation must be accounted a failure. There have, however, been more successful efforts in the present century, and these will be dealt with in the second volume.

It might seem that a minor poet, with taste, ability and leisure at command, living in Italy and associating with men of letters, would make an ideal translator of Dante; and it is surprising at first to find Lee-Hamilton's Inferno one of the poorest attempts in English. The reasons, however, are readily apparent if one reads the enunciation of his principles in the preface.

There are in the Divine Comedy three main metrical factors:

1. The spirit of the Terzina, or intellectual division of the verse into groups of three, or of multiples of three. Dante *thought* in threes and sixes, and sometimes even in nines and twelves, the groups being expressed by the punctuation.

2. The chain of the rhyme.

3. The eleventh, or as we should call it with respect to iambic verse, the feminine syllable, at the end of each line – a syllable characteristic of Italian verse in general, and without which no verse translation can reproduce the effect of the original.

Of these three factors I have preserved the first and the third, and have omitted the second. Most other translators, while sometimes preserving the second, and not always preserving the first, have disregarded the third as unimportant. Now, to my mind, the eleventh or feminine syllable is absolutely essential, if the object is to reproduce the effect of the original on the ear. And this was the view of one of the best foreign translators, perhaps the best foreign translator, of Dante – Philalethes (King John of Saxony).

The rhyme is comparatively unimportant. Its maintenance precludes the English translator from keeping the feminine syllable, and forces him to depart from closeness of meaning and literalness of expression. No rhymed translation of Dante can be more than an approximation; and the rhyme in the original is so unimportant, that he whose mind is bent upon the meaning scarcely notices it at all.

Quite apart from my own performance, of whose deficiencies I am but too fully aware, I believe that in selecting the two factors out of three which could alone reproduce in their combination the sense and sound of the original, I have adopted the only plan that can secure a comparatively satisfactory line-for-line translation.

The extent of Lee-Hamilton's aberration is clear from the penultimate paragraph, with its bland assertion of the unimportance of the rhyme; but the whole argument shows a fundamental misunderstanding of the nature of poetry. Perhaps over-indulgence in sonnet-writing encouraged the delusion that a poet selects a verse form and then thinks on matter to suit it. As for the hendecasyllable, it is characteristic of Italian verse in general because anything else is impossible. The reverse is true in English; feminine endings must be used with caution and to secure a particular effect. The idea that a translation will be more successful if it simulates the speech rhythm of the original language is a fallacy that has led astray many practitioners, both before and after Lee-Hamilton; and as we have already seen, once a prosodic theory is allowed to gain the ascendant, it seems to exert a tyranny which blinds the user to all other considerations.

Lee-Hamilton expresses admiration of Philalethes, and he unfortunately copies the most objectionable features of the latter's method.

He has, for instance, a great many lines of the type:

Into eternal dark, where heat and frost are	(III.87)
As the St. Peter's fir-cone that at Rome is	(XXXI.59)
Setting their teeth to something like a stork's note	(XXXII.36)
The hair of that curst worm by whom the world's pierced	(XXXIV.108)

Still more annoying is the continual insertion of a gratuitous 'here', 'there', 'now', etc. at the end of a decasyllable to comply with the scansion. Such lines often occur close together; in canto XIX, for instance, line 47 ends 'stake there' and line 50 'stuck there'. In canto XXIII, within a little over thirty lines, we find 'capes here – man there – earth there – cross there – pit here'. In XXV.124-9 we have:

> The erect one drew it up towards the temples,
>   And from the surplus substance that was heaped there,
>   The ears grew out of his ungarnished cheek-bone.
> What did not gather back, and was retained there,
>   Of that excess, became the face's nose then,
>   And thickened out the lips as much as needful.

Similarly in XXVI.127-9:

> Already all the stars of th' other pole now
>   I saw at night, and ours was sunk so low now
>   That it no longer rose above the sea-floor.

Often a hyphen is inserted between the two monosyllables that close the line, e.g. 'might-be', 'dead-men', 'pitch-pool', 'neck-nape', 'fang-teeth', a device that does nothing to palliate their harshness.

Awkward constructions, clumsy possessives and slovenly colloquial forms are resorted to, sometimes for the sake of the metre and at others for no apparent reason, e.g.

Who've forfeited the intellect's advantage	(III.18)
For me, who'm one, will hither summon seven	(XXII.103)
And I've the body that I've had at all times	(XXIII.96)
But 't isn't what I died for brought me hither	(XXIX.111)

Sometimes italics are used, evidently as a guide to accent, as in the endings 'where *I* was', 'to *these* here', 'by *this* time'. The third person singular of the present tense varies between '-s' and '-th' according to metrical requirements. We get diminutives for the same purpose, e.g. Francesca speaks of 'the earliest rootlet / Of this our love' (V.124-5).

The Ugolino episode starts with the unpromising line: 'He raised his mouth from the terrific morsel'.

Lee-Hamilton is in general accurate, though he often tends to weaken the vigour of the original. There are perhaps a dozen mistranslations scattered throughout, which seem to stem from an over-hasty reading of the Italian.

The press dealt with Lee-Hamilton briefly and harshly. The *Athenaeum* (12 Mar. 1898, p. 339), remarking that a succession of feminine endings is intolerable in English, described the version as 'adequate but pedestrian'. The *Saturday Review* (12 Mar. 1898, p. 370) considered it 'neither rhymed nor blank verse', thought that 'the effect is monstrous', and concluded by saying that 'Lee-Hamilton has completely disproved his theory that the feminine ending is essential to the translation of the Divine Comedy'.

The draft of Lee-Hamilton's Purgatorio is MS. d.15 of the Toynbee Collection in the Bodleian. Correspondence accompanying it shows that it was sent to Toynbee by Miss Violet Paget, the translator's half-sister, on 13 Sep. 1921, along with a letter from Signor Mario Praz, whose opinion had been sought, evidently with some hope of publication. Signor Praz's letter, dated from Florence, 8 May 1921, is eulogistic:

> ... mi pare che il pubblico inglese potrebbe trarre gran vantaggio della sua pubblicazione. Il movimento della terzina è conservato, l'ordine delle parole è altrato il meno posibile: la versione è quasi letterale. Non conosco che d'eguggite le altre traduzioni in inglese di Dante, ma questa mi sembra eccelente.

Probably Signor Praz was not at that time so well acquainted with English literature as he has since shown himself, and in any case it is always difficult to judge a version in a foreign tongue. No record of Toynbee's own opinion is preserved. The manuscript is a very untidy one, consisting of sheets from a number of cheap note-books, sewn together, full of erasures, second thoughts, marginal notes, etc. Its style shows no improvement on that of the Inferno, as III.121-35 makes clear:

> Frightful had been the sum of my transgressions,
> But Mercy Infinite hath arms so ample
> That it accepteth all that turns towards it.
> If but Cosenza's shepherd, who to hunt me
> Had been induced by Clement, at that moment
> Had by God's mercy rightly read these features,

My body's bones would to this day be lying
  There at the bridgehead, near to Benevento,
  'Neath the protection of the heavy stone heap.
Now the rain wets them, and the wind upsets them
  Outside the kingdom, by the banks of Verde,
  Whither he had them moved, with lights extinguished.
But spite their curse we never lose so wholly
  The Eternal Love, but what we may regain it
  So long as hope retaineth still some greenness.

BIBLIOGRAPHY TO CHAPTER IX

WILSTACH

The Divine Comedy of Dante. Translated into English Verse, with Notes, by John Augustine Wilstach, author of 'The Virgilians' and translator into English of the complete works of Virgil. Boston and New York: Houghton, Mifflin and Company. 1888, 2 vols.

SHADWELL

The Purgatory of Dante Alighieri (Purgatorio I-XXVII). An Experiment in Literal Verse Translation, by Charles Lancelot Shadwell, M.A., B.C.L. London: Macmillan and Co. 1892

The Purgatory of Dante Alighieri. Part II. The Earthly Paradise (Cantos XXVIII-XXXIII). As above. 1899

The Paradise of Dante Alighieri. As above. 1915

MUSGRAVE

Dante's Divine Comedy, consisting of the Inferno, Purgatorio & Paradiso. A version in the nine-line metre of Spenser by George Musgrave, M.A. The Inferno or Hell. London: Swan Sonnenschein & Co. 1893

Dante's Inferno. A Version in the Spenserian stanza, by George Musgrave, with forty-four illustrations by John D. Batten. Oxford University Press. 1933

AUCHMUTY

Purgatory. A Translation from Dante in Octosyllabic Terza Rima by Arthur Compton Auchmuty. London: Williams and Norgate (Edinburgh and Oxford). 1899

LEE-HAMILTON

The Inferno of Dante. Translated with Plain Notes by Eugene Lee-Hamilton. London: Grant Richards. 1898

POSTSCRIPT

THE reader of the foregoing pages may well feel depressed by the record of so much apparently wasted effort. Forty translators, producing among them 82 cantiche – the equivalent of some 400,000 lines of verse – and most of them consigned to the lumber room. Wasted expense too in many cases, for either the publisher or the author must have found the production of these tomes a costly and unprofitable business. Landor's lines to the pioneer of Dante translation in English,

> Cary, I fear the fruits are scanty
> Thou gatherest from the fields of Dante,

could doubtless be applied to the greater number of these translators.

About half of the forty we have found hardly worthy of serious consideration, and half the remainder as definitely of the second class, however interesting or ingenious they may be. There was, it is true, solid achievement during these 120 years, but it was mainly that of writers whose object was to help the student rather than to provide an English equivalent for the poem.

Cary, indeed, is the only translator prior to 1900 who combined poetic merit with some degree of literal accuracy. He can be criticised on many counts, but his version is established as a minor masterpiece in English, and it has been a bridge which enabled successive generations to cross at least one of the gulfs which separate Dante's time and language from our own. It is the only rendering in blank verse (as distinct from blank terzine) of any merit in the whole period, and it was not until the beginning of the twentieth century that further attempts were made to employ this medium for translating the Divine Comedy.

Of the six translations in blank terzine, all but one of which belong to the twenty years from 1850 to 1870, Longfellow's is the only outstanding one. It is made on entirely different principles from Cary's, and for a different purpose. Like Cary's it has been much criticised (often for the wrong reasons); and, again like Cary's, its historical importance has been great. It has afforded valuable guidance to many readers and assisted them in tackling the Italian. It also inaugurated the New England tradition, which continued to influence translators and students of Dante for many years, and its echoes are still heard in our own time.

Of the twenty-two translations in rhymed verse little good can be said. Fourteen of them attempt to reproduce Dante's terza rima, but not one could be called even moderately successful. The rest are 'experimental' versions of one kind or another; at least half of them are quite unreadable. We may linger lovingly over others, such as Parsons or Shadwell, even admiring some of their happier lines, but as translations of the Divine Comedy they are failures. Many of these writers in rhyme, and particularly those who used terza rima, seem sadly deficient in technical accomplishment. One feels that, however intelligently they had conned the original, they had never 'heard' it as poetry; or if they had, they showed themselves strangely ignorant of how its effects were obtained. Their prefaces in many cases indicate that they had no lack of missionary zeal. They felt that it would be good for their fellow-countrymen, who could not tackle the original, to be able to read the Comedy in their own tongue; but in their preoccupation with Dante as a moralist, a theologian or a philosopher, they tended to overlook the poetry altogether. The rhymed products of the nineteenth century can be almost entirely written off; fortunately something rather better was in store in the twentieth. Later practitioners of terza rima inherited little from their predecessors except the warning conveyed by their failures.

Although in the last decade of the eighteenth century, as mentioned in Chapter III, August Wilhelm von Schlegel experimented with terzine in which the middle lines were left unrhymed, this system, known as Schlegelian terzine or 'defective' terza rima, attained little popularity with German translators, and throughout the nineteenth century was ignored by all those writing in English with the exception of Parsons. The latter tells us that he tried it in the course of his early metrical experiments, but the only example that survives is Par. I.1-36 which appears in the 1893 volume. It was not till 1931 that a substantial translation on this principle was produced in English, since when only two other writers have used it.

Of the eight prose translations described in the preceding pages, O'Donnell's is valueless, and Sullivan's can be accorded only faint praise. The other six, however, are all worthy of commendation. Carlyle was an admirable pioneer; he was the first to tackle seriously the problem of providing adequate help for the student who wished to use a translation as a step towards the original and, as we have seen, he did his task so well that his version is still in use today. Butler, Dugdale, Vernon, Norton and Wicksteed all belong to the latter part of the century, the great era of Dante scholarship, and all acquitted themselves creditably. Dugdale is known only for his translation, so tragically interrupted, but the others were all notable contributors to Dante literature and criticism. By the time they had completed their labours the would-be student of Dante was fully equipped, and the foundations were laid for a clearer and fuller approach to his work.

INDEX

Main entries are in bold type. Casual references are not included. References to translators are listed in alphabetical order under names of periodicals.